D1623837

Management Innovators

MANAGEMENT

INNOVATORS

The People and Ideas
That Have Shaped Modern Business

Daniel A. Wren
The late Ronald G. Greenwood

New York
Oxford University Press
1998

Oxford University Press

Oxford New York
Athens Auckland Bangkok Bogotá Bombay
Buenos Aires Calcutta Cape Town Dar es Salaam
Delhi Florence Hong Kong Istanbul Karachi
Kuala Lumpur Madras Madrid Melbourne
Mexico City Nairobi Paris Singapore
Taipei Tokyo Toronto Warsaw

and associated companies in
Berlin Ibadan

Published by Oxford University Press, Inc.
198 Madison Avenue, New York, New York 10016

Oxford is a registered trademark of Oxford University Press

Library of Congress Cataloging-in-Publication Data
Wren, Daniel A.
Management innovators : the people and ideas that have shaped modern business /
Daniel A. Wren, Ronald G. Greenwood.
p.   cm.
Includes bibliographical references and index.
ISBN 0-19-511705-0
1. Businesspeople—United States—Biography.   2. Executives—
United States—Biography.   3. Industrial management—United States—
History.   I. Greenwood, Ronald G.   II. Title.
HC102.5.A2W73   1998   97-30036
658'.0092'273—dc21
[B]

9 8 7 6 5 4 3 2 1

Printed in the United States of America
on acid-free paper

To the family, friends, colleagues,
and students of Ronald Guy Greenwood

CONTENTS

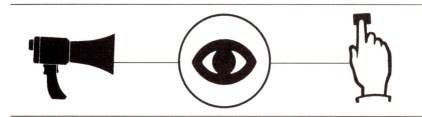

II. ORGANIZING AND MANAGING
THE BUSINESS ENTERPRISE

PREFACE

Business occupies a central role in American life: historians analyze it, journalists describe it, politicians debate it, labor unions bargain with it, novelists lampoon it, consumers buy from it, and detractors criticize its practices. Despite an occasional blemish, business furnishes everyone's sustenance in one way or another. Business touches every facet of our life, and its well-being is tied closely to the progress of the nation. From the corner merchants who bring us bread and milk to the multinational enterprise, our activities, our livelihood, and our appetites are served by business.

Part of the fascination business holds for many is its presentation of an opportunity to span the turbulent waters of social class. That is the American dream of the self-made person who rises from poverty to wealth and success. Another part of our fascination resides in our love-hate relationship with business. While business brings us our sustenance, it is feared, much as any authority figure is feared, for the power it wields over us. It is this split character of the American people—perhaps of all people—that has given business its unique flavor throughout history.

Our goal is to portray a selection of individuals whose ideas have made a difference in the way we teach and practice business management. In selecting these figures, we realize that it would be impossible to chronicle all of their activities; we could have chosen other individuals of equal stature as well. We have kept in mind an audience of contemporary managers, aspiring managers, and students of management who wish to gain a historical perspective on their profession by sketching the people and ideas that contributed to the formation of modern management.

In Part I, we trace the beginnings of American enterprise in transportation, manufacturing, communication, inventing, financing, and selling. These individuals set a pattern for others to follow as U.S. business enterprise grew. With growth came the problems of how to work smarter, to organize, to motivate, to lead, to achieve quality products, and to renew organizations through continued innovation. In Part II, selected individuals are used to portray the search for better ways to manage; these representatives played a pioneering role in shaping modern managerial practices.

A historian resides in every person insofar as we seek to understand our world and how it began. We may lack the qualities that mark a Socrates, Plato, or Aristotle, but as lovers of knowledge and understanding (that is what philosophy is all about) we want to know more so we can move on to even greater understanding and appreciation of our complicated world. This historical perspective helps us sharpen our vision of the present by using the events of the past to find more or less enduring concepts; by expanding our horizons for understanding what we see, feel, and hear; and by generating questions and alternative explanations that may not have been available to us before.

A number of individuals have helped make an idea become the reality of this book: the anonymous reviewers who helped smooth the rougher edges; Crystal Allison and Diana Randall, who helped with portions of the research; Richard A. Cosier, Dean, Michael F. Price College of Business, and Sul Lee, Dean, University Libraries, for their continuing support. Loretta Newton deserves more thanks than words can convey for using her word-processing skills to turn my scribblings into readable prose. Most of all, this book is dedicated to Regina, Ronald Jr., and Peter Greenwood and to the friends, colleagues, and students of Ronald G. Greenwood. We all miss his answering the phone: "Greenwood here."

D. A.W.
Norman, Oklahoma
February 28, 1997

PREFACE

Business occupies a central role in American life: historians analyze it, journalists describe it, politicians debate it, labor unions bargain with it, novelists lampoon it, consumers buy from it, and detractors criticize its practices. Despite an occasional blemish, business furnishes everyone's sustenance in one way or another. Business touches every facet of our life, and its well-being is tied closely to the progress of the nation. From the corner merchants who bring us bread and milk to the multinational enterprise, our activities, our livelihood, and our appetites are served by business.

Part of the fascination business holds for many is its presentation of an opportunity to span the turbulent waters of social class. That is the American dream of the self-made person who rises from poverty to wealth and success. Another part of our fascination resides in our love-hate relationship with business. While business brings us our sustenance, it is feared, much as any authority figure is feared, for the power it wields over us. It is this split character of the American people—perhaps of all people—that has given business its unique flavor throughout history.

Our goal is to portray a selection of individuals whose ideas have made a difference in the way we teach and practice business management. In selecting these figures, we realize that it would be impossible to chronicle all of their activities; we could have chosen other individuals of equal stature as well. We have kept in mind an audience of contemporary managers, aspiring managers, and students of management who wish to gain a historical perspective on their profession by sketching the people and ideas that contributed to the formation of modern management.

In Part I, we trace the beginnings of American enterprise in transportation, manufacturing, communication, inventing, financing, and selling. These individuals set a pattern for others to follow as U.S. business enterprise grew. With growth came the problems of how to work smarter, to organize, to motivate, to lead, to achieve quality products, and to renew organizations through continued innovation. In Part II, selected individuals are used to portray the search for better ways to manage; these representatives played a pioneering role in shaping modern managerial practices.

A historian resides in every person insofar as we seek to understand our world and how it began. We may lack the qualities that mark a Socrates, Plato, or Aristotle, but as lovers of knowledge and understanding (that is what philosophy is all about) we want to know more so we can move on to even greater understanding and appreciation of our complicated world. This historical perspective helps us sharpen our vision of the present by using the events of the past to find more or less enduring concepts; by expanding our horizons for understanding what we see, feel, and hear; and by generating questions and alternative explanations that may not have been available to us before.

A number of individuals have helped make an idea become the reality of this book: the anonymous reviewers who helped smooth the rougher edges; Crystal Allison and Diana Randall, who helped with portions of the research; Richard A. Cosier, Dean, Michael F. Price College of Business, and Sul Lee, Dean, University Libraries, for their continuing support. Loretta Newton deserves more thanks than words can convey for using her word-processing skills to turn my scribblings into readable prose. Most of all, this book is dedicated to Regina, Ronald Jr., and Peter Greenwood and to the friends, colleagues, and students of Ronald G. Greenwood. We all miss his answering the phone: "Greenwood here."

D. A. W.
Norman, Oklahoma
February 28, 1997

Management Innovators

INTRODUCTION

A Revolution in Industry

When we think of a revolution we think of a sudden, violent upheaval in social, economic, or political arrangements. The revolution that came to industry, however, was a series of changes that took place gradually over a half century or more. Ever since humans began to chip flints for weapons, use pierced slivers of bone for needles, employ iron plows instead of wooden ones, and use water power for grinding grain, there have been advancements in technology—the art of making tools and equipment. Although technology had been advancing for thousands of years, changes in late-eighteenth-century England marked the beginning of new technologies that developed more rapidly than ever before.

Previously, the forces that did the everyday chores of making, transporting, lifting, and so forth came from nature—human and animal muscle, wind, water. The heart of what we call the Industrial Revolution was the steam engine—a museum piece today but at one time in our history critical for economic development. For centuries, humans had known the principle of steam power—applying heat to a liquid such that it expands into a gas that carries the power to move objects. But while the principle was known, making this force serve human needs was far more difficult. Thomas Newcomen, for example, developed a steam-propelled engine that pumped water out of deep coal mines. The Newcomen engine symbolized a new age, but it suffered from numerous mechanical problems.

It was an instrument maker who was accustomed to working to close tolerances, James Watt, who developed the most efficient steam engine of that time. Watt had a workable engine as early as 1765, but he needed capital, and it was more than a decade before this engine became a commercial reality. As we shall see occurring often in business, it was the coupling of someone who had an idea with someone who had capital that brought a venture to the marketplace.

Watt's partner was Matthew Boulton, a successful maker of iron, brass, gold, and other metal products. In Boulton's Soho factory the steam engine moved from a prototype into a working engine, and the first buyer was John Wilkinson, who owned an iron works; attaching a steam engine to the bellows made the fires hotter, and thus allowed him to make stronger metal. (Wilkinson's firm, which made iron products such as swords, was the predecessor to today's company of the same name, which makes razor blades.)

How do you price a steam engine that is the best on the market? Is it the cost of eleven years of experimenting plus a fair profit? Or do you price it below cost to expand the market? In fact, neither of these approaches was used—Watt priced his engine based upon how much work it could do compared to a horse that would have been used as a source of power.

Until 1782 Watt's engines were used only to blow air for metal smelting and to pump water. His more important technological breakthrough came with an engine that transformed the up-and-down motion of the drive beam into rotary motion. This led to a host of possible new applications of steam power beyond manufacturing: to propel blades or wheels on watergoing craft, or to move the wheels of a locomotive on tracks that pulled carloads of people or freight.

The Industrial Revolution began in Great Britain and seeped slowly into the economies of other nations. In America, for example, Samuel Slater opened the first factory in 1790 in Providence, Rhode Island, but not until 1827 did he adopt steam-driven power for his looms. While American business history is characterized by such modest beginnings, the changes to come would revolutionize how products were made, sold, and transported. With growth came the problems of managing firms that had, by the necessity for capital and the accumulated resources needed for new and expanding ventures, moved beyond the grasp of a sole proprietor or a partnership. It is this growth and change, and the associated ideas and actions of individuals, that command our attention.

History is sometimes more palatable in small doses, so we invite you to let your interests guide your use of this book. If finance is your focus, you may wish to start with chapter 6, "Financiers," which provides the historical background of U.S. financial markets and discusses the activities of Jay Gould and J. Pierpont Morgan. With an inclination toward marketing, you may find it useful to turn to chapter 3, "Sellers," and read about Alexander T. Stewart, who introduced the idea of department stores, or Richard W. Sears, who brought a cornucopia of offerings to the U.S. hinterlands with his catalogs. Or try chapter 5, "Communicators," and see how the telegraph transformed information-handling technology and may have been, for that time, a more profound change than websites, electronic mail, and satellites are today. In chapter 1, "Inventors," chapter 2, "Makers," and chapter 4, "Movers," you can read of the importance of invention and innovation and how ideas are transformed into products and moved to the market.

Or you may skip to chapter 12, "Guru," and enjoy the sayings of "Chairman Peter" Drucker, the most widely quoted business author and most sought-after consultant of this age. Chapter 11, "Quality Seekers," explores how a fateful decision by General Douglas MacArthur opened the door to Japan for W. Edwards Deming and Joseph Juran; in "Leaders," chapter 10, you can survey the gamut of beliefs, from Nicolò Machiavelli to Mary Follett to Douglas McGregor, about the nature of people and examine how those assumptions guide thought and action. In chapter 7, "Working Smarter," chapter 8, "Organizers," and chapter 9, "Motivators," there are the stories of individuals who changed the way we think about organizing and managing—for instance, read the story of Lillian M. Gilbreth, who pioneered the path for women in business and earned the title "First Lady of Management."

Another way to use this book is to consider it not as a collection of histories of notable individuals but as an account of evolution, from the growth of enterprise to ideas about its organization and management. The people included here were very much like us, seeking to solve the problems they faced in their space of time. The lessons they learned can give us a vision, not of the past, but of the present. We think of steam locomotives and the telegraph as museum pieces, forgetting that they were as revolutionary to our forebears as modern technology is to us. Understanding the past may help us deal with the technology-related issues of today, and perhaps can even help us envision what our children and grandchildren will need to deal with when what we think of as modern is in turn superseded.

Taken as a whole, there is no single theme to this book; rather, it is a narrative with multiple themes as the story of American business enterprise unfolds. Beginning with a selection of inventors, we see how the process of invention and innovation changes the way we live, creates entirely new industries, and must be continuous as the competitive environment changes. Makers are those who change ideas into products for the marketplace—an evolutionary process that accompanies the shift from small- to large-scale manufacturing and then to the assembly line. Sellers take those products to market and allow us to see the sales and distribution innovations that have enabled modern consumers to live better than the monarchs of centuries before. Inventors, makers, and sellers need the movers, those who create the time and place utility; and all need the communicators, who connect the parts into a whole.

Management is an ancient practice; it had its place (and still does) in governmental, religious, military, and other types of early organizations. Yet none of these grew to the scale and scope of modern business enterprise, which needs not only to adapt ever-changing economic, social, and political forces but also to do this in a profitable fashion. So the second part of the story is about early thinkers who studied the changing nature of work and sought to make it possible for people to work more intelligently rather than just to work harder. Business enterprise succeeds only as well as its efforts are guided—and in Billy Durant and Alfred P. Sloan Jr., for example, we can see how organization, or the lack of it, spells success or failure. When we examine motivators and leaders, we see how different people view the vital activities of business and how varying ways of thinking move us in different directions. The stories of the quality seekers and of Peter Drucker remind us once more how important it is to ask the right questions and separate the trivial problems from the major ones.

The end of our story brings us back to the beginning, the importance of invention and innovation in a never steady world. Read as you like, and we hope you like what you read.

Part I

BUILDING AMERICAN
BUSINESS ENTERPRISE

1

INVENTORS

President George Washington's first annual message to Congress was given in Philadelphia, Pennsylvania, in 1790. In a plea for providing for the common defense, he said, "To be prepared for war is one of the most effectual means of preserving peace." America not only should be armed but also "should promote such manufactures, as tend to render them independent of others for essentials, particularly for military, supplies." Americans should search for inventions abroad as well as be encouraged to make "exertions of skill and genius in producing them at home . . . for there is nothing which can better serve your patronage than the promotion of science and literature. Knowledge is in every country the surest basis of public happiness." This statement, two centuries old, is as relevant to the knowledge-based society of today as it was back then.

The result of the president's plea was the nation's first patent law, passed in 1790, under the constitutional provisions of Article I, Section 8, which gave Congress the power to impose and collect taxes, borrow money, coin currency, fix standards of weights and measures, punish counterfeiters, issue patents, and "regulate commerce with foreign nations and among the several states." The first patent was issued July 31, 1790, to protect the inventor for fourteen years. Copyrights were also provided for literary and artistic works, and a 1793 Patent Law was passed to prescribe the formalities of obtaining a patent or copyright, to define the inventor's rights, and to establish a $30 filing fee.

The intent of the president and Congress in encouraging industry and the arts was clear—to establish a national economy that could be independent from its former colonial master, Britain. Efforts to develop manufactures in the colonies were discouraged by Britain, for they posed a dangerous threat to Britain's early factories. Cotton, wool, flax, and other raw materials could be sent to Britain, but textiles from these materials could not be manufactured in the United States, except for personal consumption. Britain also sought to prevent colonial industrial development by prohibiting American imports of manufacturing equipment and the emigration of skilled labor from Great Britain. Before independence the United States exported raw materials and imported manufactured goods; as a new nation, its policy was to encourage independence through invention as well as legislation.

Invention was essential for America to begin its own industrial revolution. The inventors represented here reflect a small part of the ingenuity thriving in America in the late eighteenth and nineteenth centuries. We begin with Eli Whitney, whose success transformed an industry and became symbolic of a new manufacturing age. In Thomas Edison we will see the single most creative genius in U.S. history; his ideas created entirely new industries. Together, Whitney and Edison represent the importance of the creation of knowledge through invention and innovation and demonstrate how the advancement of knowledge influences the products and services we enjoy and how we work and live.

ELI WHITNEY

Eli Whitney's America was a nation just recently emerging from its colonial status, and "Yankee ingenuity" would prove essential for it to move from an agrarian society to an industrial one. Whitney was still in college when America's first census, in 1790, showed a total population of 3,231,533, with over 90 percent of these people engaged in agriculture. The largest city was New York, with a population of 33,131; next came Philadelphia, with 28,522 persons, and then Boston, with a population of 18,300. Together, the three largest U.S. cities had a population that could comfortably be seated in a modern football stadium.

Born December 8, 1765, in Westborough, Massachusetts, Eli Whitney Jr. was the eldest of Eli and Elizabeth Whitney's four children. Eli's father had a small workshop on their farm, containing basic tools and a lathe for turning chair legs and the younger Whitney learned how to use these tools. He made and repaired violins and demonstrated his entrepreneurial tendencies early. During the Revolutionary War, he discovered that nails brought a high price and talked his father into letting him use the workshop to make nails for resale. After the war, when nails were no longer in such great demand, he noticed that women had started using long pins to keep their hats on their heads and changed his product line to make hat pins.

He aspired to a higher education, but limited family finances delayed his entry into Yale College until 1789, when he was twenty-four years old. His father pledged $1,000 for the four years at Yale, but Eli had to make up the balance of some $600 by tutoring others. At the time, Yale's curriculum provided a classical education, designed to create gentlemen for politics, the ministry, or law, but Eli was not drawn to any of these fields. Unemployed upon graduation in 1792, he was able to gain a tutor's position in the South and traveled to Savannah, Georgia, with another Yale alumnus, Phineas Miller.

Miller was the manager of the estate of the late Nathanael Greene, who was one of Washington's most trusted generals during the Revolutionary War. When Whitney's tutoring job did not develop as expected, Miller recommended him to Nathanael's widow, Catherine Greene, as a person of both mechanical ability and social graces, who would be a valuable addition to the Greene plantation. Whitney soon fell in love with the older woman, who exuded a love of life and chided the dour Whitney for not enjoying the "few fleeting years which any can calculate upon." Whitney's love was unrequited; Catherine married Phineas Miller in 1796. Whitney did not recover from this easily and did not marry until he was fifty-one, a few years after Catherine's death, but she was one of his inspirations as well as a financial backer.

The Cotton Engine

When Whitney arrived in Savannah in 1792, the main crops in the South were tobacco, which quickly exhausted the fertility of the soil, and rice, a labor-intensive grain. The cotton grown in the South had a small green seed surrounded by short fibers, and the two had to be separated by hand with great difficulty. Long-staple cotton grew in the Caribbean; its fibers and black seed were more easily separated, but less land was available for cultivation there. In England, advances in textile-making technology and the use of water-powered looms created a booming market for cotton. Woolen, silk, and linen products had their disadvantages but were more widely used because cotton production was a labor-intensive, tedious process.

One day, when other plantation owners were visiting Catherine Greene, the conversation turned to the difficulties they were having with making cotton profitable for market because of the difficulty of separating the seed from the cotton and cleaning it. Mrs. Greene referred the matter to Eli Whitney, who confessed to having seen neither cotton nor cotton seed in his life. She was sure that Eli could make a machine to separate the cotton from the seed, and urged him to do so. Eli went to Savannah and searched among warehouses and boats until he found a small parcel of cotton, which was out of season at the time, and began busying himself with the project. According to legend, the inspiration for his machine came after seeing a cat extend its claws through a wire fence to catch a chicken, only to find itself with claws full of feathers. Whitney soon emerged with a small prototype of his cotton gin (*gin* being short for *engine*).

Whitney's cotton gin was a model of simplicity; this would prove to be both a boon and his downfall. The machine consisted of a revolving drum covered with wire teeth that reached through the slats of the bin of cotton and pulled the fiber away from the seed. The fiber could be easily combed from the drum, and Whitney boasted that one person could clean ten times as much cotton as before; if the engine was turned by water or horsepower, the output was fifty times as much. And, Whitney added, no one would be thrown out of work. This tremendous increase in productivity due to mechanization eased the job of the worker, made cotton more profitable to grow and market, and made cotton goods more abundant and cheaper in the marketplace.

Whitney then constructed a larger model based on his prototype, and Mrs. Greene invited others to see the wonderful invention of her houseguest. The demonstration model worked to perfection, creating excitement about this fantastic new device. Whitney, the inventor, now had a new problem—he needed capital to start production and he needed a patent. The capital came from Catherine Greene and Phineas Miller, creating the partnership of Miller and Whitney, with capital getting top billing. Whitney headed for the nation's capital, Philadelphia, where he paid his

$30 and applied for a patent with Secretary of State Thomas Jefferson on June 20, 1793.

Feeling secure now that he had his patent, Whitney headed for New Haven, Connecticut, where he felt he could find the skilled workers who could make his gin in sufficient quantities to meet the growing demand. The problems Whitney encountered in going from a prototype to full-scale production would have tested Job—skilled labor was in short supply; there were no machine tools to make the components; in 1794 epidemics of scarlet fever and yellow fever swept New Haven; and in 1795 his New Haven Works burned, destroying raw materials, tools, machines, and half-finished gins. While he could do nothing personally about the labor shortage, the epidemics, and the fire, his ingenuity solved some of the other problems; by inventing lathes to shape the metal and tools to draw, cut, and bend the wires, he not only aided his own enterprise but also became one of the founders of the machine tool industry, which would be critical for future industrial development.

While Whitney was struggling in New Haven, Phineas Miller developed a sales strategy that would turn out to be a disaster. Mulberry Grove, the Greene plantation—its name was taken from their abortive attempt to cultivate mulberry trees to feed silkworms—was in dire financial straits and Miller needed cash. Rather than licensing the gin, Miller offered to place Miller and Whitney gins in various cotton-growing locales, and gin any quantity of green seed cotton on the basis of two-fifths pound for every one pound of cotton cleaned. Miller was asking for 40 percent of the finished good, taking even more of the growers' profit. This was not breaking precedent, since a percentage of output, although a lesser one, had been taken by millers of corn, wheat, and other grains for some time.

The reaction of their customers was an outcry about monopoly, along with a number of unprintable comments. Some who had seen the demonstration of the Whitney cotton gin realized the simplicity of its design and figured out that they could avoid paying anything to Miller by developing copies and variations of the machine. By 1797 there were at least three hundred machines that ginned cotton but were not under the Whitney patent. Since Whitney experienced great difficulty in getting production started, and Miller's sales strategy had such negative results, the Miller and Whitney firm was in trouble. When they sued for patent infringment, the cost was typically more than the award—the first settlement on which they actually received some money came in 1806, four years after the death of Phineas

Miller. Whitney lost more money than he gained with his invention, and as early as 1797 he was $4,000 in debt.

The cotton gin had consequences that were significantly more far-reaching than the financial situation of Phineas Miller and Eli Whitney, of course. The gin made cotton profitable in the South, and it also made slavery profitable. Slavery had existed in the colonies as early as 1619 in Jamestown, Virginia, and while imports of slaves were outlawed in 1808, laws rarely improve morality. By 1860, nearly one in three persons in the South was a slave, and it would take the bloodbath of the Civil War to break the bonds of slavery. Cotton was king in the South because of the cotton gin—and it was also one of the factors that made slavery a tragic blot on the nation's history.

Driven by curiosity and necessity, inventors rarely see the social consequences of their inventions, and Whitney did not live to see how the gin would influence the course of national events. By the time he died, however, cotton had become one of the leading exports for the United States and had been responsible for the creation of hundreds of mills employing hundreds of thousands of workers in New England, Britain, and elsewhere. Whitney never profited from his invention or from its contribution to the availability of an abundant supply of inexpensive cotton products.

A Twist of Fate

Although Whitney is best remembered for his cotton gin, his most lasting gift to the future arose out of his failure. Whitney's indebtedness required that he find work to keep his New Haven plant open, continue his legal battles, and pay his debts. At the time, the federal government still feared the return of the British, and possibly danger from postrevolutionary France; they sorely needed arms, and this situation provided an opportunity for Whitney. He was not a gunsmith but thought that he could design machine tools to make guns. He believed he could

> form the tools so that the tools themselves shall fashion the work and give to every part its just proportion—which when once accomplished will give expedition, uniformity, and exactness to the whole.
>
> If each . . . workman must form . . . every part according to his own fancy & regulate the size & proportion by his own Eye or even by a measure, I should have as many varieties as I have . . . part[s]. . . .
>
> In short, the tools which I contemplate are similar to an engraving on copper plate from which may be taken a great number of impressions perceptibly alike.[1]

In the United States prior to this time, muskets were crafted individually by gunsmiths in the federal arsenals at Springfield, Massachusetts, and Harpers Ferry, Virginia (now West Virginia). If a musket part broke, it could be replaced only by a remanufacture of that particular part, meaning that a defective weapon could not be fixed easily. Whitney's idea was to make the parts of the muskets, bayonets, and ramrods identical so they would fit any gun he made.

Whether or not this was an original idea of Whitney's is a matter of debate. Some credit him with the concept of manufacture by interchangeable parts that enabled what came to be known as the "American system of manufactures" and still later as the basis of modern mass production. Doubts have been raised about this, however, since some ships built in Renaissance Venice had interchangeable bows, rudders, and so on. Some European arms makers had made guns by this method also.[2] As early as 1790 a Frenchman, H. Blanc, demonstrated arms making by interchangeable parts, and Thomas Jefferson had witnessed a demonstration of this idea. What is unknown is whether this idea reached Whitney or not. We know that some English mechanics were tinkering with uniform-parts manufacture; Simeon North, Whitney's fellow Yankee, was also using this idea, and Captain John H. Hall of the Harper's Ferry armory was experimenting with uniform parts, too. Even if Whitney did not invent interchangeable-parts manufacturing, he took it further than any other person of his time and made an important breakthrough in the use of machine tools.

Whitney's Yale connections paid off once more—the secretary of the treasury, Oliver Wolcott, was an alumnus and had confidence that Whitney could deliver even though he had never before made firearms. Whitney received a federal contract to deliver ten thousand stand of muskets (a "stand" was one musket complete with ramrod and bayonet) at a price of $13.40 each, or $134,000 over a two-year period. With a $5,000 advance Whitney set forth to make four thousand the first year and six thousand the following year.

As in making the cotton gin, Whitney had to design and make the machine tools needed to make muskets. He invented, but never patented, a drilling machine, a boring machine, and a machine to make screws. The machines were water-powered, and Whitney devoted so much time and effort to building the tools and connecting them to the power source that he ran constantly behind in his production schedule.

It was three years before he could deliver five hundred muskets, and he appealed to the government for more time to complete his contract and for more monetary support: "I find that my personal attention and oversight are more constantly and essentially necessary to every branch of the work, than I apprehended. Mankind, generally, are not to be depended on, and the best workmen I can find are incapable of directing. Indeed, there is no branch of the work than can proceed well, scarcely for a single hour, unless I am present."[3] The government inspector at Whitney's site was Captain Decius Wadsworth, a Yale classmate of Phineas Miller, and he urged Wolcott to continue to advance funds to Whitney. Between 1801 and 1805 he delivered 4,500 muskets. With more and more advances of money, Whitney continued to deliver: fifteen hundred muskets in 1806, two thousand in 1807, and another fifteen hundred in 1808, some ten years after the initial contract. The nation was fortunate that Napoleon had his eye on Russia and that there was no urgent need for muskets until the 1812 War with Britain.

Eli Whitney was one among others who were advancing the concept of manufacture by interchangeable parts. Samuel Colt's revolver was made in Whitney's factory before Colt opened his Hartford, Connecticut, factory. Uniform-parts manufacture advanced into products such as clocks and watches, locks, sewing machines, pianos, and agricultural equipment. Whitney's contribution to the development of the machine tool industry was as great, if not greater, than that of any other person.

After Eli Whitney's death, on January 8, 1825, at age fifty-nine, the firm continued under the leadership of Eli Whitney Jr. and others until it was acquired by Winchester Arms in 1888. Whitney died a financial success, but that was due largely to wise investments rather than from inventing the cotton gin or making muskets.

It was an ironic twist of fate that his cotton gin made slavery profitable while his techniques of making muskets in the northern federal arsenals aided the war effort to abolish that practice. History's lesson is that inventions can be both a nemesis and a boon.

THOMAS ALVA EDISON

When Thomas A. Edison was born in Milan, Ohio, on February 11, 1847, homes and offices were lighted by gas, kerosene, or candles; correspondence was copied on James Watt's 1778 patented "copying-press" that transferred impressions from the ink on an original to another piece of thin paper; words spoken or songs sung could not be recorded for future reproduction; the size of an audience was limited by the power of the orator's lungs; the daguerreotype method of capturing images on chemically sensitized plates was only eight years old; and wood and coal created the steam that powered locomotives on America's young railroads. By the time of his death, over eight decades later, Thomas Edison had changed all of these practices and became the world's most practical and prolific inventor.

Samuel and Nancy Elliott Edison moved their family to Port Huron, Michigan, where Thomas was duly enrolled in the public schools. He disliked school and reported to his mother that he had overheard his teacher tell another that the young Edison was "addled" and any efforts to teach him would be wasted. She promptly withdrew him from the public school and he received his education at home. The too-addled-to-educate story may be true—or it may have been an inventive dodge by the young Edison to escape the classroom, because he had a strong dislike for mathematics or anything else that was not practical.

When he was fifteen Edison obtained a job on the Port Huron–to–Detroit line of Michigan's Grand Trunk Railroad, selling newspapers, books, magazines, fruits, candies, and nuts. In one of the old baggage cars he found a printing press, which he used to publish his own paper, the *Weekly Herald*, setting the type while the train was motionless in the station and printing while the train was moving. Edison's newspaper was printed on both sides of a single sheet of paper that was folded in half, and included births, marriages, and deaths that might interest his readers. For 3¢ each five hundred subscribers and another two hundred or so passengers on the train could catch up on the news and read what was probably the first newspaper ever printed on a moving train.

Edison also used the old baggage car as a laboratory to experiment with chemicals and telegraph equipment. When the train hit a large bump one day, a jar of phosphorus crashed to the floor and started a fire. While Edison was trying to extinguish the fire, the conductor entered the car, put the fire out, and threw Edison out at the next station, along with all of the lab apparatus and the printing press.

The story is often told that the train conductor was so infuriated at Edison that he boxed the boy's ears, causing him to become partially but permanently deaf in his right ear. Edison said that his hearing loss came later, when a train was pulling away from the station and he ran to jump on the last car. He did not quite make it and someone grabbed him and pulled him into the car by his ears. Edison said that when this happened he heard a crack in his ear, and from that day on he was always hard of hearing; but he did not feel badly toward the ear grabber, because he had surely saved Edison's life. In later life Edison's hearing loss would be somewhat of a handicap, but it never limited his daring.

Edison's first promotion has the ring of a Horatio Alger story. At the Mount Clemens station two rail cars came loose, and Edison saw a boy on the tracks in the cars' path. He threw down the armload of newspapers he was carrying and whisked the small boy to safety just in time. The son's father was the station agent, J. W. MacKenzie, who wanted to repay Edison in some way. Asked if he would be interested in learning telegraphy, Edison took MacKenzie up on his offer. Although he became an expert telegrapher, he bounced from job to job because of his habit of staying up nights to experiment, which caused him to doze on duty during the day—a very undesirable characteristic for that task.

In 1868 Edison took out his first patent, for an "electrographic vote-recording machine" to be used in the House of Representatives. When he exhibited the machine, the members were amazed by his fine work and ability but told him they did not want it and would not use it. Edison felt it was a perfect instrument, and the time it saved could be spent counting votes and filibustering and in carrying out other political maneuvers to rally votes or defeat legislation. Edison vowed from then on he would never again invent anything that was neither practical nor marketable.

His next invention was a universal stock ticker, which he sold to the Gold Indicator Company for $40,000. With this money, Edison now had the resources to set up a laboratory in which to conduct experiments and invent useful apparatuses.

The Wizard of Menlo Park

Edison was called the "Wizard of Menlo Park," but he debunked that idea with his much-quoted line "Genius is ninety-nine percent perspiration and one percent inspiration."[4] His process of invention was characterized by repeated trial and error, experiment after experiment, until these studies led to those flashes of insight we call inspiration. His most prolific years were from 1876 to 1887. At his Menlo Park, New Jersey, laboratory he would employ as many as fifty assistants, some of whom would later achieve high positions in the electric power generation and distribution industry, but in every project Edison was the one who inspired and drove it to completion.

His experience and expertise in telegraphy led to a contract with Western Union. He made numerous advances in this field, the most notable being the quadraplex system, which enabled four messages to be sent simultaneously in each direction over the main line. With the early Morse system, one could either receive or send; later Joseph Stearns created a duplex system for sending two messages simultaneously. Edison's advancement doubled the message-carrying capacity of Western Union without requiring an increase in the number of telegraph lines.

When Western Union recognized that Alexander Graham Bell's telephone was a competitive threat, they asked Edison to make improvements in the "speaking telegraph." How could a partially deaf man make improvements in a speaking/listening instrument? Edison held a metal plate between his teeth and connected this plate by wires to the telephone apparatus—in short, he used bone conduction to "hear" and thereby overcome his handicap. He developed a carbon-based microphone transmitter that could send and receive voice messages and was better than Bell's magneto system. Edison's microphone transmitter could also be used for public speaking, and as a result orators were no longer judged by lung capacity.

To his transmitter Edison eventually added an induction coil, which enabled long-distance telephony—in 1878 an Edison device connected New York and Philadelphia, a distance in excess of 100 miles, setting a record for long-distance service. Despite Edison's achievement, Bell was able to block those patents for fifteen years by buying Emile Berliner's carbon-based transmitter, which preceded Edison's. Edison's device was superior, but no contested patent was safe until all legal avenues had been pursued. In 1892 a federal court ruled Edison's patent valid, but by that time Western Union had sold its telephone interest and American Telephone and Telegraph had achieved a substantial market position.

Edison's work habits were legendary; he could work continuously as long as he wished and fall asleep whenever he desired. He could awaken completely refreshed after a few hours of sleep and work tirelessly in his lab until a task was done. He asked the same of his assistants, driving them relentlessly, working them from 7:00 A.M. until late, day after day. These habits played havoc with Edison's family and the families of his employees, but his compulsive drive to achieve was, as he himself noted, 99 percent of his success.

His most daringly imaginative and inspired invention was the phonograph, which, unlike his improvements of the telegraph and the telephone, had no predecessors. The phonograph (the word is from the Greek for "sound writing") grew out of Edison's insight that if the telephone could transmit sound impulses and then reproduce them in the listener's ear, why not transmit the sound to a device that would record, store, and reproduce these impulses? Edison designed and sketched such a device in 1877 and gave it to John Kruesi, one of his assistants, to build. The design was a stylus that etched sound impulses on a tinfoil covered cylinder. Two diaphragms, one for recording and one for reproduction, were used for this hand-cranked "talking machine." Edison was shocked when the system worked on its first trial: "I was never so taken aback in my life. I was always afraid of things that worked the first time."[5] His disbelief was so great that he put the phonograph aside and would not work on it until ten years later.

Edison's work in electricity was more innovation than inspiration. The force of electricity was known in ancient times, and in legend it was the Norse god Thor who loosed the thunder and lightning that sent Benjamin Franklin to go fly a kite. In the early nineteenth century the British scientist Sir Humphry Davy demonstrated two important principles: that a two-thousand-cell battery could be used to run an electric current through a small gap between two carbon rods, creating an arc of light, and that electricity had the ability to produce incandescence in substances. In 1831 Michael Faraday created a dynamo that converted mechanical energy into electrical energy as a conductor was rotated through a magnetic field. In the United States, Charles F. Brush invented an arc light, and two Philadelphia high-school science teachers, Elihu Thomson and Edwin J. Houston, developed a dynamo. The arc light was suitable for large projects such as street lighting (as an alternative to gaslight) and for providing light for erecting the Statue of Liberty in 1886.

A practical application of Davy's principle of incandescence, however, had not been realized despite numerous attempts in Europe, England, and the United States. It was difficult to create a proper vacuum within the globe, and the wick that Edison would later call the "filament" either did not glow or burned out quickly. Edison was fascinated by the work of Werner Siemens, Sir Joseph Wilson, Thomson and Houston, Brush, and others who were laying the foundations of the electric industry.

In 1878, Edison launched his experiments with financing from J. P. Morgan, his partner Eggisto Fabbri, William H. Vanderbilt, Henry Villard, and others. The Edison Electric Light Company, capitalized at $300,000 but with only $50,000 cash up front, was a low-risk investment for Edison's financiers but held the possibility of a high payout. Over a period of fourteen months

Edison solved the problem that had plagued others for years. The bottleneck of incandescence involved stepping down the high voltage that could be generated, in essence dividing it into smaller bits for home and office use. Where others had concentrated on low resistance and high voltage, Edison applied an interpretation of Ohm's law to develop a light with high resistance relative to the voltage—that is, a light that used less current to produce a glow.

He worked on pumps to evacuate more air from the bulb and tested some sixteen hundred materials for the filament—including platinum, which, if it had succeeded, would have produced a very expensive light bulb. A carbonized cotton thread filament burned 13.5 hours in 1879, and with improvements Edison increased this to 300 hours. Later cotton was replaced by carbonized bamboo, which burned 1,200 hours.

When Edison demonstrated his electric lamp at Menlo Park he created a panic on the London and New York stock exchanges as the value of gaslight companies' shares plummeted. Edison Electric Light Company shares rose to $3,500; Edison had twenty-five hundred shares and became a multimillionaire, at least on the value of his shares. Though he did not invent the electric light, he was the first to provide a practical and economical light for use in workshops, offices, and homes. But he had a problem—his light bulb would be of little use without a system to generate and distribute electricity and all of the components to accompany the bulb.

The Inventor Turns Manufacturer

Wall Street was skeptical that Edison could switch his efforts from inventing to manufacturing because he had already demonstrated his carelessness in handling financial matters. His chief financial officer, Samuel Insull, was also poor at managing cash flow. In response, Edison sold most of his electric light company shares to form the United Edison Manufacturing Company. Manufacturing was to be done in New York City, but a strike of union workers closed the plant. Edison did not care for unions and accepted an offer of land and tax concessions from the city of Schenectady, New York, to move his operations there; when the union workers decided to return to work they found that the Goerck Street building in New York City was empty.

In Schenectady Edison set out to manufacture bulbs, sockets, switches, meters, wires, and other components of a lighting system as well as to develop the means to establish power stations that would generate and distribute electric lighting. He recognized early that each light needed to operate independently, on parallel circuits; an agent from a gas lighting company once tried to sabotage a Menlo Park demonstration by short circuiting some bulbs but was foiled by Edison's parallel wiring. Edison steadily decreased the bulb's price to stimulate demand: from 70¢ each in 1881 to 34¢ in 1884, with the goal of 25¢ per bulb.

In September 1882 in New York City the switch was pulled at the Pearl Street generating station's one dynamo to turn on 400 lamps for 85 customers. At the Broad Street offices of Drexel, Morgan and Company, Edison flipped the switch that lit an array of 106 lamps. Spectacular as this appeared, only a small area of the city was lighted—to expand Edison's system, a number of generating stations would need to be built, since his generator could operate effectively over only a two-mile radius. Edison's generator used a commutator, a device for reversing the direction of an electrical current, to convert alternating current (AC) into unidirectional current, or direct current (DC). Operating at a low constant voltage of 110 to 220 volts, Edison argued that DC was safer than AC. He was in good company—noted scientists such as Elihu Thomson, Lord Kelvin, and Werner Siemens agreed that alternating current was far too dangerous for public distribution.

A different position was taken by George Westinghouse Jr., who had become financially successful inventing the air brake and signaling devices for the railroads and who, like Edison, was an inventor with no formal scientific training. He saw disadvantages in Edison's DC system and advocated eliminating the commutator to generate an alternating current of high voltage that could be sent over long distances. Then a transformer would step down the high voltage at distribution points. (The transformer could also step up the voltage for longer-distance transmission.)

As proof of the dangers of AC, Edison pointed out that New York State law permitted the death penalty by electrocution and this was done by the high voltage of alternating current. Edison's publicity of this made Westinghouse's name a synonym for electrocution in New York.

For all of his genius in many matters, Edison would never admit that AC was better. Westinghouse would win the war of the currents, but it is an irony of history that many modern electric utilities carry Edison's name—for example, Commonwealth Edison, Ohio Edison, Detroit Edison, Consolidated Edison, and in Britain, Edison and Swan United Electric Company, Ltd. But the unkindest cut of all was in manufacturing, where the Edison Electric Light Company was reorganized as Edison General Electric by

Henry Villard, then again in 1892 by J. P. Morgan as General Electric —with Edison's name removed from the company he created. Edison was on GE's board of directors but attended only one meeting; he continued to receive royalties on his patents, but he sold all of his GE stock.

The Edison Effect

Edison's first patent was issued in 1868 and his last in 1926, when he was eighty years old—over sixteen hundred patents, or one for every eleven days of his working life.[6] Many of these patents redirected industries, created new fields of research, or inspired others to advance knowledge. A few examples illustrate his inventiveness and impact:

- After ten years he returned to his phonograph, but others, such as Columbia Records and the Victor Talking Machine Company, had moved ahead by that time. Victor, based on Emile Berliner's gramophone of 1887, had seen the potential for music and recorded Enrico Caruso's voice for posterity. Edison had let the recording industry pass him by.
- The carbon transmitter for Edison's telephone became a microphone.
- The waxed cylinders and disks of the phonograph paved the way for the dictaphone.
- Eadweard Muybridge had made photos of galloping horses by a series of cameras arranged around a racetrack with the shutter for each camera tripped by the first horse that passed by. Aided by George Eastman's celluloid film, Edison saw the possibility of one stationary camera making the picture while the film moved. He never invented a projector, however; his Kinetoscope was a peep-show-type box that was first publicly demonstrated on New York City's lower Broadway in 1894 with a ninety-second film. One memorable Edison film was of the great boxer "Gentleman Jim" Corbett knocking out an unknown fighter in ninety seconds (an achievement that has often been repeated by other fighters on pay-per-view in recent years). With another person's projector, the first motion picture was *The Record of a Sneeze*; later came Edison's fourteen-minute *The Great Train Robbery*.

    Edison did not bother to patent his motion picture camera because of the $150 filing fee: "It isn't worth it," he observed.

- Electric locomotives, originally battery-powered, and the current-supplying third rail would form the basis for interurban transport.
- Edison invented a device for "multiplying letters," which he sold to A. B. Dick of Chicago and which became known as the mimeograph machine.
- For ten years Edison worked without success on an electric automobile that he hoped would be powered by a storage battery. Based upon his failure he advised a young Detroit Edison employee, Henry Ford, to focus his attention on the internal combustion engine.
- The "grasshopper telegraph," a method to send and receive messages from a moving train. Metal strips to reflect electric impulses were to be mounted on railroad cars and telegraph poles, and messages would be sent and received via wire from the nearest telegraph station. (Edison would have been quite comfortable with the idea of cellular phones!)
- He anticipated sonar with a phonograph diaphragm extended from shipboard into the water to pick up underwater sounds. Later, Lee De Forest and GE's labs would extend and refine Edison's idea.
- Edison was able to demonstrate that electrical current could be conducted in a near vacuum—a phenomenon that other scientists thought was impossible, so they called it the "Edison effect." Edison saw no practical use for this, so he *gave* the patent rights to Guglielmo Marconi. From Marconi and Lee De Forest came the vacuum tube and radio-telephony—the "Edison effect" opened the electronic age and all that would follow. Edison later remarked: "In experimenting I find a good many things I never looked for." Serendipity was one of his long suits.

By the time of his death, on October 18, 1931, in West Orange, New Jersey, Edison had influenced the development of numerous corporate research laboratories, including Bell Labs, DuPont, and General Electric. Edison would be followed by a few individual wizards of invention, such as Edwin Land, who developed the Polaroid camera, but none would ever rival the wizard of Menlo Park.

2

MAKERS

The individuals chosen as "makers," Cyrus McCormick, Andrew Carnegie, and Henry Ford, represent the development of manufacturing in America. These individuals personify the transition from labor-intensive shop production to large-scale factory production and eventually manufacture by an assembly line. McCormick gradually developed his reaper company into an international large-scale manufacturing firm. Carnegie applied the lessons of railroad management to developing the first fully integrated firm in the steel industry. Henry Ford and his associates at Ford Motor company progressed from a stationary method of production to a moving line that opened a new era in manufacturing. Together, these representatives provide a panorama of the changing scene of early American manufacturing.

CYRUS H. MCCORMICK

The Great Exhibition of the Industries of All Nations was staged in London in 1851. Encouraged by British scientists for the advancement of knowledge, it received the backing of Prince Albert, consort to Queen Victoria. It was opposed by some British manufacturers, however, who feared that the visiting foreigners would pirate trade secrets from them. The exhibition was in the specially built Crystal Palace, a structure of iron covered by 896,000 square feet of glass and occupying eighteen acres in Hyde Park. It was truly an international trade show, perhaps the first in history to attract exhibits from so many countries. Some four million visitors (more than the population of greater London at the time) were admitted during the 140 days of the exhibition to see hundreds of products from numerous nations. There were lace-making machines and furniture from France, precious metals and jewelry from the East India Company, pottery from Josiah Wedgwood, minerals and birch-bark canoes from Canada, wax models of fruit and tropical flowers from Trinidad, and marble from Greece; one of the more unique items was a physician's walking stick that contained an enema and assorted test tubes. The Americans were represented by such items as Bigelow's power carpet looms, Day and Newell's locks designed by Alfred C. Hobbs, the Sharps rifle of Robbins and Lawrence, a sewing machine by Isaac Singer, and another by Elias Howe. The Duke of Wellington praised the repeating pistols of Samuel Colt, probably wishing he had had some of those at Waterloo instead of single-shot muzzle loaders.

Each class of exhibition item had a panel of jurors to judge the relative merits of each and to pass out medals. The grain reapers were taken to the fields for the ultimate test of practicality: cutting grain. There were two British and two American models; the U.S. competitors were Obed Hussey and Cyrus McCormick. Hussey and McCormick were longtime rivals, as we will see, and each had won his share of contests in the past. On this test day, however, the Hussey machine clogged frequently and left uncut grain, while McCormick's reaper performed admirably. The British models were not competitive, and so the grand prize went to McCormick, who would make the most of this in his sales pitches in later years.

Visitors and the London press heaped praise on the Americans' skill in the mechanical arts. The American products were so successful at the 1851 exhibition that these firms began to have visions of going international. McCormick licensed the making of reapers in Essex and Vienna, Singer had branches in Paris and Glasgow, Hobbs opened a British office and factory, and Samuel Colt's armory on the banks of the Thames flew both Old Glory and the Union Jack. The Americans did not steal the British trade secrets; they began to steal their markets.

McCormick's Life and Legend

Cyrus Hall McCormick was born on February 15, 1809, the son of Robert and Mary Ann Hall McCormick, on a farm in Rockbridge County, Virginia.

Cyrus had limited formal education and most of his learning came in the workshop of his father, who was a tinkerer, mechanic, and inventor. Robert McCormick invented and held patents on a hydraulic machine, a threshing machine, a grist mill, and a blacksmith's bellows, and had been trying to perfect a grain reaper since 1809. The idea of a machine to reap grain was as old as Roman times and numerous individuals in the United States and elsewhere were working on this idea independently of each other. Cyrus grew up in this environment of inventiveness and assisted his father in various projects, including a plow to be used on hillsides.

Most authorities credit Cyrus McCormick with the invention of the reaper, but that is in doubt and may be only legend. Robert McCormick is considered by some, including Cyrus's brother, Leander McCormick, as the true inventor. According to Cyrus, he himself invented the reaper in 1831 but did not patent it because he wished to perfect it. The other side of the story is that Robert McCormick invented the reaper but became discouraged and abandoned the project; Cyrus added some minor features to his father's model and took credit for the invention.[1]

Cyrus, like his father, did not rush to the patent office. In 1834, while reading *Mechanics' Magazine*, Cyrus learned that Obed Hussey of Ohio had invented and patented a reaper on December 31, 1833. Indignantly Cyrus wrote the editor, claiming that he had invented such a machine in 1831 and that Hussey had infringed on his rights.

McCormick claimed that his reaper was different from Hussey's, and applied for a patent on June 21, 1834. Of all patents filed that year. McCormick's would have the most lasting impact. Examples of other patents of 1834 provide an insight into American industry of that time: Charles Goodyear patented "faucets for molasses gates"; James Sellers patented woven wire and frames for window coverings; Henry Blair, described as a "colored man," patented a "seeding corn planter;" Edwin Chaffee received one for making boots and shoes from India rubber; M. W. Baldwin took out a patent for a steam engine, locomotive, and cars; and John Cochran got one for a rotating-cylinder multichambered cannon.[2]

Cyrus McCormick's reaper had all of the elements that would characterize a modern one: a side-pull to allow the horses to walk outside the cutting path, a reciprocating cutting bar with guards, a divider at the end of the bar to separate the standing stalks, a reel to bring the stalks to the cutter (Hussey's patent did not have this feature), a platform for the cut stalks, and a main drive wheel. The McCormicks' reaper was a technological leap, for previously grain was cut by workers wielding a scythe, who were accompanied by binders, other workers who bound the grain into sheaves, and shockers, who stacked the sheaves to await further curing and subsequent threshing. With this labor-intensive method one reaper and two or three binders and shockers could harvest two acres of grain per day. The earlier McCormick reapers could cut ten acres a day but the one patented in 1834 could cut twenty acres a day. Less labor was required, less grain was knocked loose to rot on the ground, and productivity was increased tenfold. Since grain was a staple for humans everywhere as well as feed for animals, the reaper would influence forever how people would live.

Cyrus McCormick was diverted from a path to fame and fortune after patenting the reaper because he and Robert McCormick decided in 1836 to start an iron foundry. At the time there were many iron foundries, but their operations were small with no economies of scale, and the market was limited and geographically dispersed. Robert and Cyrus entered with little capital, were hit hard by a financial crisis in 1837, had difficulty in transporting raw materials in and finished goods out, and finally failed in the iron business. After Robert McCormick's death in 1846, Cyrus returned to the reaper and resumed his war with Obed Hussey.

Hussey was a one-eyed one-time New England whaler and tinkerer who finally set up a factory to manufacture reapers in Cincinnati, Ohio. The Hussey and McCormick reapers were near equals in technology and performance, but McCormick was a farmer himself and appeared to understand his customers better than Hussey, who never achieved that same customer orientation nor the same prowess in manufacturing. Hussey was operating in the Ohio River Valley, where agricultural activities were increasing and where the river provided an inexpensive means of transporting to market. McCormick, on the other hand, was in Virginia and relatively isolated from the fastest-growing agricultural region in America. Some McCormick reapers were being bought in what was considered at the time to be the West, and his travels to those areas convinced him that he needed to relocate his operations. His choice of a site would be a boon to him, the farmers, and his chosen city.

Chicago

McCormick was always mindful of his health, and why he chose to relocate to blustery and cold Chicago remains a mystery. When he arrived in 1848 to set up his business, Chicago had some seventeen thousand inhabitants, smallpox and cholera epidemics had taken a toll in recent years, the water supply flowed through leaky wooden pipes, the Lake Michigan water supply was tainted with effluvium, and a local newspaper complained:

> Many of the populous localities are noisome quagmires, the gutters running with filth at which the very swine turn up their noses in supreme disgust. Even some portions of the planked streets, say, for instance, Lake between Clark and LaSalle, are scarcely in better sanitary condition than those which are not planked. The gutters at the crossings are clogged up, leaving standing pools of an indescribable liquid, there to salute the noses of passers-by. . . . During the hot weather of the last few weeks, the whole reeking mass of abominations has steamed up through every opening, and the miasma thus elaborated has been wafted into the neighboring shops and dwellings, to poison their inmates.[3]

McCormick, however, was not distracted by the local hygiene but saw the advantages of lake and river transport, a developing system of railroads, a growing supply of labor, and access to the grain belt of the Mississippi River valley and its tributaries.

In his Virginia days McCormick had contracted out production to various workshops in New York, Missouri, Indiana, and Michigan and took his profits in the royalties. He had little control over what was done in these isolated shops, which he could only visit infrequently. Quality suffered and McCormick's reaper was not garnering many satisfied customers. Selling was through commission agents, and McCormick had a reputation for paying less than his competitors, but he argued that his better reapers would gain more sales, so the salespeople would make up the differences by the volume. As in manufacturing, McCormick could exercise little supervision and accountability from his sales force.

To remedy these problems he brought his brothers to Chicago and put Leander in charge of manufacturing and William in charge of sales, accounting, and purchasing. On the north side of the Chicago River a three-story factory was built that initially employed thirty-three workers, ten of them blacksmiths. This decision centralized production; the contract makers were gradually dropped, and design and quality were vastly improved. As sales improved, the factory was expanded in 1850 and employed 120 workers, mostly skilled carpenters and blacksmiths, who were capable of making 1,500 reapers a year. William hired company salespeople, who were each expected to develop a territory by hiring and training commission agents. Because the traveling sales representatives were company employees, the company had a slightly higher degree of influence over what happened with the field agents.

Better control over design, quality, production, and sales enabled McCormick's firm to become very profitable. The total cost of building one reaper in 1849 was $64.29, including all labor, materials, overhead, and administrative and sales costs. The reaper sold for $115 ($120 if bought on credit), yielding the firm a substantial markup. Cyrus held four ninths of the firm and had that share of the profits, plus a patent fee of $28 on each reaper until his patent expired. But he was not the sole beneficiary: For $115, a farmer could have a machine that had a useful life of five to ten years and harvested grain seven times faster with half the labor force. It was perhaps the best possible mutual benefit available at the time.

Feeling that his brothers could handle the home office of the firm of C. H. McCormick and Brothers, Cyrus took to the road to do battle with his formidable rival, Obed Hussey. The McCormick patent expired in 1848 and Cyrus could not get it extended, although he was able to obtain some later patents on certain features of the reaper. Without patent protection, he was more vulnerable to Hussey and other rivals, such as John H. Manny, who had developed an excellent machine that used many McCormick features. McCormick sued for infringement; in his defense, Manny employed Abraham Lincoln and Edwin Stanton and won the suit against McCormick. The young Lincoln used his $1,000 fee to finance his senatorial campaign in Illinois against Stephen Douglas in later years.

McCormick's other competitors saw the growing market opportunities and realized they could redesign old features and/or add improvements to their reapers that could compete effectively with McCormick's and Hussey's. Hussey and McCormick had numerous face-offs at state and county fairs and exhibitions such as in London in 1851 and Paris in 1855. McCormick never was concerned about the esthetics of his reaper—performance came first—but he chafed when the London *Times* described his 1851 reaper as "a cross between a chariot, a wheelbarrow, and a flying machine." Although Hussey and McCormick dominated the field, the competition heated up as patents expired and others began to compete with reapers, mowers, and other agricultural implements.

Competition stimulated McCormick to seek advantages in the market: What could he do to best his rivals? His advantage came from his skills in managing a business, many of them learned as a result of the failure of the iron foundry. In advertising his tactics were pioneering: He handed out flyers at contests and fairs; he bought advertisements in periodicals read by farmers, boasting his reaper was so good that others tried to copy it; he solicited testimonials from farmers who had used his machines (he was probably the first to use testimonials); he provided illustrations of perspiring farmers who cut grain by hand and happy farmers seated on one of his reapers; he emphasized the quality of his machine and the service by his field agents; and, in an appeal to the bottom line, he claimed the machine would pay for itself in one harvest.

Earlier sales experiences indicated that the consumer, the farmer, had to become familiar with this new mechanical reaper, which represented a dramatic break with hand cutting. To reach the farmers, the sales agents had to be brought to Chicago for a look at the factory, how the reaper operated, and how it could be maintained. Through the sales force, the farmer could learn how to use mechanical grain cutters, how to sharpen the cutting blade, how to repair the reaper, and how to maintain equipment that was often left outside throughout the year.

McCormick established a fixed price and offered a warranty (strategies unique in the reaper industry) and provided for free replacement parts. Unfortunately, model changes were made from year to year, and sometimes within a year, so parts had to be ordered for each model—not until 1880 would parts become uniform and fully interchangeable. Sales agents were expected to provide the parts and were held responsible for service as well as sales.

Recognizing the seasonality of farming, McCormick offered a installment payment plan, $30 down and six months to pay, extending credit for spring purchases with the knowledge that no payment could be made until after the harvest, provided it had been a good crop year. In bad crop years, extensions of credit without interest were made. Consequently cash flow was a perennial problem—for example, in 1858 he had accounts receivable of some $500,000, of which an estimated $200,000 would be collected, the balance becoming bad debts—yet there is no record of McCormick suing a farmer to collect a debt.

McCormick had expanded from a regional market to a national one by moving to Chicago, and soon was engaged in licensing the making of his harvester internationally. His success in selling placed greater stress on manufacturing and caused friction between Cyrus and his brother Leander, who preferred to limit production and make the products as they had done before, utilizing skilled blacksmiths and carpenters, though the market indicated that the traditional craft approach to manufacturing was inadequate. Relations between Leander and Cyrus worsened (William had died in 1865), and eventually Cyrus convinced the board of directors that Leander's position should be "vacated."

In 1880 Cyrus hired Lewis Wilkinson to replace Leander as superintendent of manufacturing. Cyrus H. McCormick Jr. became assistant superintendent, and the company became known as the McCormick Harvesting Machine Company. Wilkinson had worked in Samuel Colt's Hartford factory and for the Wilson Sewing Machine Company, both of which used special-purpose machinery and gauges for working to close tolerances so that uniform, interchangeable parts could be made. Under Wilkinson and Cyrus McCormick Jr. the firm moved from a craft shop to a large-scale mode of production. In Leander's last year as superintendent, the total output of harvesters, binders, mowers, and other agricultural implements was 20,000 units; with the new means of production, 55,000 implements were produced in 1884 and 100,000 in 1889.

Cyrus McCormick was a good citizen as well as being skilled in business. After Mrs. O'Leary's cow allegedly started the Chicago fire of 1871, Cyrus rebuilt his factory and aided others as the city rose again; he endowed four professorships at a Presbyterian seminary that was later renamed McCormick Theological Seminary; and he made substantial gifts to Union Theological Seminary at Hampden-Sydney, Virginia, and to Washington College (now Washington and Lee) at Lexington, Virginia.

He married Nancy Maria Fowler in 1858 and they had seven children, one of whom, Cyrus H. McCormick Jr., succeeded his father to the presidency of the firm in later years. McCormick was also active politically, although he often lost those battles—he backed Stephen Douglas against Abraham Lincoln, supported the efforts of Horace Greeley to prevent the War Between the States, bought the *Chicago Times* in an effort to influence his fellow Democrats to make peace rather than war, and ran for Congress but lost. He was a frugal man and persuaded Potter Palmer of Chicago's Palmer House to provide him meals at a discount. But when he tried to negotiate the fee for the surgeon who had removed a carbuncle, he was unsuccessful; the surgeon argued that his fee was small enough considering what a valuable life he had saved.

Cyrus Hall McCormick died on May 13, 1884, and the McCormick Harvesting Machine Company merged with four other agricultural-implement makers in 1902 to become International Harvester. The firm diversified into

construction equipment and trucks as well as a broad line of farm equipment. Ironically, McCormick's success in making the farmer more productive would eventually be the downfall of the firm. More-productive farmers meant that fewer were needed to feed themselves and the world. But fewer farmers mean a smaller market, and International Harvester, like numerous other agricultural-implement makers, no longer exists as a corporate entity. But in the last half century of his life Cyrus McCormick saw his reaper enable more and better implements to feed a world that was moving toward industrialization.

ANDREW CARNEGIE

Between the Civil War and 1899 Horatio Alger wrote more than a hundred books with titles such as *Bound to Rise, Luck and Pluck, Sink or Swim*, and *Tom, the Bootblack*. At least twenty million copies were sold, and the name Horatio Alger became synonymous with a success story. Alger's plots typically involved a young but poor hero who worked his way to wealth by the virtues of diligence, honesty, perseverance, and thrift. Alger's model could well have been Andrew Carnegie, born on November 25, 1835, in Dunfermline, Scotland, the elder of the two sons of William and Margaret Morrison Carnegie. William Carnegie had been a hand-loom weaver, but the coming of water-powered looms led to his unemployment and the family emigrated to America in 1848, settling in Allegheny, Pennsylvania. Andrew's first job was as a bobbin boy in a cotton mill for $1.20 per week; his next was as a messenger, delivering telegrams for $2.50 a week. The telegraph, invented by Samuel F. B. Morse a few years earlier, fascinated Andrew and he taught himself Morse code and how to operate the telegrapher's key.

When Carnegie was seventeen, another opportunity arose, a position on the Pennsylvania Railroad as the personal telegrapher of Thomas A. Scott, superintendent of the railroad's Western Division, for $35 per month. Carnegie learned fast and made his mark one day when he untangled a traffic tieup after a derailment. As he recalled:

> The railway was a single line. Telegraph orders to trains often became necessary, although it was not then a regular practice to run trains by telegraph. No one but the superintendent himself was permitted to give a train order on any part of the Pennsylvania system. . . .

One morning I reached the office and found that a serious accident on the Eastern Division had delayed the express passenger train westward, and that the passenger train eastward was proceeding with a flagman in advance at every curve. The freight trains in both directions were all standing still upon the sidings. Mr. Scott was not to be found. Finally I could not resist the temptation to plunge in, take the responsibility, give train orders, and set matters going. Death or Westminster Abbey, flashed across my mind. I knew it was dismissal, disgrace, perhaps criminal punishment for me if I erred. On the other hand, I could bring in the wearied freight-train men who had lain out all night. I could set everything in motion. I knew I could. I had often done it in wiring Mr. Scott's orders. I knew just what to do, and so I began. I gave orders in his name, started every train, sat at the instrument watching every tick, carried the trains along from station to station, took extra precautions, and had everything running smoothly when Mr. Scott at last reached the office.[4]

Carnegie's initiative earned him a promotion, and another, until by age twenty-four he succeeded Tom Scott as superintendent of the Western Division, which at the time was the largest division of the nation's largest railroad. Under Carnegie's supervision, divisional traffic quadrupled, track mileage doubled, and it had the lowest ton-mile costs of any railroad in America. On the Pennsylvania Carnegie would gain valuable experience and lessons in management as well as his first taste of the rewards of wise investments.

The system of management practiced on the Pennsylvania Railroad by Tom Scott, now a vice president, and John Edgar Thomson, the president, was the product of another Scotch immigrant, Daniel Craig McCallum. McCallum had the good fortune to be an innovator in railroad management, and also the misfortune of getting fired for succeeding. He was born in Scotland but in 1822 came to the United States, where he received some elementary schooling. McCallum left school to become an accomplished carpenter and architect before joining the New York and Erie Railroad Company in 1848. He rose through the construction ranks to become superintendent of the Susquehanna Division, where he developed an early set of procedures for that division. Faced with continuing railroad expansion, a high accident rate, and lots of lost luggage, Erie's management promoted McCallum to general superintendent in May 1854, hoping he could solve their problems. In June of 1854 the railroad workers went on strike for ten days, not for shorter hours or more pay, but to protest McCallum's system.

What could McCallum do in one month to cause such a fuss? He implemented a system based on good discipline, detailed job descriptions, frequent and accurate reporting of performance, pay and promotion based on merit, a clearly defined hierarchy of authority, and the enforcement of personal responsibility and accountability throughout the organization.

McCallum's system was successful from management's point of view, but the locomotive engineers had never forgiven McCallum for the safety rules he had devised. A six-month strike ensued and McCallum resigned, along with the company president, in 1857. But McCallum's approach to management was not lost, as Thomson and Scott applied McCallum's ideas for geographically based departments, formal lines of authority and responsibility, communications, line and staff duties, measuring performance, and cost accounting. Under Thomson and Scott, Andrew Carnegie learned McCallum's ideas about management and would put them into practice both during his railroad career and later.

Tom Scott also introduced Carnegie to the fine art of investing. He advised Carnegie to buy shares in the Adams Express Company, but, lacking funds, Andrew turned to his mother for a loan. She mortgaged her home, and Andrew invested the $500; in a few years, Adams Express was prospering and the dividends amounted to $1,400 per year—not a bad payout for the young Carnegie and his mother. Other investments followed: the Woodruff Palace Car Company (later to be merged with George Pullman's sleeping-car company); an iron foundry, telegraph and oil companies, and the Keystone Bridge Company. By 1863, at age twenty-eight, Carnegie's total income was $48,000 a year, including his $2,800 salary from the Pennsylvania Railroad.

The Iron and Steel Industry

The legendary Midas could turn any object (including the food he needed to survive) into gold. Andrew Carnegie bettered Midas; he turned iron into gold and lived to tell about it. Early on, Carnegie was involved in the iron business, owning shares in Andrew Kloman's foundry and in the Keystone Bridge Company. Thanks to his position with the Pennsylvania Railroad and his service with Tom Scott in the Secretary of War's Transportation Department during the Civil War, Carnegie came to see the value of the railroad in the war effort. The essence of Carnegie's vision was to imagine the possibilities for the iron industry brought about by the railroads' need for rails, locomotives and cars, and bridges, and, later, the need for armor plate and other iron components for ships, as well as iron for agricultural, industrial, and construction uses.

When Carnegie resigned his post at the Pennsylvania Railroad in 1865, iron was selling at $135 a ton and the industry was characterized by small-batch production (such as the iron enterprise of Robert and Cyrus McCormick, which failed) that was labor-intensive, and highly fragmented. Some firms owned the furnaces that smelted the ore into pig iron; others had the rolling mills and forges that converted the pig iron into bars or slabs; and still others took the bars or slabs and rolled them into rails, sheets, nails, wire, or whatever. Between each of these independent operations, an intermediary took the output of one and sold it to the next producer, also taking a profit for providing this service.

Britain was the world's leader in the iron industry when Carnegie began. In 1870, for example, Britain produced 5,963,000 tons, the United States 1,865,000. The British also made better steel, and U.S. railroads preferred to buy their rails abroad. When the British did make a poor-quality batch, they would call it "American iron" and sell it cheaply. Carnegie traveled frequently to the United Kingdom and often took with him U.S. railway securities to sell in the British and European markets. These trips led to a friendship with the successful London investment banker Junius Morgan, whose son, John Pierpont Morgan, was gaining prominence in U.S. financial circles and who would play an important role in Carnegie's later years in the business.

On one of his trips Carnegie saw a demonstration of Sir Henry Bessemer's process for making steel, which involved blasting air through the molten iron, resulting in a spectacular shower of sparks and, more important, the removal of more impurities, making the steel harder than earlier iron-making processes could do. After Carnegie saw the Bessemer process in operation, he had a vision of how this improved technology could be used. In 1872 he stopped his stock speculations, sold his Pullman interests, and concentrated on steel because "every dollar of capital or credit, every business thought, should be concentrated upon the one business upon which a man has embarked. He should never scatter his shot. . . . Put all your eggs in one basket, and then watch that basket, is the true doctrine—the most valuable rule of all."[5]

Carnegie was not the only one, however, to see the opportunities provided by the Bessemer process. Alexander Holley, an engineer of many talents, obtained Bessemer's U.S. patent rights; also operating under this license were companies such as Illinois Steel (later renamed Federal Steel), Joliet Steel, Cambria Iron, Bethlehem Steel, Jones and Laughlin Steel, and Pennsylvania Steel. All were larger than Carnegie's firm, were better-capitalized, and were eager bidders on contracts for all types of iron products. In the face of this competition, what advantage did Carnegie have?

His innovations in managing the business began with the construction of a mill using Bessemer converters, named the J. Edgar Thomson Works (after Carnegie's mentor on the Pennsylvania Railroad), at Braddock's Station, Pennsylvania. He hired Alexander Holley, who knew more about Bessemer's process than anyone else, to design the plant and get it operational. He acquired by merger the coke facilities of Henry Clay Frick; he employed a chemist to study the steelmaking process; he invested in a Siemens gas furnace when other steelmakers thought the initial cost was too high; and he hired talented subordinates such as William P. Shinn, who brought a knowledge of railroad accounting, and Bill Jones, an army captain during the Civil War, who served as superintendent. It was Jones who was responsible for designing and implementing the rapid flow through the plant, from the input of raw materials to the blast furnace and through the converters to the ingot-casting and rolling stages without reheating the steel. When a visiting British iron maker said he would like to sit on an ingot while he watched the work, Carnegie told him to go back to England, for in his plant no ingot was ever cool enough for a person to sit on it.

Continuous improvement was Andrew Carnegie's goal. On the Pennsylvania Railroad, Carnegie had learned McCallum's lesson about the importance of an information system that provided costs on operations. In his steel business Carnegie instituted a system of weighing in raw materials, determining costs associated with wages and materials, and gathering reports on output for each furnace. A knowledge of costs would be Carnegie's obsession and one of his reasons for success, because with this information he could make more intelligent bids on contracts and seek areas where costs could be reduced. He was able, for example, to expand his market share during the 1873–78 depression because his costs for steel rails were lower than his competitors', so he could underbid them and still make a profit.

Carnegie's success abounded. His firm supplied the steel for the Home Insurance Company Building in Chicago, the world's first skyscraper; armor plate for the navy; and locomotives, rails, and train cars. New York City's elevated railway, the Washington Monument, and the Brooklyn Bridge were all made with Carnegie steel. In the 1890s he completed the full integration of the firm by leasing the Mesabi Range to extract its iron ore deposits from John D. Rockefeller for 25 cents per ton. Carnegie's firm could take iron ore, transport it, mix it with other needed materials, and convert it into anything from iron nails to river-spanning bridges, depending on what the customer wanted.

The stain on this rags-to-riches story came in the summer of 1892 at a Carnegie mill in Homestead, Pennsylvania.

Homestead

On July 1, 1892, the interests of Carnegie and his partners were combined under the title of the Carnegie Steel Company, a firm that was capable of producing over 50 percent more steel than the annual total production of Great Britain. But with this triumph came tragedy, in the form of an event that would become a low point in the history of labor-management relations.

Carnegie had published articles in 1886 stating that workers had a right to organize unions and bargain collectively, just as producers' associations could, and that no worker could be expected to stand by peaceably if a new worker took his job; the unwritten rule of the worker, said Carnegie, was "Thou shalt not take thy neighbor's job." At the Edgar Thomson Works, Union Iron, and Keystone Bridge, Bill Jones persuaded Carnegie to put the workers on three eight-hour shifts instead of two twelve-hour ones. After Jones was killed in a blast furnace explosion in 1889, Carnegie terminated the eight-hour-shift experiment and sought to tie wages to steel prices. Workers at the Edgar Thomson site struck and the plant was shut down for five months in 1899, but Carnegie finally coaxed the workers back.

When a strike threatened one of the coke works later, Carnegie told Frick to grant concessions to the workers and not to disrupt production. Frick, who felt Carnegie was soft on labor, was indignant and never forgave him for interfering.

At the Homestead mill, 800 of the 3,800 workers were represented by the Amalgamated Association of Iron and Steel Workers, an American Federation of Labor affiliate that admitted only skilled and semiskilled workers. Carnegie was on his annual summer vacation abroad when the union contract expired on July 1, 1892, and a strike followed. The company had stood firmly against the union's position, and Frick was determined to operate without them. When Carnegie heard that the workers had gone on strike, he wired his partners, offering to come back early, but was told by return wire that this was not necessary. One of Carnegie's partners told the *New York Herald* that they feared Carnegie would give in to the union since it was "his extreme disposition to always grant the demands of labor, however unreasonable." This was not wholly true, although perhaps Carnegie's leadership would have resulted in a different outcome.

Three thousand unskilled workers stopped work along with their union coworkers, seized the plant, and took over the city of Homestead (the mayor was a union member); no one went anywhere without the approval of a Workers' Committee. In retaliation, Frick hired three hundred Pinkerton men to assail the fence and take back the mill. The Pinkertons came in barges down the Monongahela River by night, hoping to catch the workers napping. But the workers were waiting, and what followed would have been farcical had it not been for the tragic outcome:

> The battle lasted all day as the strikers kept the Pinkertons pinned down on the barges and tried to kill every last one of them. That they failed testified only to their lack of skill, not to any lack of desire. They charged the town's courthouse cannon with dynamite; it blew up. They poured oil on the river and set fire to it; the wind blew it the wrong way. They threw a lighted stick of dynamite onto a barge; it rolled into a bucket of water. They loaded a flatcar with blazing combustibles and pushed it down the track toward the barges; it derailed.[6]

One Pinkerton was killed, eleven were injured, and they surrendered late in the afternoon. They were promised safe conduct out of town by the union leaders, but the emotions of the workers and citizens could not be controlled, and mob psychology took over. The Pinkertons ran a gauntlet of sticks and stones; three more died, and the remainder were injured in some way.

The victory was brief: Pennsylvania's governor sent eight thousand state militia to recover the mill and arrest the union leaders for murder. Frick reopened the mill with seven hundred strikebreakers, and Homestead became a black mark in labor-management history. After the plant reopened, Alexander Berkman—not a worker nor a resident of Homestead, but an avowed anarchist—tried to assassinate Frick, but Frick survived. Berkman's action actually harmed the unions, since public opinion equated the Homestead bloodshed and Berkman's anarchist beliefs with the legitimate position of organized labor.

Carnegie apparently never fully understood how the times were changing. Publicly he backed Frick, but privately he felt the strike could have been settled without violence. For all of his other talents, Carnegie failed to fully realize that wages should be tied to productivity, not the price of steel; that twelve-hour shifts and seven-day work weeks were an anachronism; and that he needed to act as he spoke about workers' rights. Carnegie would recall: "No pangs remain of any wound received in my business career save that of Homestead. It was so unnecessary."

At age thirty-three Carnegie had an income of $50,000 annually. Over the next decades he concentrated on his iron and steel interests; it was not until the age of fifty-one that he finally gave up his bachelorhood to marry Louise Whitfield, by whom he had one daughter, Margaret Carnegie. By 1887 Carnegie's income was $1,850,000, and he continued to prosper.

Thanks in large part to Carnegie, the United States became the world's leading producer of steel—and no longer was American steel considered shoddy. When Carnegie started, iron rails cost $100 per ton; when he exited the business, a ton of steel rails of much better quality cost $12. Despite his success, he wished to follow the dreams of his youth: to retire and spend his energies outside of business. In 1901 Carnegie Steel was sold for $480 million to a combine formed by the financier J. Pierpont Morgan. The new company became the United States Steel Corporation and consisted of Carnegie Steel, Illinois (Federal) Steel, American Steel and Wire, American Tin Plate, and other companies as well as iron and coal mines. While this does not appear to be a large amount in today's megamerger times, the value of that deal in 1992 dollars is $7.819 billion.[7]

Accounts of Carnegie's share of the proceeds of the sale vary widely, but it is clear that he felt that the acquisition of wealth imposed a duty on its holder:

> To set an example of modest, unostentatious living, shunning display or extravagance; to provide moderately for the legitimate wants of those dependent upon him; and, after doing so, to consider all surplus revenues which come to him simply as trust funds . . . the man of wealth thus becoming the mere trustee and agent for his poorer brethren.[8]

Carnegie implemented this belief well: He provided the funds to build an estimated three thousand public libraries, purchase more than four thousand church organs, establish museums and institutes for art and music in Pittsburgh and Washington, found the Carnegie Trust for the Universities of Scotland, endow the Carnegie Institute of Technology (now Carnegie-Mellon) in Pittsburgh, establish the Carnegie Foundation as well as the Carnegie Fund for the Advancement of Teaching, build Carnegie Hall in

New York City, and build the Peace Palace at The Hague in the Netherlands, among numerous other projects. By the time of his death, on August 11, 1919, he had given away all of his wealth except for pensions to family and friends and further gifts specified in his last will and testament.

In his essay "The Gospel of Wealth" Carnegie cited the biblical admonitions about the difficulties of the rich in entering the kingdom of heaven, and to this he added, "He who dies rich dies disgraced." Andrew Carnegie did not die disgraced, and he went one up on Horatio Alger—he had made it, and then gave it away to enrich future generations.

HENRY FORD

True or false? "Henry Ford invented mass production via the assembly line." If you answered "true," read on; if your response was "false," continue reading only if you wish to discover more about an individual who played a major role in putting millions of people into the horseless carriage.

Henry Ford was born July 30, 1863, in Dearborn, Michigan, the son of William and Mary (née Litogot) Ford. By the age of sixteen Henry had developed a dislike for farming (his father's occupation) and preferred tinkering with mechanical objects. He built a kerosene-fueled steam tractor but abandoned that idea because of the danger of explosions with the fuel or the boiler. His early career led to a variety of jobs: repairing watches, working for a valve manufacturer, operating a sawmill, and working briefly for the Michigan Car Company. As early as 1885 he repaired an "Otto" engine, an internal combustion, compressed-gasoline-powered device invented in 1876 in Germany by Nicholas Otto. Henry saw a future for the internal combustion gasoline engine and developed several prototypes.

In 1896, while a night-shift engineer at the Detroit Edison Company, Ford attended a speech by Thomas Edison and afterward cornered Edison to see what advice this inventive wizard could offer. Ford recalled that Edison advised him, "There is a big future for any light-weight engine that can develop a high horsepower and be self-contained. . . . Keep on with your engine. If you can get what you are after, I can see a great future."

The automobile was still a curiosity in 1900, however. Not many people took the belching, backfiring horseless carriages very seriously, and those who did were considered daft. It was the task of men such as Henry Ford,

Walter Chrysler, Ransom Olds, William C. Durant, Louis Chevrolet, and others to redraw the face of America's map. Henry Ford popularized the automobile with auto races, and his car #999, driven by Barney Oldfield, was a sure winner.

With Detroit investors, one of whom was the mayor of Detroit, Ford formed the Detroit Automobile Company, capitalized at $150,000 but with only $15,000 in cash, in 1899. The company planned to make ten cars the first year and then gradually increase production to two cars per day. In its advertising, the company promised "that it will emit no odor . . . [and] it will make less noise than the ordinary vehicle drawn by a horse." The motor was assembled on a workbench; then the frame was placed on wooden sawhorses and the motor, transmission, springs, and axles were installed. Then the wheels, vehicle sides, seats, cushions, dash, and so on were brought to the chassis to finish the auto. The operation was labor-intensive, individual parts needed precise tolerances to fit properly (1/64 of an inch variance was acceptable), and a careful routing of work was necessary to bring the parts together. Priced at $1,000 (Henry Ford thought that was excessive), the Detroit Automobile Company was short-lived, dissolved by a sale of its assets in 1901. From this firm, however, the Cadillac Motor Car Company would later emerge.

Failures in the automobile industry were not unusual at this time and most ventures failed to get past the start-up stage. In 1900 the auto industry made 4,192 cars; of these, 1,681 were steam-powered, 1,575 were electric, and 936 were gasoline-powered. Henry Ford's commitment to the internal combustion engine clearly put him in the minority with respect to where the industry was headed. It is not surprising that Ford's supervisor called him a "dreamer" when Ford left a secure future in a public utility, Detroit Edison, in 1899 to venture forth on the muddy, rutted, potholed, uncharted roads of the United States.

Technology and legalities shaped the emerging auto industry. Steam-driven vehicles needed frequent stops for water and fuel and a long wait preceded any trip so that the proper pressure could be obtained. Electric (battery-powered) motors seemed promising and were placed experimentally in taxicabs operating in New York City, Boston, Philadelphia, Washington D.C., and Chicago. The batteries were very heavy, had to be replaced after every trip, and became a joke among passengers who had to ride with the "Lead Cab Company." (Perhaps the phrase "get the lead out" originated under these circumstances.) The gasoline-powered car manufacturers were thwarted by an 1895 patent held by a lawyer, George B. Selden. Selden was never able to raise the capital to build an automobile, but he collected royalties from all firms that used his patents in gas-powered vehicles. Henry Ford held out and fought a half decade of legal battles before a circuit court of appeals held that Selden's patent did not apply to Ford's four-cycle engine because it was patterned after the earlier "Otto" design. Without patent bondage and with superior performance on the road, the gasoline-powered cars began to dominate the industry.

The Assembly Line

The failure of the Detroit Automobile Company did not stop Ford. In 1903 he raised $28,000 in cash from new partners and formed the Ford Motor Company. His shareholders included John Gray, a Detroit banker; Alexander Malcolmson, a Detroit coal dealer; James Couzens, Malcolmson's secretary and the man who would become the business brain of Ford Motor; John F. and Horace E. Dodge, machinists who had previously built engines and chassis for Ford, and others. Controversy soon arose, as Ford wanted a reliable, low-priced car while Malcolmson wanted a higher-priced, six-cylinder vehicle. Ford bought out Malcolmson in 1906 for $175,000 (substantially more than Malcolmson's 1903 investment).

Ford was now the majority shareholder and proceeded with his Model N, a light, rugged vehicle built of tough vanadium steel. Sales of the Model N encouraged Ford to design his Model T, which was introduced in 1908. Base priced at $825, the four-cylinder, twenty-horsepower, 1,200-pound hand-cranked vehicle was a success, selling over ten thousand cars in its first year. With new orders arriving, Ford realized the need to expand production and began plans for his Highland Park plant, just outside of Detroit, to replace the old Piquette Avenue plant.

In the early manufacture of carriages, railroad cars and engines, and automobiles, the assembly was stationary; that is, the parts were brought to the frame and subassemblies were done by workers at their workbenches. Components were moved to the next stage by carts, hoists, or various techniques. Henry Ford, like other manufacturers, at first used the stationary assembly process, but this procedure was slow and labor-intensive—for example, to assemble 189,000 chassis in 1913 required five hundred assemblers and a hundred parts handlers.

The evolution of a continuous-flow process to assemble automobiles provides an early example of what would be called today *kaizen*, continuous improvement toward a goal. The initial effort was the flywheel magneto, assembled as it moved by the workers on a conveyor. Previously, there were twenty-nine workers, each at a bench, who each did an entire assembly, averaging about twenty minutes per assembly, or between twenty-seven and thirty magnetos in nine hours for each worker. After changeover to a moving belt, the assembly was divided into twenty-nine operations performed by these twenty-nine workers spaced along the belt. The average assembly time dropped to thirteen minutes per magneto, then to seven minutes, and finally to five minutes.

Henry Ford was initially skeptical, but the results were proof that the conveyor line worked. Next came moving lines for the motor and then the transmission, all with successful results. By 1913, three feeder lines (magneto, motor, and transmission) could produce more subassemblies than the final assembly could tolerate, creating a stockpile of parts. The solution was a motorized capstan that dragged a line of chassis along the floor, parts were added as it flowed, and the feeder and assembly lines were synchronized. Mass production by an assembly line was an evolution by trial and error, not a single event, and the product of teamwork, not a single creator. The team consisted primarily of Peter E. Martin, the factory superintendent; Charles E. Sorensen, Martin's assistant; Harold Wills, draftsman and toolmaker; Clarence W. Avery, who had been Henry Ford's high-school manual training teacher; and Charles Lewis, a first-line supervisor. As a team member recalled: "Henry Ford is generally considered the father of mass production. He was not. He was the sponsor of it."[9]

The results were impressive. In 1909, by stationary assembly, Ford produced 13,840 autos; by progressive stages in the moving assembly method, output in 1914 was 230,788 vehicles; and in 1916, 585,388 autos were produced. Prices were driven downward as productivity increased: in 1909 a fully equipped Model T touring car was priced at $950; in 1914, $490; and in 1916, $360.[10] This tremendous increase in productivity suggests that Henry Ford was using scientific management, then in vogue due to the writings of Frederick W. Taylor and Frank B. Gilbreth. Critics of scientific management often see Fordism and Taylorism as the same thing, but they were not. When asked directly, Ford denied "any systematic theory of organization or administration, or any dependence on scientific management."[11] Taylor never saw Ford's assembly line, but when Gilbreth visited, he observed that the workers were required to "adjust to the line" rather than designing the line to fit the worker. That was the difference between the assembly line and scientific management—the former was conveyor-paced, the latter worker-paced. Where Taylor or Gilbreth would ask how much coal a worker could shovel, or how many ingots of pig iron could be hauled, Ford would be asking whether a hoist or conveyor could be found to do that job.

The rapid growth in sales and production strained the company's ability to gather the multitude of parts from numerous suppliers, and Henry Ford created an innovative answer to this situation. Ford claimed that he reduced his overhead from $146 to $93 per car by 1922 by paring the office staff, changing the first-line supervisors' span of control from five to twenty workers, and taking out 60 percent of the telephones, but, most of all, by doing what Henry Ford called "speeding up the turnover":

> We discovered, after a little experimenting, that freight service could be improved sufficiently to reduce the cycle of manufacture from twenty-two to fourteen days. That is, raw materials could be bought, manufactured, and the finished product could be put into the hands of the distributor in (roughly) 33 percent less time than before. We had been carrying an inventory of around $60,000,000 to insure uninterrupted production. Cutting down the time one third released $20,000,000.[12]

By the time Ford built the River Rouge plant, he had developed an integrated firm that included ore fields, coal mines, a railroad, ore and coal boats, and timberlands. By careful production forecasting and coordination, Ford could have raw materials arriving where they were needed and when they were needed, reducing the costs of storage of inventory. It was Ford who discovered the "just-in-time" system of production and inventory handling. From the receipt of raw materials until finished goods, Ford had anticipated how flows could be planned and coordinated to minimize inventory. Taiichi Ohno, creator of Toyota's just-in-time system for assembly, acknowledged that the idea came from reading about Henry Ford's experiences.[13] While Ford Motor may be remembered for the moving assembly line, that innovation would have had less of an impact if the notion of moving inventory had not been developed as well.

The "Five-Dollar Day"

In addition to meeting the raw material needs of the plants, increased production also meant that more workers had to be hired. Compounding the problem was a high employee turnover rate, not just at Ford but other companies in Detroit. The company had another problem—the workforce consisted of 71 percent foreign-born workers from twenty-two different national groups. Southern and eastern Europeans were the majority and included (in order from high to low percentages) Polish, Russians, Romanians, Italians and Sicilians, Austro-Hungarians, and Germans. Few of these spoke English, making communication difficult for supervisors and coworkers. To lessen the problem, Ford Motor started an "English School" so that diverse work group members would be able to communicate.

Reducing the high turnover rate of employees posed a different problem, and Ford and his employment manager, John R. Lee, started a program to reward workers not for meeting production standards but for staying on the job and following Ford's rules. In January 1914 Ford announced a *minimum* wage of $5 per day, instead of the previous $2.50 per day, and a reduction of the workday from nine to eight hours. A portion of this $5 per day consisted of wages, and the remainder represented "anticipated profits," paid in advance provided the worker had been in the company's employ for six months. In addition, to be eligible, married men had to be living with and taking good care of their families; single men over the age of twenty-two had to prove their habits of thrift; and men under age twenty-two and women were eligible if they were the sole support of a next of kin.

The five-dollar day set the floor and scaled all other wages upward. This shocked the Detroit employers and was denounced as "economic madness," "industrial suicide," and "socialism." Packard Motor Car's president complained, "We [Packard] are not running a philanthropic business like you." Henry Ford answered the critics by saying that the five-dollar day was not philanthropy but good business: "An underpaid man is a customer reduced in purchasing power. He cannot buy. . . . There can be no true prosperity until the worker upon an ordinary commodity can buy what he makes."

A company study done in March 1913 indicated that 71 percent of the turnover for that month was caused by "five-day men," workers who were absent from work for five days or more without informing the company about the reasons for their absence. Ford's plan, in part, was directed at these floaters who worked briefly, collected their wages, and moved on. With respect to employee turnover, the results of the new wage plan were dramatic, reducing average monthly turnover from 31.9 percent in 1913 to 1.4 percent in 1915. Further, more and more workers earned the full amount: 60 percent were eligible at the beginning; 87 percent at the end of one year; and 98.5 percent at the eighteen-month mark.

There was concern that the easy money of a $5 minimum would lead the workers to dissolute living. A sociology professor at the University of Michigan commented: "The great trouble with the vast majority of our laborers is that they do not know how to spend their wages judiciously. If they receive $5 a day, the likelihood is in the majority of cases that it will all be spent when the next pay day comes and . . . [nothing more will be left] than before [i.e., when the minimum was $2.50 per day]." Ford agreed: "When we first raised the wages to five dollars a day, we had to exercise some supervision over the living of the men because so many of them, being foreign born, did not raise their standards of living in accord with their higher incomes. That [supervision] we entirely gave up when the need had passed." The supervision that Ford referred to was the establishment of a Sociology Department that employed some 100 advisers who visited the workers' home to ensure that their homes were neat and clean, that they did not drink too much, that their sex life was without tarnish, and that they used their leisure time profitably. This sociological experiment lasted but three years and ended when Ford told Samuel S. Marquis, then head of the department: "There is too much of this snooping around in private affairs. We'll change this from a Sociology Department to an Education Department." Thereafter, the home visits stopped, and the Ford Motor Company turned its attention to education. The Sociology Department was an abortive experiment but eventually found that the problem was in employee education, not in social work. In all, Ford's vision combined affordable transportation, increased wages, and a concern for worker well-being. Different circumstances were coming, however, throwing a cloud over Ford's vision.

Changing Times

Henry Ford was a successful pioneer in the automobile industry, but business conditions changed while Henry stayed the same. Ford had a disdain for "experts": "I never employ an expert in full bloom. If ever I wanted to kill opposition [competition] by unfair means I would endow the opposition with experts. They would have so much good advice that I could be sure they would do little work." Ford factories had no organization chart, no specific job descriptions, no line of authority, and few job titles; Ford once threw his finance chief into panic when Ford visited the accounting department and dumped all of the files, commenting on the overabundance of red tape and records.

Table 2.1

Ford vs. General Motors

	Ford Motor		General Motors	
	Units produced	Market share (U.S.)	Units produced	Market share (U.S.)
1912	78,440	21%	49,696	13%
1917	785,432	42%	203,119	11%
1923	2,090,959	51%	798,555	20%
1926	1,442,950	33%	1,234,850	28%

Ford also lacked the ability to keep good managers, reducing any chance to build a strong management team. James Couzens, who provided the financial wizardry while Ford tinkered, left the company in 1915; Norval Hawkins, who was instrumental in Ford's sales and dealer relations, resigned to work for Alfred P. Sloan Jr. at General Motors; William S. Knudsen, acknowledged as a production whiz, also went to GM and became a star; the Dodge brothers left to form their own company; and John R. Lee, who could have helped with the human problems, left; only the durable Charles Sorensen stayed for forty years.

In hiring Harry Herbert Bennett, an ex-prizefighter and a willing yea-sayer, Henry Ford gave industrial relations in the auto industry a recurring bad name. Bennett hired ex-convicts and rough, tough guys to keep the unions out of Ford Motor. Bennett hired the entire University of Michigan football team for one summer to keep order, but also to practice on company time. Ford never awakened from his dream that all people wanted was an inexpensive, reliable, basic automobile. His advisers told him of the changing times, but he saw the issue as production when General Motors saw it as organization and marketing as well. Table 2.1 summarizes the data that should have told Ford that GM was ready to go in the passing lane.

In 1927–28 Ford closed down (except to make spare parts) to retool for the Model A. While closed, other auto makers boasted that they were hiring Ford's best salespeople. Ford was unconcerned: "I know that some people think that salesmen make a car. We believe that a car, if it is good enough, will make salesmen." Henry had a stroke in 1938 at age 75, but held the reins tightly. His son, Edsel, preceded Henry in death (1943), and finally the family convinced Henry to relinquish control to Edsel's son, Henry II, in 1945. One of the first moves of Henry Ford II was to fire Harry Bennett, signaling a new era for Ford.

The Model T "Tin Lizzie" inspired poems (with apologies to Rudyard Kipling):

> Yes, Tin, Tin, Tin,
> You exasperating puzzle, Hunka Tin,
> I've abused you and I've flayed you,
> But by Henry Ford who made you,
> You are better than a Packard, Hunka Tin.

Jokes:

> Why is Henry Ford a better evangelist than Billy Sunday?
> Because he's shaken hell out of more people than Billy ever did.

Bumper stickers:

> Barnum was right.
>
> You may pass me big boy, but I'm paid for.
>
> Follow us, farmer, for haywire.[14]

The Model T wizard died on April 7, 1947, having seen more than twenty million "Tin Lizzies" cross the finish line. Ford was a visionary, yet an eccentric; innovative, but stubborn; he defied business advisers, while being an example of how competitive enterprise works; and he was a tinkerer, yet his works revolutionized the automobile industry, created new giants in glass, rubber, steel, and petroleum, and changed the way the world lived.

3

SELLERS

Trade is as ancient as humankind, but its evolution from bartered commodities to plastic debit and credit cards is a story with many chapters. Before the eighteenth century the lack of rapid transport and communication established barriers to trade, restricting it to local markets or creating long periods of time between the shipment of a product and its receipt at some distant point. Steam power brought transport by rail, on inland waterways, and across the seas, enabling the more rapid exchange of goods over greater distances. Communication improvements, such as the telegraph and the telephone, provided for information exchanges that facilitated the expansion of trade.

Although advances in transport and communication were available, the channels of distribution remained largely unchanged. Few manufacturers had a sales force; rather, they sold through commission agents or jobbers who were specialized wholesalers. There were import houses, wholesalers, and retailers to bring products to the consumer. In isolated rural areas, peddlers and "drummers" took products to country general stores or from door to door. Small town merchants specialized in furniture, hardware, boots and shoes, dry goods, jewelry, groceries, and other products.

Growing urbanization would transform traditional ways of getting products to the consumer. The earliest department stores appeared in the largest cities: London, Paris, and New York. Most of these were begun by specialized merchants who grasped the opportunities to diversify their product assortment and group similar goods into departments under one roof, consolidating the management of the store under one person or partners.

In London the earliest stores were James Shoolbred's, Harrod's, and William Whiteley's. In Paris there was the Petit Saint-Thomas, where Aristide Boucicault learned merchandising, the Ville de Paris, and the Bon Marché, all apparently beginning in the late 1830s or early 1840s as dry-goods stores.[1] Boucicault and Paul Videau acquired the Bon Marché in 1852 and Boucicault bought out his partner in 1869 to create the Maison du Bon Marché (meaning "house of bargains"; one could put it in modern terms as "everyday low prices").

Some consider the Bon Marché as the first department store, but there is evidence to suggest otherwise. Shoolbred's in London opened its doors in 1817, and U.S. merchants had beginnings before Bon Marché. Bon Marché was, however, the first to have a female general director of a large department store. After the deaths of Aristide and their only child, Aristide Jr., Marguerite Boucicault inherited the store in 1879. She was not prepared for general management but kept in touch with the daily business through her managing associates. She had the foresight to provide for the future of Bon Marché by increasing the firm's capital through selling shares and for these shareholders to elect future directors, thus avoiding the fate of many family firms. When she died in 1887, Bon Marché had gross sales of 123,000,000 francs (approximately U.S. $24,600,000 in 1887) and was the leading department store on the Continent.

Those selected to represent the "sellers" in America are Alexander T. Stewart and Richard W. Sears. Stewart was a dry-goods merchant who is generally credited with beginning the first department store and was more certainly the one who provided the best example of this means of merchandising in the late nineteenth century. Sears took an unclaimed shipment of watches and began the most successful mail order house in the nineteenth century; his successors turned Sears, Roebuck into the most successful retail store chain during much of the twentieth century. Together, Alexander T. Stewart and Richard W. Sears characterize the major changes in selling strategies that made modern America.

ALEXANDER T. STEWART

In 1790 the three largest cities in the United States were New York, Philadelphia, and Boston; the common thread among these cities was their natural ports, which encouraged trade and immigration. In these cities were the import houses, agents, wholesalers, and retailers who carried out the exchange of commodities and products from the eastern seaboard for manufactured goods from Britain and the Continent. What we call the department store grew out of these trading establishments, particularly those dealing in dry goods: laces; cloth from silk, linen, wool, and cotton; ribbons; thread; hosiery; shawls; and so forth.

In 1823 an Irish immigrant, Alexander Turney Stewart, brought a selection of Irish linens and laces for sale in this great marketplace of New York City, which had grown to nearly 180,000 citizens. Some sources say he acquired his initial inventory with an inheritance from his maternal grandfather, but it is more likely that it was a combination of some cash down payment and the balance on credit—in either case, it was a wise investment. He opened for business on September 1, 1823, at 283 Broadway in a shop that had a 12.5 foot frontage and was 30 feet deep.[2] Numerous other dry-goods merchants operated in this area with stores about the same size as Stewart's. The secret to success—then as now—was to find the right goods at the right price and to increase the inventory turnover. His first ad in the *New York Daily Advertiser* contained a brief notice: "A.T. Stewart, just arrived from Belfast, offers for sale to the ladies of New York a choice selection of Fresh Dry-Goods at Two Hundred Eighty-Three Broadway." Clearly he had a market segment in mind.

After his marriage to Cornelia M. Clinch, they lived in the rear of the store until his mercantile success enabled them to move to larger quarters. He relocated his business to a larger shop at 262 Broadway in 1827, and then in 1830 to 257 Broadway, where he would spend the next sixteen years. There his neighbor was Charles L. Tiffany's store, Tiffany and Young at 259 Broadway. At the 257 Broadway store he began to arrange his merchandise by similarities, or by "departments," such as carpets and oilcloth, bed linens, cloaks and shawls, and so forth.

While Stewart's operation was not a department store with a full line of goods as we know it, it was a prototype for a new form of retailing: grouping similar goods into departments, all under one roof for convenient shopping, with each considered a distinct entity having its own sales staff and daily accounts of sales and cash. The department managers reported to Stewart, who was also responsible for buying new merchandise, but as his store's assortment increased he hired buyers for each department.

The lower end of Manhattan also spawned other dry-goods merchants who would departmentalize: Aaron Arnold and James Constable opened

Arnold Constable in 1825 on lower Broadway; Samuel Lord and George Washington Taylor formed Lord and Taylor in 1826, located on Park Row just off Bowery; and in 1858 Rowland H. Macy opened "uptown" on West Fourteenth Street at Sixth Avenue. Located on major thoroughfares with public transport nearby, these early stores were forerunners to a transformation in the selling of merchandise.

The Marble Palace

As Stewart's successes mounted, he built the architectural marvel of its time—the "Marble Palace" at 280 Broadway. Opening in 1846, its Broadway frontage of twenty-six marble columns ran between Reade and Chambers streets. The four stories (a fifth was added later) were faced with marble, and each floor, including a basement, had its merchandise arranged by departments. Rising the full height of the interior, a glass-domed central rotunda (not too far from the modern concept of a galleria) provided natural lighting and ventilation. Chandeliers provided artificial lighting, and the counters and shelves were constructed of maple and mahogany.

Plate glass windows, six feet by eleven, were imported from France for the first floor front and later added to other entry sides. Great fears abounded about thrown objects and the damage they could do to these costly windows, even though this never happened. Despite the opportunity to use the windows for displays, Stewart never used them for that purpose. Another quirk of his was to never put his name on any of his stores, believing that people would hear about his store and find it (in modern terms, "If you build it, they will come."). His advertising was descriptive and unimaginative—a paragraph or two in the city papers announcing the arrival of some choice new merchandise, or a "must go" advertisement to clear slow-moving inventory. Since advertising is considered essential to selling success, and A. T. Stewart never followed that path, how can his continued prosperity be explained?

Stewart took two early initiatives to shorten the distribution channels: international purchasing offices and backward vertical integration into the ownership of manufacturing facilities. He established purchasing offices in every major textile center in Ireland, England, and France to buy directly from the factory for import to the United States; in 1872 A. T. Stewart's imports accounted for 10 percent of all import duties paid at the Port of New York. By purchasing abroad, Stewart no longer had to rely on distress or closeout sales and could eliminate the commissions paid to manufacturers' sales agents. These savings would in turn be passed on to the customer.

Stewart also moved to acquire mills in the United States and abroad. He acquired the Woodstock Woolen Mill in Vermont and other woolen mills for carpets, flannels, and blankets; a cotton mill in Manchester, England; a linen factory in Belfast, Ireland; a lace curtain factory in Nottingham, England; and others. The factories could provide the goods Stewart wanted at the quality and price he desired, and eliminated another factor in the chain of distribution, the wholesaler. A. T. Stewart was thinking vertical integration and global business over a century before these ideas would become popular.

Successful ideas in retailing are readily copied, and due credit for these innovations is difficult to pinpoint. Some of Stewart's ideas may have been borrowed, and some were the product of his experience in the business. What appears to be unique to Stewart was how his policies formed a *system*.[3] His influence on other retailers such as J. L. Hudson (Detroit), Fred Lazarus Jr. (Columbus, Ohio), and John Wanamaker (Philadelphia and later New York) is one measure of the recognition and esteem he enjoyed. Marshall Field of Chicago took pride in being hailed as "the A. T. Stewart of the West." Some of Stewart's retailing principles would be found in other stores across the land, such as:

- No misrepresentation of merchandise. Stewart said, "I do business to establish a principle. It is the principle of truth. I am in a state of constant warfare to prevent what are called white lies being told in my establishment." For example, he fired a salesperson who told a customer that some calico cloth was colorfast when in fact it was not. Honesty in merchandising was the principle—and somewhat unique, considering some practices of that period.
- One price. Although many lay claim to this policy to replace haggling over price, as early as 1832 Stewart advertised: "In order to save time and prevent trouble, no deviation from the prices asked, on the regularity and fairness of which our customers and the public can fully rely." He made exceptions for markdowns to clear out slow-moving inventory and for promotional sales. In his early experience he found that negotiating a price was time-consuming and often led to unhappy customers and browbeaten salespeople.
- The salesperson as key point of contact for the store. Stewart made it a practice to select people who could sell as well as make an attractive

appearance to the public. Clerks were not allowed to sit down, except during break periods, in order to appear attentive to customer needs, and numerous floorwalkers helped with directions and information for the customer. At the Marble Palace and later at his Astor Place store, Stewart provided indoor toilets for the ladies, writing desks, and comfort areas. Customer-oriented marketing is not an idea that originated in the twentieth century.

- Quantity buying for cash. This gave Stewart the ability to take discounts on merchandise purchased and allowed him to lower prices at the store.

- Selling for cash. Although Stewart would occasionally extend credit to preferred customers, his basic policy was cash only.

- Low markup. To increase the volume of sales and stock turnover, Stewart kept prices low. "Ten percent [markup] and no lies!" was his standard, rather than charging what the market would bear. Stewart was the highest volume retailer of his time—$2,500,000 in sales at retail in 1846; in 1865, $8,000,000; and $12,000,000 in 1873. Not until 1896, twenty years after Stewart died, did another retailer exceed $10,000,000 in retail sales in a single year.

- Merchandise returns and refunds. These were allowed, although he would discount all returned goods ten percent to discourage frequent or whimsical exchanges of merchandise.

- Wholesaling. He imported more than he could sell at retail and began selling to other merchants. His largest customer was Wanamaker and Brown of Philadelphia, predecessor to John Wanamaker and Company. In 1865, for example, Stewart's total sales were $50,000,000, with $42,000,000 of that coming from his wholesaling operations.

- Cash boys. Before the invention of pneumatic tubes, cashboys were floor runners who took the money and sales bill to a central cashier, returning with the receipt. All large-scale retailers followed this practice. One noteworthy cash boy was William Claude Dunkerfield of Philadelphia's Strawbridge and Clothier. Dunkerfield quit the firm as pneumatic tubes came into use, turned to vaudeville, and changed his name to W. C. Fields.

- Mail order. Realizing that America's interior communities did not have the advantage of stores such as his, Stewart began newspaper advertising in other cities describing his wares and stating "Samples sent free." His mail order department would send the requested samples of cloth and the price per yard and the customers would return the sample they desired with their money (cash only) for their goods to be shipped. Although A. T. Stewart never published a catalog, as others would do later, he realized the potential of a market beyond the large urban areas.

In 1862 Stewart opened a second store covering one square block bounded by Broadway and Fourth Avenue between New York's Ninth and Tenth Streets. Called the "Cast Iron Palace" because iron provided the superstructure, it had eight floors, each covering about two acres, with a large rotunda that enabled a person on the top floor to look down the entire height of the store. In this store Stewart came the closest he would come to a modern department store by adding a line of "Yankee notions" (pots, pans, and related ironware) to his thirty departments of silks, calicos, gloves, laces, hosiery, shawls, carpets, and so on. Only three floors were used for sales, while the other floors were for making ladies' wear, upholstering, storage, and offices. Six steam-powered elevators, three for freight and three for customers, served one of the earliest tall buildings in New York City.

Continuous organ music entertained the shoppers at the Cast Iron Palace, and John Wanamaker called it the "Greatest Store in the World."[4] "I got it at Stewart's" was a statement of satisfaction and prestige by his customers. Carriages of the rich and famous often drew up at the store, and Mary Lincoln refurnished the White House with materials purchased at Stewart's. Stewart stretched his cash-only policy for Mrs. Lincoln, and at the time of President Lincoln's assassination she had $27,000 charged to their account.

Following the Founder

Then as now, the death of the founder of a family business can lead to unpleasant outcomes. Alexander T. Stewart died on April 10, 1876, short of his seventy-third birthday, leaving most of his estate to Cornelia Clinch Stewart because there were no surviving children. In addition, there were various bequests to others, including over $300,000 to be distributed (based on seniority) among his two thousand employees.

Over the years Stewart had many "partners" in profits, but he kept the ownership. His partners in profit at the time of his death were Henry H.

Hilton and William Libbey, who owned less than 2 percent of A. T. Stewart and Company. Libbey had been with Stewart for some ten years and was considered a shrewd businessman, although he was not a merchant of A. T. Stewart's caliber. Hilton was Stewart's lawyer and his friend—though this latter would turn out to be less than true after Stewart's death.

Hilton was bequeathed $1,000,000 for "managing, closing and winding up" Stewart's estate. Twenty-four hours after the funeral, Hilton told Cornelia Stewart he would "relieve her of the worry" of the business if she granted him a general power of attorney. In Hilton's case this power corrupted, and his first step was to buy A. T. Stewart and Company, except for the Astor Place property, from Mrs. Stewart for $1,000,000—which was also the amount of his bequest. In short, Hilton acquired much of the business at no out-of-pocket cost, even though the goods in inventory were estimated to be worth $12,000,000, and a fair market price for the company would have been in excess of $20,000,000.

History rarely records such a disastrous partnership as that of Hilton and Libbey. The mills deteriorated, and all but three were sold at a loss; store sales declined. Hilton and Libbey tried to penetrate the Chicago market but lost badly to Field and Leiter, the predecessor of Marshall Field and Company. Stewart's will provided for a "working woman's hotel," which Hilton built for $3,750,000 only to see it close fifty-three days after opening because the rent was more than working women could afford. The Grand Union Hotel at Saratoga Springs, New York, was part of A. T. Stewart's real estate holdings, and Hilton (no relation to the later Hilton hoteliers) closed it to Jewish registrants. Jesse Seligman, the senior partner in a leading investment bank and a prominent member of New York's Jewish community, was one of those denied admittance to the Grand Union after numerous years as a guest. He called for a boycott of the store by Jewish customers, who were a substantial clientele, and by Jewish suppliers of clothing and textile products to A. T. Stewart stores. The Grand Union was no longer considered grand.

It took Hilton and Libbey some six years to liquidate what the merchant prince had built in a lifetime. The Marble Palace was remodeled into an office building and sold. In 1882 A. T. Stewart and Company was liquidated, and Libbey received $1,000,000 and Hilton $5,500,000 for the remnants of a much more valuable collection of properties. The Astor Place store was an exception, however; it was not sold as a property by Cornelia Stewart, and her heirs would later sell it to John Wanamaker. Wanamaker paid his respects to the man who had greatly influenced his life by advertising his store as "Formerly A. T. Stewart and Company." Eventually Wanamaker sold the building, and it stands today as condominium apartments named Stewart House.[5] It is doubtful that the occupants and passersby make a connection between that dwelling and its former glory.

Stewart's obituaries called him the "merchant prince of New York," but his influence was more far-reaching. Increasing urbanization in America in the last half of the nineteenth century spread the "grand emporiums" from coast to coast and border to border. The great names in department stores—Macy's; Gimbel's; Wanamaker; Hudson; Strawbridge and Clothier; I. Magnin (the first department store founded by a woman, Mary Sue Magnin, and named for her husband, Isaac Magnin); May; Rich's; Neiman Marcus; Jordan Marsh; Carson, Pirie and Scott; and Marshall Field—are merely a sample of the legacy of Alexander Turney Stewart.

RICHARD W. SEARS

"The great price maker"; "Send us no money"; "With cash, we pay the freight." These were advertising phrases that reached out to rural America and captured a market that was eager for the products available in urban areas. The idea of ordering by mail was not new: Benjamin Franklin issued a catalog in 1744 offering a list of six hundred books that could be ordered by mail. A. T. Stewart, R. H. Macy, John Wanamaker, and Charles Tiffany had mail order departments that targeted primarily the inland cities of America. The Larkin Company had a catalog for ordering soap, tea, coffee, and extracts; Butler Brothers of Boston offered hardware; and National Cloak and Suit (later renamed National Bella Hess) was also in the mail order business, specializing in certain product lines with urban markets in mind. In 1880 72 percent of America's population was classified as rural, and this market was relatively untapped. Aaron Montgomery Ward and his brother-in-law, George R. Thorne, pioneered the idea of a general-merchandise catalog that was targeted for the rural market. Ward began his career as a clerk for Field, Palmer, and Leiter (predecessor to the Marshall Field Company) and launched his catalog business with one-page flyers, followed by a catalog of a broad range of merchandise in 1874.

By 1887 Ward advertised twenty-four thousand different items in a 540-page catalog. Like other mail order firms, Ward had to gain the trust of customers who relied on the printed page to tell them what they needed to know about a product. Ward received an endorsement from the National Grange of Patrons of Husbandry, an agrarian group that promoted the interests of farmers, which helped create this image of trust. "Cheapest Cash House in America" and "Satisfaction Guaranteed—Or Your Money Back" were slogans intended to promote the reliability of doing business with a distant supplier by mail order.

Born in Stuartsville, Minnesota, in 1863, Richard Warren Sears came to the mail order business by a different route. At the age of sixteen he learned telegraphy (like Carnegie and Edison) and used this to advance his career on the Minneapolis and Saint Louis Railroad, becoming station agent at North Redwood, Minnesota. In this position he could read the numerous mail order catalogs that passed through and become familiar with prices and markup from the bills of lading.

A consignment of watches from a Chicago jeweler was refused by the North Redwood jeweler and Richard Sears was given the opportunity to buy them for $12 each. Sears knew this was a good price and that watches carried a high markup, but he also knew that he could not sell all of these gold-filled watches in the small town of North Redwood. He wrote other agents on the line that he would sell them for $14 each, "subject to examination," COD. These watches retailed for $25 and Sears told the agents that they could keep any profits over his price. The watches were sold through the agents and they asked for more. In the first six months of this venture Sears netted $5,000, and left the railroad to establish the R. W. Sears Watch Company in Minneapolis in 1886.

After a year in Minneapolis he moved his business to Chicago, where he felt he had a more central location and superior communication and transportation facilities. Sears expanded his product assortment to include jewelry and silverware, and requests for watch repair started appearing. To take care of this side of the business, he hired Alvah Curtis Roebuck, an Indiana farmboy who had learned watch repair through a correspondence course. Sears and Roebuck parted company in 1889 but joined forces again in 1893 to form Sears, Roebuck and Company, with "and company" being represented by Sears's sister, Eva, who held one share of stock.

Catalogs

While the railroad and the telegraph provided the support system of transportation and communication that enabled the mail order business to succeed, the U.S. Post Office also played a large role. John Wanamaker, an admirer of A. T. Stewart and a successful merchant in Philadelphia, was appointed postmaster general by President Benjamin Harrison in 1888. Wanamaker promoted "rural free delivery" (RFD) but that did not become law until 1896, after Wanamaker had left his government post to return to retailing by adding the former A. T. Stewart store in New York to his interests. Further, second-class postage came into use and allowed catalogs to be mailed for 1¢ per pound to anyone, rural or urban. Later (in 1913) the creation of parcel post provided a less expensive way of shipping compared with what freight express companies were charging. Mass-market advertising and distribution on a national scale was enabled by advances in transport, communication, and a more favorable postal rate structure.

Mail order catalogs reached customers who would be very unlikely to have such a cornucopia of products available to them otherwise. By 1893 the Sears, Roebuck catalog offered firearms, sewing machines, organs and pianos, bicycles, clothing, athletic equipment, wagons, seeds, stoves, books, men's and ladies' hats, patent medicines, and tombstones. The catalog encouraged the shopper to compare the Sears, Roebuck price with that of their local merchant. Sears did not see urban department stores or other mail order houses as his primary competitors; rather it was the local merchants—the hardware retailers, farm implement dealers, jewelers, music stores, booksellers, and other local vendors—who would be consulted when the customer compared prices. On the cover of the 1897 catalog, for example, Sears, Roebuck and Company stated "This book tells just what your storekeeper at home pays for everything he buys [and this catalog] will prevent him from overcharging you on anything you buy from him."

Sears emphasized price in all advertising copy and urged the shopper to compare Sears with other sellers, so there should be no reason to wonder why local merchants fought Sears, Ward's, and other mail order firms in the U.S. Congress when issues such as parcel post, RFD, and second-class mail arose. Both Sears and Ward adopted the practice of sending their catalogs in a plain brown paper wrapper to disguise them from local merchants, whose stores often also served as the local post office; perhaps it also suggested to the customer that this package included material that others should not see.

The Sears, Roebuck catalog was advertised in daily and weekly newspapers, especially those that reached the farm market. Sears himself wrote as much copy as possible when the catalog was smaller and was not hesitant to use the give-aways to draw the reader's attention: for example, "Free 36 pieces of glassware" if the customer sent $16.50 for $30 worth of groceries (a product line that was soon dropped). In patent medicines, the catalog made a disclaimer that Sears, Roebuck could not recommend "any particular preparation" and knew nothing of "the formulae or ingredients." If unintended symptoms occurred, the catalog recommended consulting a "skilled physician." The catalog continued by offering Dr. Wilder's Quick Cure for Indigestion and Dyspepsia, Brown's Vegetable Cure for Female Weakness, the Wonder Heart Cure, and the Seroco Cure for the Tobacco Habit.

After the passage of the Pure Food and Drug Act of 1906, Sears waited five years before inserting a disclaimer regarding these patent medicines:

> We have . . . selected from the great array of preparations found on the market a list of proprietary remedies, which from their popularity would appear to be reliable, and which we believe may also be depended on to do as much as is reasonable to expect of such remedies. . . . Our desire to protect our customers against the possibility of being disappointed as to the results likely to be obtained has led us to be very conservative in our claims for all of these products.

In the fall of 1911 Sears, Roebuck established a laboratory for testing the quality of various products. After consultation with pharmacists and the American Medical Association, the laboratory director influenced the formulation of a new policy regarding advertising patent medicines:

> Therefore we have decided to restrict our line of drugs and medicines to those officially approved by the leading drug and medical associations of the country. . . . From among the preparations that experience shows are of most value, we have selected a few simple remedies that we believe may be of use in the household. In presenting this list we wish to be understood as not urging the purchase of any medicine that is not needed. Again, if any of our customers have need of more than a few simple home remedies, such as those listed, we are frankly of the opinion that they should consult their family physicians rather than waste either time or money experimenting with drugs, whether patent medicines or any other.[6]

The laboratory was responsible for testing all chemical products, textiles, tools, and other products both for their quality of performance and to see that no product was described falsely in the catalog copy. For example, if clothing advertised as "all wool" was determined after testing to be three-fourths cotton, the catalog description had to be changed. If, after testing, the lab determined that the clothing was all wool, the catalog could reflect that. Sears was the first mail order firm to start a textile testing laboratory and one among a few other companies that were starting quality checking labs and developing product specifications and standards.

Richard Sears had a knack for writing advertising copy and for promoting the catalog as well as the products it sold. "Send no money" proved to be an irresistible lure for Sears customers, while Ward's was still asking for money with an order. In addition to advertising in the catalog, Sears was the nation's largest mail order advertiser and maybe America's largest advertiser: In 1898, the firm spent $400,000 on advertising, and ten years later the amount was $3,500,000.[7]

Both Sears and Ward's distributed their catalogs for free, and all mail order firms competed to increase their circulation. Sears was more innovative with his "Iowaization" plan. He shipped two dozen catalogs to each of his best customers in Iowa and asked them to distribute them to their neighbors. The names and addresses of those who received those catalogs were to be sent to Sears, Roebuck and they, in turn, would send the distributors premiums based on how much was ordered by the new catalog holders. The plan was so successful that Sears "Iowaized" the nation, distributing 318,000 in 1897 and over 6,500,000 catalogs ten years later. Sears's tactic bears a remarkable resemblance to more recent systems of selling household products through distributors who enlist others to sell for them and receive a percentage of their sales as well.

Richard Sears was a great promoter, using installment sales for big-ticket items; truly offering a money-back policy if the customer was dissatisfied; using COD; spearheading the "Iowaization" tactic; and segmenting his catalogs by geographical territory (for example, catalogs distributed in colder climates would feature snow boots and tire chains, while areas with milder winters would not see these items in their catalog but would see more swimsuits). In one instance, however, he was too successful, when he began a customer profit-sharing plan that gave coupons for certain amounts of purchases. These coupons were redeemable for premiums and the 1905 catalog had fourteen pages of items that could be obtained in exchange for coupons. The coupons carried no expiration date, but Sears estimated that fewer than half of these coupons would be redeemed. In 1904 unredeemed coupons amounted to over $230,000. The 1905 results also alarmed the auditors since some $260,000 in coupons had been redeemed but over $300,000 for 1905 were still outstanding, constituting a potential future liability of over $500,000 for 1904 and 1905. The auditors insisted that a reserve fund be established and the unredeemed coupons be treated as a charge against earnings. In 1906 these liabilities continued to accrue at a greater rate, and 1907 saw the end of this plan. It was a great idea for promotion, but Sears was persuaded not to try to remedy it but to drop the plan because of the constant and ever-increasing squeeze on earnings.

A national financial crisis in 1893 and a business decline the following year made Alvah C. Roebuck apprehensive about the firm's future. The company's liabilities were three times its assets, and Roebuck decided to sell his interest to Richard Sears for $25,000. Aaron E. Nusbaum, who had made $150,000 from his soda pop and ice cream concession at the 1893 World's Columbian Exposition in Chicago, had invested this money in a venture to make and sell pneumatic tubes for use in sales transactions in department stores. He called on Sears and failed to make a sale, but he liked what he saw in the operations. Sears offered Nusbaum a half interest in Sears, Roebuck and Company for $75,000. Nusbaum conferred with his brother-in-law, Julius Rosenwald, about sharing this investment. Rosenwald was a manufacturer of men's clothing and had sold ten thousand suits to Sears, Roebuck. He knew that the company could sell in large volumes at a low price with a small markup and be very profitable.

Rosenwald agreed to invest, and Sears sold him and Nusbaum more stock, which enabled each to own one third of the company. The lawyer who drew up the charter of incorporation in 1895, Arnold Loeb, took four shares of stock valued at $400 in lieu of a fee; by 1918, Loeb's four shares were worth $400,000.

The period 1895–1900 was one of rapid growth: $750,000 in sales in 1895 and $10,000,000 in 1900, surpassing Montgomery Ward and allowing Sears, Roebuck to become the dominant mail order firm. With such growth, numerous problems surfaced: there were delays and mistakes in filling customer orders; returned merchandise piled up; cash dwindled; and the organization suffered from inexperience and a general lack of coordination.

Otto Doering, the plant superintendent, saved Sears, Roebuck and Company, aided by a new building on a forty-acre tract on Chicago's west side. Doering's solution to the mounting number of customer orders was a scheduling system that could handle a hundred thousand orders per day. Briefly, upon receipt each customer order was assigned a shipping bin number along with a date and a fifteen-minute time window for that order to be filled, packed, and shipped. "Mixed" tickets, orders that required routing to more than one department, were a major problem that was solved by sending each department involved the stock number, the bin number, and the targeted day and time window. If a department failed to be on time, it was fined fifty cents and charged the cost of shipping the short item separately.

Doering's system treated each order as a "batch" that was divided, assigned to the responsible departments, filled, and then reassembled at the shipping point. It involved thousands of orders each day, each representing numerous pieces of paper that in turn represented numerous items of merchandise, large and small. Although it is difficult to conceive of this operation without modern technology, Doering's system worked and reduced back orders, late shipments, and errors in shipping and billing.[8] When we think of just-in-time inventory management, we should remember Otto Doering as well as Henry Ford.

The Sears-Rosenwald-Nusbaum partnership succeeded for a while, but there were continuing sources of friction. Sears was the promoter and aggressive for expansion; Rosenwald was the systematizer who wanted to improve operations; and Nusbaum was a burr under both Rosenwald's and Sears's saddles as a fence sitter who would defer to their decisions but say "I told you so" if things went wrong. Nusbaum also irritated his partners by finding fault and nagging others; he felt that criticism rather than praise kept people on their toes.

Sears's frustration mounted, and eventually he told Rosenwald, "Someone's got to go—you and Nusbaum can buy me out, or you and I will buy Nusbaum's shares."[9] Rosenwald had to choose family ties or the company, and he chose the latter. In 1901 he and Sears bought Nusbaum's interests for $1,250,000, a substantial gain over the $37,500 that Nusbaum had invested.

The Rosenwald-Sears team continued to broaden the scope of the catalog offerings, opened branch offices in New York City (1902) and Dallas (1906), and acquired interests in the companies that were suppliers. Sears, Roebuck followed the policy of taking a major share of a supplier's output but never all of it (so that the supplier had to remain competitive outside of Sears's purchases), and leveraging the price down by volume purchasing. For instance, the Sears, Roebuck top-of-the-line sewing machine sold for $17.55 in 1897 but only $7.65 in 1900. By 1906 Sears, Roebuck owned sixteen factories as suppliers, Sears and Rosenwald owned 95 percent of the shares of the company, and sales reached $49,000,000. Two decades after taking an unwanted shipment of watches, Richard Sears was a multimillionaire.

A business downturn in 1907 slowed Sears, Roebuck's growth and sales dropped to $47,000,000—not a substantial decline, but this first interruption in the firm's expansion led to a fundamental difference of opinion between Sears and Rosenwald over strategy. Sears had been very effective in merchandising and felt that the way out of the slump was more aggressive promotion to sell more and more. Rosenwald defined the problem in belt-tightening terms, and in his view Sears, Roebuck needed to refine and extend Doering's scheduling system so as to balance orders received with orders shipped and reduce back orders, returned merchandise, and complaints. Sears, on the other hand, would be happy if nine of ten orders were correct and shipped on time. Since about a hundred thousand orders were being received each day, this meant that some ten thousand orders per day would be delayed or short-shipped. To Rosenwald this undermined the customers' confidence in the company, with long-run damage to its mission to have performance equal promise.

Their differences were not resolved, and Sears sold his interest to the investment firm of Goldman, Sachs for $10,000,000. Sears was made a member of the board of directors, attended one meeting, and quit as a wealthy but embittered man.

Richard Sears had succeeded in building the nation's leading mail order establishment by tapping a prosperous rural market that had fewer choices before the catalog; by filling his catalog with a vast array of goods; by buying in volume and stressing quality, satisfaction, and low prices; by a liberal returned-goods policy; and by heavy promotion and advertising. In brief, the Sears, Roebuck catalog was the rural customers' department store. After the death of Richard Sears in 1914, *Printers' Ink* paid him this tribute:

> R. W. Sears was a mail-order man, had the mail-order viewpoint, knew how to use advertising space, knew the value of copy, knew the conditions surrounding mail-order publications, and he succeeded in a big way because he possessed those qualities to a greater degree than any other mail-order man who ever lived.[10]

When President Franklin D. Roosevelt was asked what one American book he would want every citizen of the Communist USSR to have, he said, "The Sears, Roebuck catalog."[11] Nothing illustrated better the consumers' choices in a market economy.

Counters

Julius Rosenwald was correct in his assessment of what Sears, Roebuck and Company needed to do to recover from the 1907–1908 depression. Afterward, a growth spurt increased Sears, Roebuck's sales sixfold from 1908 to 1920, and earnings increased threefold during that period. The mail order market was maturing, however, and other firms such as Spiegel, Bella Hess, and L. L. Bean (for Leon Leonwood Bean) were entering the game to challenge Ward and Sears, Roebuck. Two other trends indicated change. First, the rural population declined from 72 percent in 1880 to 54 percent in the census of 1910. Second, chain stores were on the rise, following the Great Atlantic and Pacific Tea Company, which had pioneered chain stores in groceries (1859), and variety chains such as F. W. Woolworth (1879), which was followed by the McCrory, Kress, and Kresge chains. James Cash Penney founded his first Golden Rule store in 1902, and W. T. Grant opened in 1906. By 1920 J. C. Penney had three hundred stores targeting smaller towns and cities rather than the rural market, illustrating a keen perception of the demographic changes. Neither Ward nor Sears, Roebuck had demonstrated any interest in retail outlets, while J.C. Penney, W. T. Grant, and others were expanding. An unusual blend of circumstances would bring about a substantial change, however.

The Kansas City, Missouri–born Robert Elkington Wood was a West Point graduate (class of 1900) who served in the Philippines before being assigned to help with the logistical problems of constructing the Panama Canal. His talents were recognized early by the first superintendent of the Panama Canal Company, John Stevens, who had learned his administrative skills under the tutelage of James J. Hill of the Great Northern Railroad. Stevens was succeeded by Colonel (later General) George W. Goethals in 1907, and Wood stayed and played a key role until the project was completed in 1915. Under Stevens and Goethals, Wood learned lessons of inventory management, logistics, forecasting, and leading people. Digging the "Big Ditch" was the largest construction project of that time, and Wood gained experience that would shape his career and the future of merchandising.

Wood supervised construction projects for E. I. Du Pont de Nemours and Company after his release from his Panama Canal responsibilities. America's involvement in World War I brought him back to active duty to serve under General Douglas MacArthur in coordinating the movement of supplies and troops. Wood was promoted to brigadier general in 1918 and was named acting quartermaster general to provide logistical support for the Allied Expeditionary Force.

Peace brought General Wood to civilian life and a position as vice president of merchandising for the Montgomery Ward Company. He was hired by Robert J. Thorne, who had served as a civilian on Wood's staff during the war and whose family had a majority interest in the firm. A steep but brief depression in 1920–21 brought about a financial reorganization of the Montgomery Ward company with the Thorne family being bought out by a syndicate formed by J. P. Morgan and Company. Robert Thorne was replaced by Theodore F. Merseles, formerly general manager of the National Cloak and Suit Company, a successful New York City mail order house.

Wood's biographer says "there was a widely circulated myth (probably grounded in fact)" that Wood read the *Statistical Abstract of the United States* while he was confined in the infirmary in the Panama Canal Zone for a minor ailment.[12] It makes a good story, but there is indeed evidence that Wood was keenly aware of demographic statistics and saw J. C. Penney moving into smaller towns and cities. The statistics would also have shown a declining rural population and increasing urbanization as well as other statistical information such as the increasing number of automobiles being sold and roads and highways being constructed and paved.

Reading something like a statistical abstract does not prompt action until the occasion permits it. The 1920–21 business downturn prompted Wood to open outlet stores *within* Ward's four mail order plants in Chicago, Kansas City, Fort Worth, and Portland to move the inventory. Two other stores were opened in Aurora and Springfield, Illinois, under the name George Lane Stores, to move out distress goods. The George Lane Stores produced miserable results, but those associated with the Ward name were successful. It is possible that it was this experience and reading the *Statistical Abstract* that led Wood to write this memo entitled "The Past, Present, and Future of Ward's" to Merseles:

> I originally tried to extend the house sales as an aid to our mail order business. I think in itself it can be developed to a very large and profitable business without interfering with our mail order business and aiding it in many ways. With the assistance of house sales I think we can make progress in the turnover of our mail order business that we have not dreamed of. . . . The keenest competition of all that we have to face is the chain store competition. . . . There are two weak spots in connection with the chain stores, the first being that with the exception of the old established grocery chains like the A&P they have no distributing warehouse system. . . . Many of these chains have not had the foresight to so group their stores as to work out a good system of warehouse distribution.
>
> I feel that if we are so inclined, we can beat the chain stores at their own game—that we have certain advantages which they do not possess and that

we can easily and profitably engage in the chain store business ourselves with a relatively small amount of capital. We have four splendid distributing points; we have an organized purchasing system; we have a wonderful name, if we choose to take advantage of it, and we ought to be able to build up our organization as good or better than the chain stores themselves and without harming our mail order business. . . .

We should experiment carefully and just as soon as we feel sure enough of our ground to go ahead, we should go ahead as rapidly as possible.[13]

In modern terms, Wood's memo would be a strengths, weaknesses, opportunities, threats (SWOT) analysis of Ward's competitive position in retailing.

Merseles rejected Wood's idea on the basis that the outlet stores would cannibalize the mail order business and move Montgomery Ward from the rural base that formed its primary market into uncharted territory. Merseles was successful in revamping Ward's catalog and in improving mail order operations. He did not share Wood's vision, however, and by 1924, for reasons that are not entirely clear, he saw Wood as someone who could oust him—indeed, talk in Chicago and the merchandising trade placed Wood in a position of "greater visibility in the business world than Merseles."[14]

In late September, 1924 Robert Wood left for a hunting trip in the West. He received news by telegram that he had been fired (maybe this explains why some executives are reluctant to take vacations). When he returned to his Chicago office it had been searched and his files seized, including the plans and drawings for the retail stores that he had proposed.

Wood was not out of a job for long and was hired by Julius Rosenwald as vice president of Sears, Roebuck's factories and retail stores. When Sears, Roebuck's president, Charles Kittle, died suddenly in 1928, Wood took over a company with mail order sales of $206,000,000 and profits of $14,000,000. Wood retired as chairman of the board in 1954, forty years after the death of Richard W. Sears. The company that Sears had started with a shipment of watches was the world's largest merchandising company, with $3,000,000,000 in sales, and $141,000,000 in profits, 200,000 employees, 11 mail order plants, 570 catalog sales offices, and 694 retail stores in 1954.

The lessons of Sears, Roebuck are those of defining and reforming the purpose of the firm as the times change. Richard W. Sears was able to take an assortment of products through the catalog to the rural market, a relatively untapped segment of the population. When Sears, Roebuck needed to tighten its belt in tough times, Julius Rosenwald made it a more competitive enterprise. As the rural market waned, Robert E. Wood reformulated its mission into retail outlets without harming the mail order business.

4

MOVERS

John Henry was a li'l baby, uh-huh,
Sittin' on his mama's knee, oh, yeah.
Said: "De Big Bend Tunnel on de C. & O. road
Gonna cause de death of me,
Lawd, Lawd, gonna' cause de death of me."...

Cap'n says to John Henry,
"Gonna bring me a steam drill 'round,
Gonna take dat steam drill out on de job,
Gonna whop dat steel on down,
Lawd, Lawd, gonna whop dat steel on down."...

John Henry started on de right hand,
De steam drill started on de lef'—
"Before I'd let dis steam drill beat me down,
I'd hammer my fool self to death,
Lawd, Lawd, I'd hammer my fool self to death."...

De man dat invented de steam drill,
Thought he was mighty fine.
John Henry drove his fifteen feet,
An' de steam drill only made nine,
Lawd, Lawd, an' de steam drill only made nine....

> John Henry was hammerin' on de mountain,
> An' his hammer was strikin' fire,
> He drove so hard till he broke his pore heart,
> An' he lied down his hammer an' he died,
> Lawd, Lawd, he lied down his hammer and he died.[1]

The tale of John Henry and numerous other songs and poems illustrate the romance and tragedy of America's railroads. "Wreck of the Old 97," by D. G. George; "The Gospel Train," by an anonymous writer; "Casey Jones," by T. L. Liebert; "Homesick Blues" and "Freedom Train," by Langston Hughes; and "The Wabash Cannonball," by the Delmore brothers, are glimpses of a way of life that is long gone but not forgotten. Few songs about internal combustion engines or rockets have been woven into American life as much as songs about the railroad era, which the poet Robert Frost said touched "far into the lives of other folk."

Although other means of transportation now get us there more quickly, the building of the railroads represented an era of expansion into new lands, the availability of new products, and opportunities to travel to dreamed-of places. Britain's George Stephenson built the first locomotive, and Britain's early railroads, such as the Stockton and Darlington, led the way in long-distance travel by rail. America's railroad development was different, however, because no other nation had such a vast expanse of virgin land, a growing population to be moved, and fewer customs and political barriers to block travel. In no other land did the railroads play as substantial a role in economic development, social change, and the emergence of different political arrangements.

Colonists from Britain traveled three months in cramped and swaying quarters aboard sailing ships to settle along the eastern seaboard of America. Travel beyond the Appalachian Mountains was difficult and dangerous, but one could travel by horseback or in Conestoga wagons, the forerunner of the covered wagons of the plains, from Philadelphia to New York City in two days. Turnpikes with beds of rock or logs were one way of travel, and most roads were privately financed, although local or state funds were sometimes available. One, the Cumberland Road, ran from Cumberland, Maryland to Wheeling, West Virginia; the Philadelphia-to-Lancaster Pennsylvania Pike was completed in 1792. Turnpikes were expensive to build and maintain, and it typically cost thirty cents per ton-mile to ship freight on them—often transport costs were more than the selling price of the freight.

River and canal transportation made use of nature's own paths to move products and people. George Washington and his friends put their money in the Potomac River Company in 1784, and in 1817 the most famous canal of all, the Erie, was authorized. It ran 364 miles from Albany to Buffalo, New York, and touched off a craze of canal building throughout the country. River travel was one-way downstream until American ingenuity in the persons of Robert Livingston and Robert Fulton came to the rescue. In 1807 the steamboat *Clermont* made a trip from New York City to Albany, New York, a distance of 150 miles, on the Hudson River in thirty-two hours. Steamboats soon came into wide use on inland waterways and provided key services to many cities.

While waterways and turnpikes made possible the extension of the national market, a new scheme of travel was on the horizon. Unlike canals and pikes, the early railroads were entirely privately financed, although land grants and subsidies would come later. The railroads were resisted by vested interests in the canal and pike business, and also by well-meaning citizens who feared them and found no sanction for them in the Bible. One Ohio school board went on record as opposing the construction of a railroad through their community because it "was a device of Satan to lead immortal souls down to Hell." Some railroads were taxed to provide funds for canals, and some were sued for damages when canals lost revenues to the iron horse.

Despite the resistance, the web of tracks continued to grow, probing the interior of lands where nature had furnished no natural pathways. The Baltimore and Ohio had thirteen miles of track in 1827, and in the period 1830 to 1840 many lines were built from one city to another. By 1840, America had 3,326 miles of canals and 2,818 miles of railroads; by 1850, railroad trackage exceeded 5,000 miles, in contrast to approximately 3,700 miles of canals. Between 1850 and 1860 all states east of the Mississippi River were connected by some 30,000 miles of track, and one could travel all the way from New York to Chicago in three days. Companies such as the Erie, the Pennsylvania, the Western and Atlantic, the Chesapeake and Ohio, and the Baltimore and Ohio were moving westward, and few towns were out of earshot of the train's whistle.

It is difficult to choose representatives of America's railroad movers from an abundant list, such as John Murray Forbes of the Michigan Central and later the Chicago, Burlington, and Quincy; the "Big Four" of the Central Pacific—Leland Stanford, Collis P. Huntington, Mark Hopkins, and Charles

Crocker; the Denver and Rio Grande's William J. Palmer; Erastus Corning of the New York Central; John W. Garrett of the Baltimore and Ohio; and the list could go on and on.

James J. Hill and Edward H. Harriman have been selected to represent the movers here because they were builders as well as consolidators of railroad systems. Hill was a visionary who saw the railroad as a means of regional economic development and of connecting the North American continent to the relatively untapped markets and products of the Orient. Harriman represents the financial capitalists who saw the need to consolidate and build an interconnecting system of railroads to provide low-cost, efficient service. Together, Hill and Harriman represent the problems and the promise of American railroads.

JAMES J. HILL

Missing the last westward-bound wagon train was a pivotal point in the life of James Jerome Hill. Hill was born on September 16, 1838, in Rockwood, Ontario, Canada, the son of James and Anne Dunbar Hill. James Hill was successful enough as a farmer that they were able to send the young James Hill to Rockwood Academy, a Quaker-sponsored private school. His favorite subjects were history and geography, and he read what was available on India and the mysterious countries of the Orient.

A childhood accident with a bow that snapped and reversed the arrow into his right eye left him visually impaired. He clerked in a grocery store for four years to support the family after his father died, and at age eighteen he set out to realize his childhood dreams of visiting the Orient. In Atlantic ports he tried to find work to pay his passage on a ship to the Orient. Unsuccessful, he thought he would have better luck sailing from a Pacific port, so he headed overland westward. When he arrived in St. Paul, Minnesota, he found that the last wagon train of that year had left for Oregon a few days before.

Stranded in St. Paul for the winter, he clerked for a firm that served riverboats that came up the Mississippi River as far as they could, then discharged their freight for portage by wagon to connect with other riverboats that traveled up the Red River of the North to Fort Garry (modern Winnipeg, Manitoba). The territory surrounding the Red River of the North was a growth area for hard winter wheat, furs shipped to Fort Garry by the Hudson Bay

Company, and wood that became building lumber or firewood for the steamboats. Northward flowed groceries, dry goods, farm implements, and other necessities.

As a freight forwarding agent, Hill could see the inefficiencies of overland transport between the Red and Mississippi Rivers. He tried to enlist in the First Minnesota Volunteers when the Civil War began but found that no one wanted a one-eyed soldier. He turned back to the growing town of St. Paul (population 4,000) and began an entrepreneurial career by supplying wood for the locomotives of the St. Paul and Pacific Railroad. The St. Paul and Pacific connected St. Paul eastward to the Chicago, Milwaukee, and St. Paul and the Illinois Central. He built warehouses that facilitated the off-loading of steamboats onto wagons and formed a partnership with Norman W. Kittson to establish the Red River Transportation Company, which would provide transport and storage services from St. Paul to Winnipeg.

One historian described the early railroads as "little more than a teakettle on wheels pulling a few oblong wooden boxes on spindly iron rails."[2] This was an appropriate description, but these spindly rails were not bound by nature's passageways such as rivers and canals. Investors saw the emerging possibilities, and Jay Cooke received a federal charter to build a railroad from Duluth on Lake Superior to Seattle, Washington. In 1870 the Northern Pacific Railroad began construction but would reach only as far as Fargo, North Dakota, before the financial panic of 1873 brought the house of Jay Cooke down. Cooke had also planned to extend the branches of the St. Paul and Pacific into Canada, but that venture fell too in 1873.

One of the crippling features of America's early railroads was that they were built for the profits, either from the bonds or shares to be sold or from padding the construction costs. James J. Hill's approach was different. He saw the railroads as tools of regional economic development, with profits to follow from operations in those areas. With his partner, Kittson, and two Canadians, Donald Smith and George Stephen, who was president of the Bank of Montreal, the St. Paul, Minneapolis, and Manitoba Railroad was formed. This line was chartered and existed on paper only, but it sold stocks and bonds to purchase the assets of the bankrupt St. Paul and Pacific, which was soon renamed. The line was extended northward, and bumper crops of wheat plus availability of transport soon made Minneapolis the grain-milling-and-processing capital of the United States. In turn, Hill and his partners became millionaires.

Westward Ho!

Hill poured his profits into fulfilling his dream of trade with the Orient. Hill was not the only person to have this dream, however: Henry Villard picked up the pieces of Jay Cooke's Northern Pacific in 1881 to extend the line to Seattle to connect with Villard's Oregon Railway and Navigation Company and provide it with an outlet to eastern U.S. markets. The Northern Pacific reached the Pacific in 1883 but had a cost overrun of $14,000,000 and a debt of over $19,000,000. Villard began to employ agents in eastern U.S. ports to meet immigrants on incoming ships, as well as agents at British and European ports to sell emigrants on the idea of settling in areas served by the Northern Pacific.

While Villard built with the hope of attracting settlers later, Hill took a contrarian strategy of building gradually, attracting settlers, and then building further westward. Villard built to get federal land grants, but Hill was buying land in North Dakota and Montana, especially in the copper-rich area around Butte, Montana. He also hoped to attract settlers by advertising cheap land where there were lush forests, abundant water, and deposits of minerals. He gave free bulls to ranchers who wished to improve their breeding stock; prizes were awarded for the best-quality grain that was shipped on the Hill line; for $10 settlers could ride to their claims; small-business owners were offered inexpensive lots to build upon; and Hill kept freight rates low to encourage shippers. His goal was to build incrementally to the Pacific and thereby gain access to the Orient.

To compete effectively, Hill observed, meant that "the birth and growth of our commerce with the Orient would depend absolutely upon a favorable transportation rate. Having to meet the competition of the world, we must sell more cheaply and deliver more satisfactorily than the rest of the world."[3] Hill's first westward step was the Montana Central, completed in 1886 and connecting the St. Paul, Minneapolis, and Manitoba with Great Falls, Helena, and Butte (Montana), a new total track distance of 1,175 miles. From the southwest spur to Butte, Hill built northwesterly with a line called the Seattle and Montana Railway Company that reached Seattle in 1893. Hill and his partners now had a line that ran from Seattle eastward to Lake Superior—he renamed this aggregation of railroads the Great Northern Railway.

The signature train of the Great Northern was called "The Empire Builder," the name that others had given to James J. Hill. The Great Northern was a well-managed line that had lower operating costs per mile, less debt, sturdier track and roadbed, and better locomotives and rolling stock than the Northern Pacific. The Great Northern was the only line that never missed a dividend and never went bankrupt during the financial upheavals of the late 1800s and the early 1900s.

Once he reached the Pacific, Hill realized his dream of trade with the Orient—trade that would roll over his lines to the eastern markets in days rather than the four to six months that were necessary for a ship to round Cape Horn and arrive in eastern ports. He made Seattle his headquarters and received news that the Nippon Yusen Kaisha shipping line was negotiating with officials in San Diego to make that city its port of call. He rallied his backers, including Frederick Weyerhaeuser, the Northwest's lumber pioneer, and convinced the Japanese firm that Seattle was a better location.

Hill's efforts, more than those of any other single person, established American trade with Asian countries in the late 1800s and early 1900s. In 1896, the United States exported $7,700,000 worth of goods to Japan; by 1905 the figure was $51,700,000. Imports from Japan rose from $25,500,000 to $51,800,000 in the same period.[4] As Hill commented:

> The market was opened, the opportunity accepted, our trade with the Orient, no longer a dream, became a splendid fact, as the statistics show. In the ten years between 1893, when the Great Northern reached the coast, and in 1903, the exports of the Puget Sound customs district increased . . . nearly 540 per cent. In those years our exports to Europe increased 50 per cent . . . to South America a little over 30 per cent. . . . At this rate it seemed that the bulk of trade of the Orient was ours for the taking.[5]

Hill had dreamed, and had mastered his dream.

Merger Myopia

In 1893, the Great Northern reached Puget Sound and another financial crisis put the Northern Pacific into its second receivership. Hill saw the possibilities of consolidating the interests of these two railroads that reached from the Great Lakes to the Pacific and served seven northwestern states. To his longtime friend and fellow investor, George Stephen (now knighted as Lord Mount Stephen), he sent a detailed reorganization plan that showed the economies that could be obtained from such a merger. With Edward Tuck representing the Chase National Bank, a financial plan of reorganization was formulated.

Between 1869 and 1875 Minnesota, Illinois, Iowa, and Wisconsin had passed state laws called granger laws, which regulated railroads, grain elevators, and storage warehouses in the interest of midwestern farmers. Minnesota law expressly prohibited "the consolidation of parallel lines," and Hill's attempted merger of the Great Northern and the Northern Pacific was blocked by a lawsuit filed under the Minnesota statute. A circuit court dismissed the case, but the U.S. Supreme Court granted an injunction in 1896.

Thwarted by the Court, Hill and his associates found no prohibition against their ownership of the two lines independently and began to buy Northern Pacific securities. J. Pierpont Morgan was also interested in the plan and he and his associates and the Deutsche Bank of Berlin subscribed $50,000,000 to a merger that was not a merger. The Great Northern and the Northern Pacific became functionally one railway under one management but were still legally separate entities.

Hill wrote Morgan that they had accomplished their objective, which "was to bring together as nearly as possible the general policy of the Northern Pacific and the Great Northern so that both companies could be operated . . . [to] preserve their mutual independence . . . [and to] discharge all its duties to the public . . . [and] avoid unnecessary expenditure of money either in building new lines or in the operation of existing lines."[6] Hill added that this new way of operating the lines as one had already reduced operating expenses $50,000 per month, and more savings could be expected.

The Great Northern and Northern Pacific alliance demonstrated that the consolidation of lines held the potential of greater long-run savings, but public policy was taking a more myopic slant. The granger laws were superseded by the Act to Regulate Commerce (better known as the Interstate Commerce Act) of 1887, which created the Interstate Commerce Commission. This act prohibited rebates, discrimination between long- and short-haul charges, and pooling and other traffic agreements, and it contained other provisions that regulated railroad operations. The Sherman Anti-Trust Act (1890) was not aimed at railways specifically but prohibited combinations and conspiracy in restraint of trade in corporate affairs. Neither of these acts was very effective, but they illustrated the changing political climate that would have an impact on the future of U.S. railways. As James Hill would comment later:

Take the Northern Securities Company for example. It contemplated no power and had no power under its charter to operate a railroad. . . . The courts asserted that it had the power to restrain trade; that the power to do a thing is as objectionable as the doing of it; that is to say, that since with your hand you may kill a man, it is against public policy for a man to have hands.

So the Northern Securities Company went out of business. What has been the result? . . . To the public, no difference at all except that it has missed the advantages which the simpler and more businesslike plan would have secured.[7]

Pools, agreements, trusts, or other semblances of an alliance, whether they led to improved railroad operations or not, became suspect.

In this climate of growing governmental scrutiny we find James J. Hill and his financial backer, J. P. Morgan, doing battle with Edward H. Harriman and his financial wizard, Jacob Schiff, of Kuhn, Loeb, and Company. Harriman's side of the story will follow, but for the Hill-Morgan interests it was an opportunity to gain control of the Chicago, Burlington, and Quincy (known as the Burlington). The Burlington had 7,922 miles of line from Chicago to and through Illinois, Missouri, Iowa, Kansas, and Nebraska, with one branch connecting with the Denver and Rio Grande in Colorado and northern branches extending into South Dakota and Wyoming. For Hill and Morgan, this would bring their interests into the prosperous Midwest with an outlet to Lake Michigan.

Harriman and Schiff also saw that their interests in the Union Pacific and the Southern Pacific could be served in the same manner. Hill and Morgan moved first, however, and soon controlled 97 percent of the Burlington's capital stock, blocking Harriman and Schiff. In Hill, Harriman had met his match. Unable to obtain the Burlington, Harriman started buying Northern Pacific; if he could gain control, he would have its share of the Burlington.

Hill and Morgan were slow to realize what Harriman and Schiff were doing, and Harriman had a majority of the preferred stock and was forty thousand shares short of a majority of common stock before Hill and Morgan acted. They bought more common stock, driving share prices to a high of $1,000, and Hill postponed the Northern Pacific's annual meeting in order to retire the preferred stock before Harriman could use his votes to change the board of directors. The buying war between the Hill-Morgan and the Harriman-Schiff interests created the stock market panic of May 9, 1901. Peace was finally restored—but the reader will need to await the story of Edward H. Harriman to find this part of the tale (clue: look for the Northern Securities Company and President Theodore Roosevelt).

James Jerome Hill had a life beyond boardroom battles. In August 1867 he married Mary Theresa Mehagan and they eventually became the parents of ten children, seven girls and three boys. He was a family man and delighted in endowing a Roman Catholic seminary in St. Paul that was dedicated to his wife. One of their sons, Louis W. Hill, took over the presidency of the Great Northern when Hill retired in 1907; by that time Hill's railroads served an area containing over 1,500,000 people. Hill loved hunting and fishing; he also collected art by an emerging school of young artists who would become known as the French Impressionists. He believed that real talent would rise to the top and refused to provide two years of financial backing to a young American artist who promised to give Hill all of the paintings completed during that period of time—Hill was right, the artist was Rockwell Kent.

By the time of his death on May 29, 1916, this Canadian-born one-eyed visionary had reshaped the American Northwest.

EDWARD H. HARRIMAN

Edward Harriman stood about 5 feet 4 inches tall and weighed about 130 pounds, and it has been said that he "looked more like a clerk than the latest Napoleon of the railways . . . his chin had a pugnacious thrust to it, his eyes gleamed with energy . . . and he walked with a jockey's bow-legged jaunti-ness."[8] Off the job, he was a devoted family man, but at work he was a brusque dynamo who hated wasting time and money. Like Napoleon, he hated to retreat even though sometimes it would have made sense.

Edward Henry Harriman was born February 20, 1848 in Hempstead, New York, the son of a Columbia University–educated Episcopalian clergy-man, Orlando Harriman, and Cornelia Neilson Harriman. The Harriman household combined piety and poverty, and Edward left home at the age of fourteen to escape poverty, although he never forgot piety, at least in his pri-vate life. His first job was as a runner in the stock exchange house of D. C. Hays and involved the carrying of securities from the Hays office to other bankers and brokers. Since there were no electric tickers to provide stock and bond quotations at that time, these messengers also carried from place to place pads of paper upon which were written current prices of various securities and buy and sell offers. Wall Street slang for this job was "pad shover," and Harriman proved to be a good pad shover since he could quote prices from memory rather than having to consult the pad.

By the time he was twenty-two years old Harriman realized his future was in finance. He borrowed $3,000 from his uncle, Oliver Harriman, and bought a seat on the New York Stock Exchange. He opened a modest office on the third floor of a building at the corner of Broad Street and Exchange Place. As a runner he had made numerous acquaintances who were to become his clients—one of them, Richard Schell, a noted speculator of that time, hated to climb stairs and offered to pay Harriman's rent if he would move his office to the first floor. Harriman did and gained the Schell account as well as that of Schell's brothers, who were connected to the New York Central Railroad and were friends of Cornelius Vanderbilt. Horatio Alger could well have based his heroes on the life of Edward Harriman because his hard work, thriftiness, and trustworthiness brought him numerous clients such as August Belmont Sr., Vanderbilt, Jay Gould, and the investment adviser to the Equitable Life Assurance Society.

Harriman was content to be a broker and take his commission until he noted a run-up in the price of shares of railroads whose primary freight business was hauling anthracite coal. He sensed an attempt to corner the market and knew that the real value of these stocks was below the market price. He made his first move as a speculator by selling short, that is, promising to sell stock (which he did not currently have) at a future price that was below the going market price. In brief, he became a bear, speculating that by the time he had promised to deliver in the future, the share price would drop and he could buy and deliver, perhaps at a gain.

Harriman was right: A mysterious Wall Street speculator known only to historians as "Deacon" White was trying the "corner."[9] White failed to get the shares he needed, share prices fell, and Harriman gained $150,000 by selling short. Buoyed by his success, he tried a bear campaign on the Delaware and Hudson Railroad, but his antagonists in this case were the deep pockets of the Astors, and Harriman lost the $150,000 he had gained previously.

Although Harriman remained prosperous thanks to his brokerage commissions, his marriage in 1879 to Mary Williamson Avery, daughter of the president of the Ogdensburg and Lake Champlain Railroad Company, would move him more deeply into the railroad business. Harriman served on the board of directors of his father-in-law's railroad and expanded his interests in railroads beyond finance to managing them. With partners, he bought the Lake Ontario Southern, reorganized and modernized the line, and sold it to the Pennsylvania Railroad at a substantial profit as the Sodus Bay and Southern line.

His success with the Sodus Bay and Southern convinced him that America's railroads were in need of reorganization and modernization. Many railroads had been built as speculative financial ventures or to obtain land grants, but this had been done without regard for the long-run maintenance and economic performance that would provide transportation service at a profit. In 1885 he left E. H. Harriman and Company, turning the business over to his brother, William M. Harriman, and began using his financial expertise on the railroads. In that same year he bought the eight-thousand-acre estate of James Parrott, situated forty-five miles north of Jersey City and ten miles west of the Hudson River in Orange County, New York. He renamed the estate Arden; Arden House later became the property of Columbia University and today provides the setting for a highly regarded executive development program.

Another of Harriman's successes in railroad reorganization was the Illinois Central, the belt of railroad lines that ran west as far as Sioux City, Iowa; north to Madison, Wisconsin; southeast to Cincinnati, Ohio; and south to New Orleans, Louisiana, with branches to St. Louis and Memphis. As head of finance, Harriman began to acquire the funds to modernize the Illinois Central and to purchase or form alliances with connecting railroads. The Illinois Central's president, Stuyvesant Fish, credited Harriman with the survival and success of the line: During Harriman's tenure passenger rates declined from 2.42 cents per mile to 1.84 cents between 1883 and 1909; freight rates per ton-mile decreased from 1.43 to .6 cents over the same period.[10] Harriman alone could not have done this, but his policies of modernization and more thorough connections with other railroads led to decreased rates and increased revenues, making the Illinois Central a top performer that would succeed during the financial panic of 1893 while 156 other lines became bankrupt or were placed under a receivership.

The Union Pacific

Advances in selling and making products would not have been possible without similar progress in transportation. Binding the nation together with a web of steel had been a dream before the Civil War. The cessation of hostilities made it possible for a new dream that would perhaps provide balm for old wounds. To get to the golden promise of California, the seeker had three choices: three months in a covered wagon across Indian Territory, deserts, mountains, and plains; six months in a ship (a clipper could do it in four) around Cape Horn and its stormy seas; or by ship to the Isthmus of Panama, a traverse across land and by river through malaria-ridden jungles, and then by ship again up the coast. The Golden Lorelei attracted people by all three means. Some made it; some did not.

In 1862 a charter was granted the Union Pacific Railroad to build westward from Omaha, Nebraska, and the Central Pacific was to build eastward from Sacramento to meet the Union Pacific. Because of the rugged Sierra Nevada, the Central Pacific met with difficulties, and Congress instructed the Union Pacific to keep going west until it connected with the Central Pacific. The two lines finally met May 10, 1869, at Promontory Summit, near Ogden, Utah. A golden spike commemorated the joining of East and West—the nation was united. Other coast-to-coast lines were to follow: the Southern Pacific, the Northern Pacific, the Great Northern, and the Santa Fe. One could travel from the Atlantic to the Pacific in only one week.

This westward dream clashed with financial reality in 1893 when the Union Pacific filed for bankruptcy and was placed in receivership. J. P. Morgan and his associates were asked to undertake the task of financial reorganization, but they refused, calling the Union Pacific "a rusted streak of iron" that ran through sparsely populated mountains and deserts. Kuhn, Loeb, and Company undertook the task, with Jacob Schiff to head the effort; Harriman saw more promise in the West and resigned his financial position on the Illinois Central (although he stayed on its Board of Directors) so that he could invest in the Union Pacific.

The Union Pacific had been in an uncertain condition since its inception, as a result of financial scandals regarding its construction, and it was estimated that at least half of its stock was "watered," that is, bloated by exaggerated expenses. When Harriman took over, the Union Pacific's track was old; it had been built haphazardly so as to meet construction deadlines; light iron rails had been used, maintenance had been neglected, and the curves were short and the grades steep. Each of these factors contributed to a slow, uncertain flow of cross-country traffic.

To gain firsthand knowledge of the Union Pacific, Harriman put together a special train that would travel westward from Omaha with an observation platform in front and a locomotive pushing from the rear. Harriman mounted the observation platform and visited every station from Omaha to Portland, Oregon, and back, stopping occasionally to inspect the track or the signals, or to talk to the employees. Harriman, as one historian noted, "must have risked one of history's most profound combinations of wind-

and-sun burns" in that late spring and early summer of 1898.[11] But, when he finished, no one knew the Union Pacific better than Edward Harriman.

Immediately he embarked on an improvement plan that would cost some $160,000,000—at a time when the entire U.S. federal budget was $561,000,000.[12] The Union Pacific bored an eighteen-hundred-foot tunnel through a granite mountain to turn twenty-one crooked miles into eleven straight ones; built a bridge across the Great Salt Lake to save a 147-mile trip around it; laid miles of new, stronger steel track; abandoned seldom-used tracks; scrapped older locomotives and bought newer, faster, more powerful ones; acquired nearly five thousand new steel freight and passenger cars to replace the wooden rolling stock of the past; and installed block signals for increased safety over five thousand miles of track.

Harriman turned the Union Pacific around. Freight tonnage tripled; the rate of return on capital increased 44 percent from 1898 to 1909; freight and passenger rates declined; a passenger could ride from San Francisco to New York in 71 hours and 27 minutes in 1906; and Union Pacific stock rose from 44⅜ to $219 per share (stock and commodity prices will be quoted in dollars and fractions of a dollar rather than in dollars and cents). With greater carrying capacity in steel rail cars, stronger locomotive power, and better track, the amount of traffic could be increased substantially without significantly increasing the ratio of operating expenses to revenue. As a modern manager would say, it was a matter of "throughput." Harriman had demonstrated that an investment in improvements could lead to faster, safer, and more profitable operations.

Harriman's strategy for acquiring and improving the Southern Pacific Railroad was essentially the same. The Central Pacific was the extension of the Union Pacific from Ogden, Utah, through Sacramento to San Francisco, and was built by the "Big Four," Collis P. Huntington, Leland Stanford, Charles Crocker, and Mark Hopkins. This group also owned the Southern Pacific, and when Harriman wanted the Central Pacific to upgrade its tracks to match his Union Pacific improvements, he was rejected. By 1884 the Big Four owned less than 30 percent of the Central Pacific and Southern Pacific stock, however, and the death of Collis P. Huntington in 1900 made 400,000 of the 2,000,000 shares outstanding available for sale. Those shares were valued at $100,000,000, and Huntington's heirs were anxious to sell.

Harriman moved quickly and obtained the Union Pacific board's vote (which was not difficult, since he ran the board as Napoleon ruled his generals) that issued $100,000,000 in 4 percent bonds convertible in five years to

Union Pacific stock. Now Harriman controlled the Union Pacific, Central Pacific, and Southern Pacific, which formed a railroad that extended from Seattle in the northwest to San Diego in southern California, then east through Yuma and El Paso to Fort Worth and to connect with the Illinois Central in New Orleans, as well as eastward from San Francisco to Omaha. If a person traveled every mile of a Harriman line, the distance would have been twenty-five thousand miles, the longest interconnecting railroad system in the United States.

The Union Pacific's compliant board rapidly followed Harriman's request for approval to spend $18,000,000 on improvements for the Central Pacific and $41,000,000 for the Southern Pacific. Chicago became the headquarters, and the operations, maintenance, auditing, purchasing, and traffic offices were centralized there. The traffic capacity was increased, the track improved, and from 1901 to 1908 passenger rates declined 22 percent and freight rates declined 6 percent. John W. "Bet-a-Million" Gates, no slouch as a speculator and appraiser of property values, said that Harriman's consolidated Union Pacific, Southern Pacific, and Central Pacific created "the most magnificent railroad property in the United States."

Having carried his Central Pacific, Southern Pacific, and Union Pacific lines to good economic performance, Harriman set his eyes on a terminus in Chicago, the line headquarters, which would also complete a box of lines that connected with the Illinois Central in both the north and the south. The Chicago, Burlington, and Quincy Railroad (Burlington) became his target for acquisition because it essentially ran parallel to the Union Pacific from Denver to the Missouri River and also terminated in Chicago. Burlington stock was widely held and in 1900 Harriman formed a group of financiers to buy Burlington: Jacob Schiff represented Kuhn, Loeb, and Company; James Stillman of New York's National City Bank, was included (hence establishing a Rockefeller connection), as was George J. Gould, the son of and eventual successor to Jay Gould, who had died in 1892.

The Harriman group thought 200,000 shares would be enough to control the Burlington and started buying Burlington stock in small batches and through intermediaries so as not to reveal their goals nor run the price up too fast. With Kuhn, Loeb buying, some 80,300 shares (less than 9 percent of the shares outstanding) had been acquired by late July 1900, but at a cost of $10,000,000. The stakes were becoming too high and acquiring the desired total of 120,000 shares would cost more than the Harriman group wanted to pay, so buying ceased in July of 1900.

Kuhn, Loeb had camouflaged the purchases so skillfully that no one realized that Burlington stock was in play. In the fall of 1900, James J. Hill decided that he wanted the Burlington to reach Chicago, so he allied with J. P. Morgan and his associates, still not knowing of the Harriman group holdings. Morgan was as clever as Kuhn, Loeb in buying, and Burlington stock prices rose, but not so much as to signal others that action was occurring.

Harriman's group saw Burlington's prices rising and sold 60,300 of their shares at prices ranging from $130 to $140⅝ which Morgan's buyers absorbed without either Harriman or Schiff being the wiser. The Harriman buying pool disbanded, dividing the remaining 20,000 shares among the members of the group. It was not until March of 1901 that Harriman realized that Hill and Morgan were after the Burlington; now the battle was between these two great railroaders, Hill and Harriman. Harriman arranged a meeting with Hill through a mutual friend, the financier George F. Baker. The meeting was brief: Harriman, on behalf of the Union Pacific, offered to provide a third of the money necessary to buy the Burlington in return for a one-third interest. Hill, knowing he had Morgan money behind him, refused to discuss the offer. Harriman has been quoted as terminating the meeting with the statement "Very well, it [Hill's refusal] is a hostile act and you must take the consequences."[13] Hill did not realize the force that he had set in motion.

Unable to buy into the part of the Burlington that was in Hill's Northern Pacific pocket, Harriman made one of the most audacious moves in financial history—he went after the Northern Pacific shares! If he could control the Northern Pacific, he would also have its share of the Burlington.

Smug in their defeat of Harriman, Morgan had sailed for Italy to shop for artworks and Hill had gone to the Northwest to relax as well as catch up on business affairs in Seattle. While Hill and Morgan were away, Harriman instructed Schiff to start buying Northern Pacific. The stock price rose from $112 to $149¾ in one week, and this signaled the stock was in play. The speculators pounced: The bears felt that the price would drop since the intrinsic value of the Northern Pacific was less than what it was selling for, while the bulls speculated that there would be a further rise in price because the Burlington would add substantial value to the Northern Pacific. Neither Hill, Morgan, nor any of their associates realized what was happening. The Northern Pacific sold 13,000 of its shares that were being held by the company, and Morgan and Company sold 10,000 of its shares—with all of these shares headed to Harriman's Union Pacific pocket.

By Friday, May 3, 1901, Harriman had a majority of Northern Pacific's preferred and was 40,000 shares short of a majority of Northern Pacific's common stock. On Saturday, Harriman was ill and unable to go to the office. He knew the stock market closed at noon on Saturdays so he sent a message to Kuhn, Loeb for Schiff to execute such an order. Schiff, a devout Jew, was at the synagogue on the Sabbath, so a Kuhn, Loeb junior partner delivered Harriman's message there. Schiff did not feel that Harriman needed the extra 40,000 shares; he also reasoned that such a purchase attempt would drive the price to an impractical level. He therefore told the messenger that the order should not be initiated.

Meanwhile, Hill had returned to Seattle and learned of the run on Northern Pacific's shares; he wired Morgan in Italy for authority to buy 156,000 shares of common in order to block Harriman. On Sunday, Morgan wired his office to buy the Northern Pacific shares when the market reopened Monday. Harriman learned on Monday what was happening and bought no shares after the Morgan order hit the trading floor. By Wednesday, Northern Pacific common was $1,000 a share.

What followed was the insolvency of about half of the Wall Street brokerage firms as the bears tried to deliver. There was a general sell-off of other shares to cover their losses: for example, U.S. Steel dropped from $46 to $24; the Atchinson, Topeka, and Santa Fe Railroad from $76 to $43; and the Delaware and Hudson from $163 to $105. The contenders called a truce: Neither Harriman, Schiff, Hill, Morgan, nor the bankers desired to bankrupt their Wall Street colleagues and those who had been buying and selling Northern Pacific shares. Fifteen prominent banks formed a $20,000,000 fund to relieve the distressed money market; others, including Morgan and Company and Kuhn, Loeb, and Company, agreed not to call for delivery of short-sold Northern Pacific shares; Hill and Harriman agreed to release enough shares to allow the bears to cover their deliveries at $150 per share. What was called the "Northern Pacific panic" passed and stock market order was restored, but Harriman had missed out on control of the Northern Pacific by a mere 40,000 shares because the buy order was not placed. Out of this, however, a landmark case in American business history would follow.

The Northern Securities Company

Financial chaos had been avoided, but the question of the Northern Pacific was still undecided: Hill interests had a majority of the common stock, while Harriman had a majority of the preferred and of the *total* Northern Pacific stock if preferred and common were combined. Hill and Harriman settled their differences in November 1901 by chartering the Northern Securities Company in corporation-friendly New Jersey as a holding company for the shares of the Northern Pacific, the Great Northern, and the Union Pacific. The Hill interests held twelve seats on the board of directors, and Harriman's group had three positions; with 23 percent of the stock of the Northern Securities Company, Harriman had 20 percent of the board but no officer position. Hill was clearly at the throttle of the greatest railroad combination in history.

When President William McKinley was shot and subsequently died on September 14, 1901, he was succeeded to the presidency by Theodore Roosevelt, a reform-minded Republican. Roosevelt promised some "trust-busting," and the Northern Securities Company provided a grand opportunity. The State of Minnesota filed a suit against Northern Securities as a "conspiracy in restraint of trade" that was illegal under the Sherman Act. In March 1902 the Justice Department joined the suit, and in 1904, by a 5 to 4 vote, the Supreme Court ruled Northern Securities a trust and ordered its dissolution.

This case would set a far-reaching legal precedent; one historian concluded that the Supreme Court's ruling established the principle "that great concentrations of power are bad in and of themselves. In the Northern Securities case, the American fear of great concentration of power triumphed over evidence that great power had been greatly used. A mutilated eagle is a sorry sight, but at least he cannot soar above the pedestrian beings who clipped his wings."[14]

The divided court reflected its uncertainty about corporate power. In Justice John Marshall Harlan's majority opinion: "It need not be shown that the combination, in fact, results or will result, in a total suppression of trade or in a complete monopoly, but it is only essential to show that . . . [it] tends to create a monopoly." So "tendency," whatever that meant, was sufficient. The great dissenter Justice Oliver Wendell Holmes expressed the minority opinion: "Great cases like hard cases make bad law . . . because of some accident of immediate overwhelming interest which appeals to the feeling and distort the judgment. . . . [this] makes what previously was clear seem doubtful, and before which even well settled principles of law will bend."[15]

How do you unscramble an omelette? Northern Securities stock was issued as the basis of what the Hill and Harriman lines had put in, but getting it back out was another problem. Harriman wanted the *value* of the

Union Pacific stock back, while Hill wanted to prorate the stock on the basis of *percentage* of Northern Securities without regard for what had been invested. After a series of legal skirmishes, Hill won and Harriman's Union Pacific wound up with less than it had invested.

Was Hill the winner? The Union Pacific received some Great Northern and Northern Pacific stock in the settlement, and when that stock rose in price after the dissolution, the Union Pacific sold it, making some $58,000,000 in the process. Harriman had turned a loss into a gain, but he would make two strategic mistakes afterward: one, he incurred the ill will of President Theodore Roosevelt; and two, he turned the Union Pacific into an investment company as well as a railroad.

Harriman had been a staunch supporter of the Republican Party and of Theodore Roosevelt in his successful campaign for the governorship of New York, and later as a vice presidential candidate on the McKinley ticket. When Roosevelt sought the presidency in 1904 Harriman raised $250,000 for the campaign, including $50,000 of his own money. In return, President Roosevelt agreed to appoint Chauncey Depew, a friend and colleague of Harriman, as ambassador to France. After the election, Roosevelt reneged on his promise, saying that he needed Depew in the Senate rather than in France. In 1906 Harriman was again asked to raise money for Republican congressional candidates, but he refused. Two months later the U.S. attorney general initiated an investigation into the activities of the Union Pacific.

Harriman made a second mistake that provided the powder for President Roosevelt's antitrust musket. Harriman dominated the Union Pacific board, and he used the Union Pacific's profits from the stock sales after the Northern Securities breakup and another $72,000,000 in Union Pacific cash to invest $130,000,000 in seven other railroads that reached to the Atlantic coast. The Union Pacific's holdings were a minor part of these rail lines, but there was the possibility of Union Pacific influence on those lines. The charge was that the Union Pacific was a combination in restraint of trade, under the provisions of the Sherman Anti-Trust Act of 1890. To add to Harriman's discomfort, President Roosevelt joined the fray by publicly calling him a "wealthy corruptionist," "an enemy of the republic," and "a malefactor of great wealth." Political commentators and cartoonists characterized Harriman as the "little giant" who ruled the nation's railroads.

Did Harriman rule America's rails? True, the Harriman lines were the longest, with 25,000 miles of track, but in 1906 two thirds of America's railroads were under the management of seven groups: Harriman's 25,000 miles; "Morgan roads," which also comprised 25,000 miles; the "Vanderbilt roads," 22,000 miles; the "Hill lines," 22,000 miles; William H. and James H. Moore's Rock Island and Santa Fe group, with 25,000 miles; "Gould roads," running 17,000 miles; and a "Pennsylvania" consortium with 20,000 miles.[16] Of all these lines, only Harriman's came under investigation, strongly suggesting that President Roosevelt's political motives outweighed any actual tendency toward concentration by Harriman's Union Pacific.

Edward H. Harriman's death, on September 9, 1909, came one year after Henry Ford brought out his Model T and some six years after Orville and Wilbur Wright had demonstrated the possibilities of powered flight. Steam still propelled the trains and ships, and over-the-road cargo-carrying trucks were a decade away. The railroads were still big business, and Harriman had built a great, if not the largest, railroad system.[17]

He is remembered, unfortunately, as Theodore Roosevelt and the media depicted him. Rarely does anyone see his benefactions: a boys' club on the East Side of Manhattan that he financed in order to get youth off the streets and into more enlightening activities such as summer camps; providing 1,600 carloads of food and medicine freight free to those injured in the San Francisco earthquake and evacuating 225,000 refugees from that tragedy, again at no charge; saving the Imperial Valley of California from disaster when the Colorado River flooded, by restoring its natural channel; sponsoring scientists and naturalists such as John Muir in explorations of Alaska and the Sierra Nevada; and creating a ten-thousand-acre national park on the Hudson River near his Arden House.

What can we learn from Edward Harriman? One, he was ruthlessly efficient in business and as cold as the glacier in Alaska that bears his name; two, his domination of the Union Pacific board of directors both served and destroyed the best interests of his shareholders—he did not own the Union Pacific, but used it eventually as an investment bank, not as a railroad; and three, he allowed himself to get too deeply involved in politics and "loosed the dogs of war" (paraphrasing William Shakespeare), which came to bite him.

On the positive side of the ledger we find a powerful person who transformed a substantial portion of America's railroads. First, he was a keen appraiser of railroad property and bought low to remake the transportation network—for example, the Illinois Central as well as the Union Pacific. Second, he put his railroad properties into first-class operating condition, upgrading the carrying technologies used and reconstructing the rails themselves. He did not buy railroads to resell them at a profit, as many of the period did, but added value by creating greater transport capacity, lower costs, and better service. Third, he recognized the need to consolidate a number of disjointed rail lines into a system that could be operated more efficiently, and in that way he was far ahead of actions to consolidate railroads that followed over half a century later. Finally, he leveraged his capital well—his style was to issue convertible bonds, and investors recognized that under Harriman's management these bonds would appreciate substantially when they were later converted into stocks. We will allow Harriman to sum up:

> Accumulation of money must come with success in developing enterprises and should be looked upon only as evidence of the success of the undertaking. The satisfaction lies in the fact that the enterprise *is* successful and will be of permanent benefit to humanity. Without capital it could not be begun, or carried on after completion.[18]

5

COMMUNICATORS

In 490 BC, Pheidippides carried the news of the Greek victory over the invading Persian army at Marathon to Athens, a distance of some twenty-two miles, in three hours. It is told that this messenger gasped the news to his audience but then fell dead of his exertion. The story of this early messenger illustrates the primitive reliance on humans, animals, or other natural forces for communicating over long distances. Messengers and commerce appear hand in hand historically, representing the reliance of business on means of communication. Indeed, Mercury, the Latin god of commerce, portrayed as wearing a winged hat, was also the messenger of the gods and the god of eloquence.

Other than a national network of railroads, no development had as much impact on U.S. business in the nineteenth century as the telegraph. The telegraph enabled a rapid exchange of messages over long distances, quickly and cheaply, connecting buyers, sellers, and transporters. Without the telegraph, a national and international market would not have emerged as quickly as it did. The communication revolution began with Samuel F. B. Morse and his telegraph, a quantum leap in information technology. Ezra Cornell built and promoted the telegraph, and he saw the need for consolidation, but fell prey to the intrigues of an emerging industry. Finally, Alexander Graham Bell represents another advancement in communicating over distances, the telephone, which came to rival the telegraph. Bell was an inventor, but, more important, he was also an entrepreneur.

SAMUEL FINLEY BREESE MORSE

The forces of electricity and magnetism were known since ancient times but it was not until the early 1800s that Hans Christian Oersted discovered that electricity could travel by wire and produce a magnetic effect at a terminal. By switching the current on and off a magnetic charge or discharge could be effected. Other scientists such as Michael Faraday, James Maxwell, Alessandro Volta, and Sir William Thomson (Lord Kelvin) became interested in this phenomenon, but it appears that André-Marie Ampère was the first to suggest that electro-magnetism could be used for "distance signaling."

Scientists in Britain and Europe were working on transmitting electromagnetic impulses by wire in the 1830s. While in Europe a young portrait painter and inventor, Samuel F. B. Morse, became intrigued with these ideas, especially Ampère's distance signaling. Morse was born in Charleston, Massachusetts, on April 27, 1791, the son of Jedediah and Elizabeth Ann Breese Morse. Samuel studied "natural philosophy," which included classes in electricity and chemistry, at Yale College, but his ambition was to be an artist.[1] It was his trip abroad in 1832 to seek portrait commissions that brought him into contact with the scientific work there.

Returning from Europe, Morse devised a code of dots and dashes that represented letters of the alphabet. These marks would appear on a moving strip of paper at a terminal in response to electromagnetic impulses sent by wire. Morse developed the idea in 1832 but did not patent it until 1837 as the electromagnetic recording telegraph. In that same year William Cooke and Charles Wheatstone obtained a British patent and installed thirteen miles of wires on poles along the Great Western Railroad, a German named Steinheil demonstrated distance signaling from Munich to a nearby village, and others were gaining patents. A great legal battle was about to begin.

The First Message

Initial capital came from Alfred Vail, the son of a successful iron works owner in Morristown, New Jersey. Vail had seen Morse demonstrate his telegraph, saw its potential, and borrowed money from his father for a one-fourth interest in developing it. In 1838 Morse strung three miles of wires and transmitted the message "A patient waiter is no loser" throughout the interior of the Speedwell Iron Works.

Morse and Vail wished to demonstrate further the telegraph and sought financial support from Congress. The plan was to insert insulated copper wires in lead pipes that would be laid in a trench to be dug between the dual track lines of the Baltimore and Ohio Railroad between Baltimore and Washington, D.C. Morse was appropriated his estimated cost of $25,420 and he began his original plan with a young mechanic, Ezra Cornell, inventing a ditch-digging machine that would also cover the pipe after it was installed. Early in the project, it was discovered that the lead pipes leaked badly, allowing water to soak through the insulation and disrupt the electrical flow.

After considerable discussion it was decided to follow the British example and place the wires on poles. More money was needed for poles, hole digging, pole insulators, and so on, so Morse went back to Congress, finally getting his total appropriation increased to $30,000. Morse may have been the first federal contractor to incur a cost overrun.

Construction was finally completed, and the first telegraphic message over a longer distance was transmitted from the chamber of the U.S. Supreme Court in Washington, D.C., to Baltimore, Maryland, a distance of some forty miles, on May 24, 1844. The message was from the Old Testament: "What hath God wrought" (Numbers 23:23).

Once demonstrated, the problem was what to do to further develop the telegraph. Congress appropriated $8,000 to operate the telegraph and placed responsibility for it in the postmaster general's office. Morse offered his patent rights to the government for $100,000. This notion was rejected by the postmaster general, Cave Johnson, who had earlier pronounced the telegraph as "unworthy of the notice of sensible men." In its first year of operation the Washington-Baltimore line lost money, reinforcing Johnson's opinion that the telegraph's revenues could never "be made equal to its expenditures" under any circumstances. Johnson's myopia brought history's good fortune—the telegraph would be a private enterprise and not part of the U.S. Postal Service.

Connections

Morse formed the Magnetic Telegraph Company, appointed a former postmaster general, Amos Kendall, as his attorney and business manager, and spent the next ten years defending his patent, refining his invention, and traveling and promoting the telegraph. There were numerous rivals in the United States and abroad, but the Morse patents of 1837, 1840, and 1846 stood legal test after test until the U.S. Supreme Court upheld Morse's rights in 1854.

The Magnetic Telegraph Company had started the business, but Amos Kendall was licensing the Morse patent to numerous others, who began to build lines across the United States to the Mississippi River. In 1855 there were an estimated twenty-five electric telegraph companies in various locales. Messages were not cheap: 50¢ for ten words, and 5¢ for each additional word, rates that were affordable primarily by commercial ventures. The report of an 1855 committee indicated the changes that were occurring:

> The advantages to be derived from the adoption of the Electric Telegraph, have in no country been more promptly appreciated than in the United States. A system of communication that annihilates distance was felt to be of vital importance, both politically and commercially, in a country so vast, and having a population so widely scattered. . . .
>
> Distances are now to be measured by intervals, not of space, but of time: to bring Boston, New York, and Philadelphia into instantaneous communication with New Orleans and St. Louis—In the operations of commerce, the great capitals of the North, South, and West are moved, as it were, by a common intelligence; information respecting the state of the various markets is readily obtained, the results of consignments may be calculated almost with certainty, and sudden fluctuations in price in a great measure provided against.[2]

Typically built along railroad rights-of-way, the telegraph and the railroads formed the earliest connections to integrate transportation and communication. On the New York and Erie, for example, the telegraph line was built in 1848 and used for dispatching trains. When Daniel McCallum became superintendent of that line in 1854, he developed information management to what was probably the highest state of the art for the times. He used the telegraph to make operations safer as well as to facilitate administration by requiring hourly reports to show the position of every train in the system, daily reports on passengers and cargo, and monthly reports to give management statistical accounts for planning, rate making, and control.

In 1854 a submarine cable crossed the Gulf of St. Lawrence to connect Nova Scotia and Newfoundland. Morse bragged that now Europe was "within six days of America," that is, the telegraph to Newfoundland and six days on a steamer to Galway, Ireland. October 1861 saw the completion of the first transcontinental line, joined in Salt Lake City—the express ponies could now retire. After five failures, Cyrus W. Field completed the Atlantic transoceanic cable in 1866, bringing San Francisco just a lightning flash away from Europe. Despite the speed of telegraphy, messages still had to be encoded, transmitted, and decoded by humans at the receiving point, where Mercury's messengers still delivered them to the addressee.

Samuel F. B. Morse died on April 2, 1872, his patents upheld and his invention honored throughout the United States, Britain, and Europe as the world's standard for telecommunications. No one could have imagined that from the message "What hath God wrought," a century and a quarter later the signal would be "That's one small step for a man, one giant leap for mankind."

EZRA CORNELL

The visionary leader of the fledgling telegraph industry was Ezra Cornell. Cornell was born on January 11, 1807, in Westchester Landing, New York, to Elijah and Eunace Barnard Cornell. Ezra Cornell had a modest education, spending most of his time in his father's pottery shop and learning carpentry and mechanical skills. In 1828 he heard of a prospering town that was connected with the Erie Canal by Lake Cayuga. He moved to Ithaca, New York, where he labored as a mechanic and eventually became manager of a flour and plaster mill. When the mill was converted to textiles, it failed, and young Cornell was out of a job. Fortunately he heard that there was need of a good mechanic to help with the construction of a telegraph line.

Cornell devised a ditch-digging machine for Morse's Washington-to-Baltimore line before it was decided to string the wires on poles. That then became Cornell's job, and he did much of the early construction work for Morse's Magnetic Telegraph Company, such as building the New York–to–Philadelphia line by devising a way to cross the Hudson with a submarine cable that connected the New Jersey side (at Fort Lee) with Magnetic Telegraph's main office at 10 Wall Street. New York city was Magnetic Telegraph's hub for connecting the early lines, but the Morse patent was being licensed by numerous others. One line went westward from New York to Harrisburg to Pittsburgh; another ran from New York to Boston; and John Butterfield, a former stagecoach line operator, was licensed to connect New York, Albany, and Buffalo.

Cornell saw the flurry of activity and formed a partnership with John James Speed Jr., a colleague from his flour mill days, to raise capital and build lines under the Morse patent. One line would follow the New York and Erie Railroad, but this venture would turn out to be a near disaster. The lead and brimstone (sulfur) insulators failed frequently, and a winter storm felled the wires and poles that crossed the Hudson River below Newburgh. That telegraph line went bankrupt, but Cornell's financial reorganization was renamed the New York and Western Union Telegraph Company. He also built another line that connected Buffalo, Cleveland, Detroit, and Milwaukee and called it the Erie and Michigan Telegraph Company. He took in another partner, Jeptha Wade, and two other ventures followed: the Ohio, Indiana, and Illinois Telegraph Company, and the Southern Michigan Company. Others were building as Cornell was doing and the industry was spreading north to Canada, west to St. Joseph, Missouri, south to New Orleans, and numerous places in between. By 1852 three rival systems were operating under the Morse, Bain, and House patents.

Patent Rivalry

The Morse system was the most commonly used and would eventually buy out the electrochemical printing process that the Scotch scientist Alexander Bain had invented. An 1846 patent by Royal E. House of Vermont was another matter—it was similar to the Morse invention but escaped patent infringement because it printed differently. The Morse printer recorded dots and dashes on a moving paper strip and a telegrapher had to decipher the message. House, however, had devised a printer that decoded the dots and dashes and inscribed the message in Roman letters on the moving tape.

Competition among the various lines that were built was very intense; price was used as the primary weapon, and at one time a ten-word message could be sent for 10¢. These tariffs were still too high for social and personal uses, so commerce and newspapers were the primary customers. While the price was right, the service was terrible: Messages coming from one line had to be copied or deciphered, then recopied for transmission over another company's line. Delays were common and users complained that they could never find out which line was responsible should a transmission error occur.

The confusion was caused by the lack of connections as well as overlapping lines. Users could choose, for example, a Morse line from New York to Troy to Buffalo, or a Bain line from New York to Buffalo, or a House line from New York to Buffalo. Someone could send a message to Cincinnati on a Morse line via Baltimore and Pittsburgh, or on a House line via Buffalo. Differences in tariffs and questions concerning reliability made choosing the right service difficult.

Early in the expansion of the industry Cornell saw the need for consolidation of these competing lines. Long-distance signaling required a smooth routing through the system if the customer was to have economical, efficient service. Cornell felt that his eight-hundred-mile Erie and Michigan line would "be a link in the chain of lightning that will vibrate between the Atlantic and Pacific oceans transmitting the will of nations across our continent."[3] His vision was sound, but a series of events would prevent his accomplishment of this Atlantic-to-Pacific chain of lightning.

Hiram Sibley had made his money in banking and real estate and entered the telegraph business as a partner in the New York and Mississippi Valley Printing Telegraph Company, formed in 1851. Like Cornell, Sibley had visions of expansion, and the company built a line from Buffalo to St. Louis and intermediate connections. Licensed under the House patent, Sibley and his partners' line became a worthy rival of the Cornell-Speed-Wade lines. Sibley thought the New York and Mississippi Valley Printing Telegraph Company should be the pivot point, while Cornell thought the Erie and Michigan line should be.

Here the intrigue began. Cornell was bedridden with severe stomach pains and unable to personally oversee his lines. When doubts were raised about Cornell's ability to lead, his primary partners, J. J. Speed and Jeptha Wade, decided they needed to take charge of their affairs. Their motives differed: Speed had lost a substantial amount of money in a railroad venture and faced other debts; Wade had had heated exchanges with Cornell over Wade's role—he wanted to be a senior partner, to have a larger share of the profits, and eventually to succeed Cornell. In 1854 Speed and Wade met secretly with Sibley and his partners.

For $50,000, Speed and Wade sold their entire telegraph interests, including their Erie and Michigan stock, and their rights to future use of the Morse patent. Sibley now had a hold on Cornell's linchpin, the Erie and Michigan, as well as the patent rights to stall westward expansion by Cornell. Cornell was not surprised that Wade had sold out, because he knew Wade's ambitions. Speed was a different matter, and when Cornell asked him why, Speed replied: "To make money, by God." Cornell wrote that he had both a Judas and a Benedict Arnold in his ranks.

The year 1855 brought pain of a different sort for Ezra Cornell. While riding in a hot railroad coach he had the window open and his arm resting casually on but protruding out the window. At a narrow bridge his elbow was hit and numerous bones broken: a doctor at the next town set the arm, but the pain never fully went away. Once more Cornell had to be away from his business; revenues were down, and creditors and shareholders were putting on the pressure. Cornell's failing was that he had built so much of the business about himself that his absence endangered the survival of the various lines. He never thought Wade would become an effective manager, and Speed had jumped the rails—there was no one capable of taking Cornell's place.

Cornell realized he was beaten; more stomach problems and a painful arm were enough to convince him that his active days in the telegraph business were over and that he would never fulfill his dream of connecting the Atlantic to the Pacific with lightning. In the fall of 1855 Cornell met with the Sibley group to surrender his control of the Erie and Michigan line and his Morse patent rights. In return, Cornell got a seat on the New York and Mississippi Valley board, retained nearly one sixth of the consolidated company's stock, and had the privilege of naming the reorganized venture the Western Union Telegraph Company.

Western Union

Hiram Sibley became president of Western Union; he would be succeeded in 1865 by Jeptha Wade. Sibley moved aggressively to consolidate the telegraph industry, and the "Treaty of Six Nations" in 1857 created an alliance of six companies that controlled all traffic from Newfoundland to the western borders of Minnesota, Iowa, Missouri, Arkansas, and Louisiana.[4] In time, these "nations" would become principalities in service to the king, Western Union. The consolidation of interests was essential, however, to providing long-distance through traffic. A new means of telecommunicating was appearing on the horizon and a new competitive era was to begin.

Ezra Cornell retired to Ithaca, New York, to family and philanthropy. He and Mary Ann Wood Cornell had three daughters and four sons; one of the sons, Alonzo, later became governor of New York State. The New York State Agriculture College at Ovid, New York, closed in 1861 but was rescued by Cornell, who was a trustee and agreed to donate three hundred acres of land and $300,000 if the college moved to Ithaca. High above Lake Cayuga, Cornell University opened in 1868.

Ezra Cornell died December 9, 1874, with his vision of a chain of lightning from the Atlantic to the Pacific implemented by others.

ALEXANDER GRAHAM BELL

George Bernard Shaw's *Pygmalion*, better known to musical-theater goers as *My Fair Lady*, was inspired by Alexander Bell, a shoemaker and Shakespearean actor who founded a school in London to cure stammering. His son, Alexander Melville Bell, continued the family interest in eloquence, spent his life as a teacher of the deaf, and sought to invent an artificial speaking machine to assist the deaf. Melville and Eliza Bell's son, Alexander (the *Graham* was added later to avoid confusion with other Alexanders) was born March 3, 1817, in Edinburgh and continued the family interest in speaking and hearing disabilities. The family moved to Brantford, Canada, near Lake Erie, in 1870.

The young Bell began teaching the deaf in New England, finally opening a school for the deaf in Boston. Among his first pupils was George Sanders, son of the prominent leather merchant Thomas Sanders, and Mabel Hubbard, who had been struck deaf by scarlet fever at age four. Gardiner Greene Hubbard, Mabel's father, was a prominent Boston lawyer. Hubbard and Sanders were interested in Bell's experiments with the transmission of sound and became his financial backers. Thomas Augustus Watson (no relation to the Watsons of IBM) was a mechanic in the electrical machine shop of Charles Williams Jr., of Boston, who was approached by Bell in 1874 to assist in developing a transmitter and receiver that would use electric current to "shape sound." These four were to form the Bell Patent Association: 30 percent each to Bell, Hubbard, and Sanders, and 10 percent to Watson.

"Electric Speech"

While Bell was experimenting with what he called "electric speech," Elisha Gray, an electrician and inventor, was working on a similar problem, although neither knew of the other's work. Gray had started a factory with E. M. Barton in Chicago to make electrical and telegraphic equipment, and the partnership of Gray and Barton would eventually become the Western Electric Company. Gray visited the Western Union Telegraph Company in May, 1874 to demonstrate his speaking instruments but stimulated no initial interest.

While Gray was forging ahead, Bell fell in love with Mabel Hubbard. Bell's work languished, and Mabel's father, who was worried that Bell was not financially capable of supporting his daughter, told Bell that if he could finish and patent his speaking machine, permission to marry would be granted. Bell and Watson returned to the lab with renewed vigor, and Bell filed his patent on February 14, 1876, just hours before Elisha Gray filed his claim. It would be almost a month, however, before Bell transmitted the first intelligible telephone message to his assistant: "Mr. Watson, come here, I want you."[5]

Sanders and Hubbard became impatient for a quick payout now that the patent was filed and a working instrument had been demonstrated. The major player in the industry was Western Union, which was financially strong and already wired throughout much of the United States. William H. Vanderbilt, son of Cornelius Vanderbilt, was in financial control, and William Orton, former commissioner of internal revenue under President Andrew Johnson, was president of Western Union.

Orton had seen Bell's models demonstrated earlier, but when Orton found out that G. G. Hubbard was providing financial support to Bell, Orton told Bell that Western Union "will never take up a scheme which will benefit Mr. Hubbard."[6] The Orton-Hubbard disagreement had begun five years earlier, when Hubbard had testified before a Senate committee that Western Union was a monopoly that set its rates too high. Hubbard proposed that a new private corporation be chartered, the U.S. Postal-Telegraph Company (with Hubbard as one of the incorporators), that would set up telegraph facilities in every post office and charge about half of what Western Union charged. Orton defended Western Union vigorously and never forgave Hubbard for his testimony against the company.

Hubbard evidently did not realize that Orton was antagonistic and in 1877 offered to sell the interests of the Bell Patent Association to Western Union for $100,000. Printed accounts differ with respect to Orton's refusal of the offer; some have Orton saying that it was a "toy" or a "scientific curiosity"; others have him commenting, "What can we do with such an electrical toy?"[7] Thomas Watson, who had $10,000 (his 10 percent share) riding on the outcome, was less direct but closer to the event: "[Western Union] evidently had no faith in the future of the telephone for they refused to buy the patents and wouldn't even make an offer for them. I was . . . disappointed when the President of the Telegraph Company finally and somewhat contemptuously turned down our offer."[8] Watson felt, however, that the Bell

Patent Association had the last laugh, because two years later those same patents were worth $25,000,000.

Western Union was Goliath, capitalized at some $40 million, while the Bell Patent Association was David, capitalized at $300,000, when Western Union refused to buy the patents. The Bell group owned no factory and had no sales force, and their financial position was precarious. Orton's decision was based largely on his feelings about Hubbard—and would change the course of history.

Western Union's rejection of the Bell patents turned Alexander Graham Bell into an entrepreneur, and the Bell Telephone Company was formed on July 9, 1877, to replace the patent association. (Two days later he married Mabel Hubbard after the Hubbard family was finally convinced that he could support their daughter.) Bell took to the road to promote his instrument and his approach was unique—he charged people 50¢ to attend his lectures. Watson was not in the hall but stationed at a distance of five or so miles away, connected by wire to Bell's apparatus in the hall. On request, Watson would talk to Bell, or sing to the audience, which was astounded at hearing someone talking from a distance.

At least two things beyond thrilling the audience were gained from Bell's lecture tours: one, a decision that the instruments should be leased rather than sold, thus becoming an asset to raise capital and enabling the company to upgrade and service the equipment; and two, the money that Bell received from the audiences provided the working capital needed to expand the business.

The Bell Telephone Company contracted out its manufacturing to Charles Williams's Boston workshop, where Thomas Watson continued to work on Bell's instrument. Sales were developed by licensing agents for district market territories and their job was to sell, set up the poles, string the wires, install the equipment, collect the rents, and maintain service. The Bell partners' income was royalties from these licenses, and every territory was an adventure as the electric speaking telegraph went to market.

Bell's telephone consisted of small, heavy wooden boxes that used electrical impulses to move the human voice over a grounded iron wire. One could either speak or listen, waiting for the other person to stop, perhaps saying "over," before you could send. Rain and snow disrupted a signal that was not too strong in the first place. The principle of telephony was that the human voice vibrating in a magnetic field induced an undulating current that was transmitted to a similar magnetic field in a distant receiver, with a resulting vibration of the same pitch being reproduced in the second device. Founded on this principle, Bell's patent would survive some six hundred challenging lawsuits (some from instruments superior to his) and be upheld by the U.S. Supreme Court.

The early phones were sold in pairs and made a connection between those two instruments only. The first pair was sold to the banker Roswell Downer, of Boston, for connecting his office to his home in Somerville, some three miles away. Bell used some very basic promotional strategies to develop sales: Downer, for example, was given a month of free service for installing the telephones, and all early users were given discounts to lease a pair of lines. Differential pricing—$40 a year for business and $20 a year for a residential lease—was used on the assumption that business users would make more frequent use of the telephone than residential ones.

Bell also emphasized the advantages of the telephone over the telegraph: rapid contact and exchange with another person; the personal touch of another human voice; and the privacy afforded, since no one had to encode, decode, and deliver messages. Bell the inventor had become Bell the entrepreneur, the promoter.

Even though some 5,200 telephone pairs had been leased by 1877, Bell saw the limits of this site-to-site paired connection. He was behind others, however, in how to overcome this problem. The first commercial exchange was created by the owner of a burglar alarm company who connected his bank clients directly to his office so that they could ring him in case of an emergency. He also realized he could connect one banker to another within his system—and he observed that "with the third telephone circuit in my office I could hear that their conversation was successful" (becoming perhaps the first telephone eavesdropper). Bell's first central switchboard went into operation in 1878 in New Haven, Connecticut. No longer tied to a connection, a person could ring central and be connected by the operator to anyone else who had a telephone. Bell visualized connecting one central switchboard to those in other cities, but that would come later.

Goliath Regroups

The telephone was beginning to look like something that could compete with the telegraph, and the sleeping giant Western Union began to make some countermoves. Although William Orton's antipathy toward Hubbard had prevented an early acquisition of the Bell patents, Western Union began to use its substantial resources to acquire patents such as Joseph B. Stearns's duplex device for the telegraph, which allowed two messages to be sent simultaneously in each direction over the main line, and adopted it to the telephone. Orton also contracted with Thomas Edison to make improvements in both Gray and Bell's devices, and the inventive genius provided a quadraplex system to better Stearn's system and a microphone transmitter that could send and receive and was superior to Bell's magneto. Western Union also acquired one third of the Western Electric Company as well as the patents of Amos E. Dolbear, another of the hundreds of those who challenged the Bell patents in the courts.

Edison's instrument had a lamp-black carbon transmitter that operated to vary the pressure on the lamp black at each sound vibration. By adding an induction coil, he boosted the distance for telephoning—an Edison phone connected New York and Philadelphia, a distance of over 100 miles, in 1878, setting a record for long-distance service. In 1879 Western Union had a greater competitive advantage than the Bell Telephone Company—patents for improved instruments for multiple messages and longer distances, experience in the business, the wires in place, an impregnable financial position, and a stable of inventive personnel. Western Union formed its American Speaking Telephone Company in 1877 to compete with Bell, yet abandoned the field two years later. Why?

The Deal of the Century

Western Union's entry into the telephone business led to more competition, through rate cutting to get subscribers and through the drive to build more central exchanges. Bell Telephone needed more capital and, as so often happens, money makes the decision. William H. Forbes, son of John Murray Forbes, who had made a fortune in trade with China and in New England railroad companies, provided an amount of capital that neither Sanders nor Hubbard could raise. In return, Forbes became president of the National Bell Telephone Company. Theodore N. Vail, who started his career as a telegrapher, like Edison and Andrew Carnegie, was hired as general manager. Vail was a nephew of Alfred Vail, who was Samuel Morse's first partner, and T. N. Vail would lead the telephone company in later years. The original Bell patentees, although represented on the board, were shunted aside when it came to dealing with Western Union.

Under advice of its chief counsel, George Gifford, Western Union began to have second thoughts about the telephone business: Bell's patents were winning in the courts over Gray's claims, and Edison's patents had been delayed by other legal maneuverings. Gifford, perhaps also fearing federal action if Western Union had both the telephone and telegraph markets, counseled that the Bell patents were more likely to be upheld (as they were), leaving Western Union with less protection from infringement litigation.

Another storm cloud for Western Union was Jay Gould, financier par excellence, who had gained control of the Union Pacific Railroad and its telegraph subsidiary, the Atlantic and Pacific Telegraph Company. Gould was also building lines and making contracts with other railroads, such as the Baltimore and Ohio, that owned their own telegraph lines. Gould formed the American Union Telegraph Company to compete with Western Union and also started buying Western Union's stock.

Western Union was now at war with Jay Gould, justly fearing that Gould could merge with Bell, increasing the strength of both, or that Gould could acquire Bell licenses to enter the telephone business. To cover one flank, Western Union began negotiations with National Bell to get itself out of the telephone business.

The final agreement divided the telecommunications industry: Western Union would have the telegraph, Bell the telephone. Bell was to confine its operations to within fifteen miles of any central office and would pay Western Union a 20 percent royalty on rental income for every telephone in service. In return, Western Union relinquished all of its phone patents, its fifty-six thousand telephones in fifty-five cities, and all phone assets and equipment. By mutual agreement, neither was to encroach on the other's line of business until 1896 (an agreement that National Bell would violate in 1885 by reorganizing as American Telephone and Telegraph and developing intercity service).

For Western Union it was the deal of the century. They could concentrate on the telegraph business, fight Gould (except on this point they lost, as he eventually gained control of Western Union), and sit back and collect royalties on all telephones without having to market, install, or service them. For example, in 1881 Western Union collected $200,000 on telephone rentals, and before the agreement expired in 1896 it would receive some $7,000,000 in royalties.

National Bell shareholders reaped a bonanza—stock that Graham Bell struggled to sell for $10 a share a few years earlier steadily rose from $110¼ a share in June 1879, when rumors began that Western Union would exit the telephone business, to $997½ a share with news of the final agreement. It was also the deal of the century for Bell, as it shook off its major competitor and could now concentrate on developing the telephone business.

Aftermath

Second-guessing Western Union's decisions would be too easy from a modern vantage point because history tells us what happened in the telecommunications industry. In 1879, however, the telephone was a relative novelty, affordable mostly for business use and limited in range and in the quality of signal delivery. The telegraph, on the other hand, connected the United States with Europe, and plans were in place to make connections with Latin America and, over the Bering Strait, with Russia and Asia.

In 1879 the telegraph was the fastest, most dependable known means of long-distance communications. At the time it would have been difficult to foresee the coming leaps in electromagnetic technology—for example, Elisha Gray's 1888 and 1891 patents for a "telautograph" for facsimile writing and drawing for transmission and reproduction over the telegraph. Guglielmo Marconi was only five years old in 1879, and wireless messages were still the stuff of science fiction. National Bell had not yet renamed itself as the American Telephone and Telegraph Company, and it would be almost three quarters of a century before a young Royal Air Force officer, Arthur C. Clarke, would conceive the idea of using an earth-orbiting satellite for distance messaging.

The later part of Alexander Graham Bell's life was devoted to science; he was a cofounder of the publication *Science*, a regent of the Smithsonian Institution, president of the National Geographic Society, a promoter of powered flight (although the Wright brothers beat him to it), and inventor of a "photophone" that transmitted speech via a ray of light and an audiometer that measured sound levels. With the audiometer, for example, one could identify children with defective hearing and enable them to get proper classroom placement. With the audiometer Bell's name became part of our language in the word *decibel*.

In tribute to Bell after his death on August 2, 1922, all telephone service was stopped for one minute.

6

FINANCIERS

Early American business organizations were sole proprietorships or partnerships and were financed out of the pockets of individuals. There were no securities such as stocks or bonds required for these types of firms, but an early financial market in government securities arose as early as 1789. There was no organized trading, and transactions occurred in New York City coffeehouses—the most well known one was the Tontine Coffee House—and there was a "curb" market, a meeting place on the street where buyers and sellers could make their transactions.[1] The New York Stock Exchange (NYSE) was formalized in 1863; it moved to 11 Wall Street in 1865, and it installed a telegraphic stock market ticker in 1867.

America's first big business, the railroads, required amounts of capital that were beyond the means of an individual or partners. The stocks and bonds of various railroads hastened the formation of the NYSE as a means for investing or selling these equity and debt instruments. While some, including James Monroe and Thomas Jefferson, frowned on the trading of securities, considering it a form of "legalized gambling," without such a securities exchange mechanism, raising capital for large scale enterprise would have been a difficult, if not impossible, task.

Money and banking have also had a checkered past in American business history. The Continental Congress had authorized the printing and issuance of Continental notes, or Continental dollars, but paper money lent itself readily to the printing-press method of financing government operations. The Revolutionary War was financed in such a manner—and galloping inflation was the result. As the value of the dollar declined to the point that it became worthless, another quaint American phrase appeared: "Not worth a Continental dollar."

Debasement of the currency such as this has led to the rise and fall of nations, and the U.S. Congress used its constitutional power to minimize this danger by putting money on a bimetallic standard, a system where values were based on a ratio of gold to silver. At first, the ratio was 15 to 1; that is, one ounce of gold was the equivalent of fifteen ounces of silver. This ratio was arbitrary, and people hoarded gold and silver and made their exchanges in paper money. By 1860 there were some nine thousand different kinds of paper bank notes (local, state, and federal) in circulation.

Banking was also a hot political issue in America. As secretary of the treasury, Alexander Hamilton sought a national bank like the Bank of England. It would lend money in times of distress, collect taxes, transfer funds to foreign nations, and act as the fiscal agent for the government (although it was not the same role as that of central banking today). Amid cries of "Unconstitutional!" the bill creating the First Bank of the United States passed Congress. This bank lasted until 1811, when its charter was not renewed. In 1816 a Second Bank of the United States was chartered, and in 1823 it came under the capable leadership of Nicholas Biddle. This venture was successful until the administration of President Andrew Jackson, who had a long-standing antipathy toward banks in general. After a long political battle Jackson succeeded in abolishing the bank in 1836.

There was still no central bank of the United States in 1861, but the need for one remained. In 1864 the National Bank Act took a large step forward, partly fulfilling the earlier dreams of Hamilton and Biddle. The act provided the procedures by which banks were to be organized and chartered, specified initial capital requirements, and governed reserve requirements and the issuance of bank notes. This act did little to control credit and currency, and it was not until 1914 and the passage of the Glass-Owen (Federal Reserve) Act that a system of national banking was established.

Within this slender financial framework the work of the providers of capital and the users of capital began with the intermediaries of stock brokerage houses and investment banks. There were few rules about how to play this game. The NYSE had few formal rules; trading information was not public knowledge; there were no federal nor state oversight commissions; and what happened in the exchange of securities was often "street talk" or unsupported rumors. It is difficult for us to understand how this type of financial world existed on such a paucity of regulation and public knowledge. Two representatives of this age, Jay Gould and J. Pierpont Morgan, provide a mere blink into the intricacies of corporate finance in America's late nineteenth and early twentieth centuries.

JAY GOULD

The individual who became known as "the most hated man in America" and the "Mephistopheles of Wall Street" was born May 27, 1836 in Roxbury, New York, the son of John and Mary More Gould.[2] The baby Gould was frail and weak and the family delayed naming him for a week, thinking that he would not survive. Jason "Jay" Gould did survive, but life was hard on John Gould's farm. Jay's mother died when he was five; John Gould remarried, but Jay's stepmother died; John tried again, but the second stepmother also died. From the age of nine Jay was cared for by his five older sisters, and in adult life the men of Wall Street thought Jay Gould effeminate since he preferred domestic life, reading, gardening, and flowers to golf, drinking, and fast yachts; Jay Gould was not a large man, what he lacked in size was compensated for by his quick mind and fierce need to achieve.

Jay was too frail for farm work, but he obtained an elementary education, worked as a store clerk, learned to survey land, and later formed a partnership with Zadock Pratt to operate a tannery, which prospered. Pratt offered to buy out Gould for $10,000 or to sell his share to Gould for $60,000. Gould surprised Pratt by obtaining $60,000 from Charles Leupp and David Lee, leather merchants of New York City, with one third of the tannery going to each new partner for $30,000 apiece. Gould now owned one third of the tannery with no money out of his pocket, and in later years he polished his skills as a master in leveraging other people's money.

The tannery partnership would not be a pleasant one, however. Leupp, who was described as having wild mood swings (perhaps manic-depression, in modern terms), committed suicide. Lee and Gould did not get along well and at one point Lee seized the tannery, turning it into an armed fortress while Gould was away. Gould did not buy the idea that possession was nine tenths of the law and hired some men to attack the tannery. When the shooting stopped, Gould's efforts had succeeded, but Lee turned to the courts. In the course of seven years of litigation, the tannery business was abandoned, and although Lee had received a $3,500 judgment earlier against Gould, Lee would finally settle for $1. The lesson for Gould was that he could use the courts to delay and delay until his opponent came to terms, and he would employ this tactic often in his business career.

Jay Gould was not idle while he battled David Lee in court. He learned that Rutland and Washington Railroad bonds could be acquired for ten cents on the dollar, and this became his entrée into America's expanding network of railroads. The Rutland and Washington had never been a good performer, and Gould decided to become a hands-on manager: "I took entire charge of that road. I learned the business and I was President, treasurer, and general superintendent. . . . I gradually brought the road up and I kept at work. . . . In the meantime my bonds had become good, and the stock also; so that I sold my stock for about 120."[3] With his added knowledge of railroads and how they could be managed, Gould soon became more interested in Wall Street and the possibilities it held.

It is likely that the Rutland and Washington created another opportunity in Gould's life by bringing him into contact with Daniel Miller, a successful New York City merchant who also dabbled in railroad securities. Daniel Miller admired Gould's business skills and introduced him to his daughter, Helen. The Millers were members of the elite Murray Hill society, and Jay Gould jumped social classes with his marriage in 1863 to Helen Day Miller. With marriage, Jay now had a family, something that he had not truly experienced in his youth. Jay and Helen Miller Gould's family would grow to six children, and Jay would be a faithful, loving husband and a doting father. This model family life in their Fifth Avenue home would be a marked contrast to the reputation he gained in business on Wall Street.

How to Gain a Bad Reputation

No casting director would ever select Daniel Drew, James Fisk Jr., and Jay Gould to play the parts they did in an economic drama that came to be known as the "Erie Wars." Daniel Drew had earned the dubious reputation of creating the practice called "watering stock" when he had purchased a herd of cattle with an enlistment bonus he had received from his Civil War army days. In transporting the herd to market, he fed them salt to make them thirsty, and then offered them all the water they could drink; he then sold at a very large profit some temporarily overweight cattle.

The New York and Erie was one of the older railroad lines; it connected New York to Lake Erie and the ports east and west from there. Drew had been buying shares of the Erie, finally gaining a position as treasurer, and from his inside position printing new issues of stock, selling it short, and then unloading his shares and watching the price plummet. Under Drew the Erie became known as the "scarlet lady of Wall Street." Cornelius Vanderbilt had also been buying Erie stock, hoping to add another connection for his New York Central Railroad. The shot heard around Wall Street occurred when Drew and Vanderbilt went to war over the Erie.

The battle was joined by two others of whom the Street knew little: Jim Fisk and Jay Gould. Fisk was the polar opposite to Gould; Fisk loved life in the fast lane, kept a mistress, golfed, drank over par, and was a bon vivant on Wall Street in the brokerage firm of Fisk and Bolden. Gould, on the other hand, was a relative unknown on the Street who had become a partner in the small but respectable brokerage firm of Smith, Gould and Martin.

Vanderbilt distrusted Drew, correctly so, and was able to secure the services of a Tammany Hall creation, George C. Barnard, a judge on the New York State Supreme Court. Judge Barnard enjoined Drew and the Erie board of directors from issuing any further stock or convertible bonds, and the injunction included the removal of Drew from his treasurer's office. To help solicit proxies, Drew had been joined by Fisk and Gould, and together they created an executive committee to act in periods between Erie board meetings. As the executive committee, they ignored the injunctions and asked the board to authorize an issuance of convertible bonds for railroad "improvements." The board approved this, and it soon became apparent that convertible bonds represented stock in the making. The bonds were converted and Vanderbilt, unaware of who was selling, was buying all he could. Drew, Fisk, and Gould still had some unissued bonds and, with the market still strong, dumped them on the market. This time the market price dropped slightly and Vanderbilt realized he was being duped.

Vanderbilt returned to Judge Barnard and got a contempt-of-court ruling against the unholy trinity. Fearing arrest, Drew, Fisk, and Gould gathered up the accounting records and the money and fled to Jersey City, where they holed up in the Taylor Hotel, promptly dubbed "Fort Taylor" by the press because the hotel was well protected by their hirelings. While Gould missed his family, Fisk brought Josie Mansfield, his mistress, across the Hudson River and put her next door to him.

A New York receiver was appointed for the Erie, and Gould knew they could not do any further business in New York. The Erie receiver was Peter

B. Sweeney, another Tammany Hall figure, and Gould would have to deal with him later. Meanwhile, the New York state legislature had proposed a bill to legalize the issuance of convertible bonds. Vanderbilt led the fight to oppose this bill and it was defeated in the lower house, adding to the fire-power of Vanderbilt and his Tammany Hall colleagues. Gould realized this created additional jeopardy for their cause, and he returned to New York to be arrested. He was, but was released on bail by Judge Barnard. Gould then headed for Albany to make a case for the Drew-Fisk-Gould side.

And what a case he made! It was a suitcase full of the proceeds from a hundred thousand illegally issued shares of Erie stock. Gould began to spend the money to acquire the votes to force passage of the bill legalizing convertible bonds. Vanderbilt knew how the game was played and dis-patched his own agents with money to Albany. Reporters told of the legisla-tors scurrying back and forth between Gould's room and Vanderbilt's agents to get a higher bid for their vote. It has been estimated that Gould spent between $300,000 and $1,000,000 in gifts to the legislators, but in later years he responded that he did not remember: "You might as well go back and ask me how many cars of freight were moved on a particular day."[4] As the bid-ding rose, Vanderbilt withdrew, many voters changed sides, and the New York State Assembly legalized convertibles in a landslide vote. It takes two to tango but with a little more money you can obtain a chorus line.

Gould's interests had won. In the aftermath, Vanderbilt dropped his law-suit in return for some $3,500,000 in cash and bonds plus a $1,000,000 "bonus"; Peter B. Sweeney, the receiver who had nothing to receive, was paid $150,000 to soothe his itchy palms; two Vanderbilt associates received $500,000 each to repay them for their losses that came from selling Erie short; and Judge Barnard deferred any hearing on the charges that had been brought earlier, and then dropped the charges altogether.

Daniel Drew, weary of war, secretly appealed to Vanderbilt for a compro-mise. When Gould and Fisk heard of this, they appointed Tammany boss William M. Tweed and the soothed Peter B. Sweeney to the Erie board, and with them came the friendly court presence of Judge Barnard. Gould and Fisk used their added power to elect Gould president of the Erie and to send Drew packing.

A second incident added to Gould's reputation as a manipulator. The Gold Standard Act of 1862 had fixed the price of gold at $100 for 4.7 troy ounces of gold. Specie payments, that is, payments in gold coin, had been suspended by the government, and domestic transactions were conducted in paper currency, especially federal bank notes, called "greenbacks" because of the vivid color on the reverse. International transactions, such as wheat, cotton, and other products sold abroad, however, had to be settled in gold. This gold had to be converted to paper currency for domestic use, creating a potential disparity between the price of gold and greenbacks. To facilitate international trade, a Gold Exchange, called the "gold room," was established on William Street, near the New York Stock Exchange. In the gold room, gold could be bought and sold through brokers to settle international accounts.

Traditionally, people prefer gold to paper money, so gold sold at a premium. That is, $100 in gold could command differing amounts of greenbacks depending on the ups and downs of the market. The price of gold was stated in terms of how many greenback dollars could be acquired for 4.7 ounces of gold; for example, $100 in gold might bring someone $130 in greenbacks, or more, or less.

To protect themselves, exporters would use gold room brokers to hedge by selling short. For instance, a merchant would sell wheat to a European buyer when gold was at $130. Consummation of international transactions could take up to two weeks because of loading, shipping time, and so on. Within these two weeks, the price of gold could go up or down, putting the merchant at risk. To sell short, the merchant would borrow gold from a broker and sell it on the exchange for, say $129 for delivery at some agreed-upon future date.

If the price of gold went down, the merchant had protected his market position. If gold was $128 when the transaction was completed, the merchant could buy on the market at $128 and cover his short sale at $129. If gold went up to $132 during the period when the transaction was being completed, however, the merchant would have to buy at $132 to deliver at $129, thus incurring a loss. The result of all of these fluctuations in the gold market was that buyers and sellers were constantly watching the market, trying to anticipate what was going to happen. Speculation on commodities or stocks was (and is) a risky business.

In the summer of 1869 gold was selling at $135 and it was expected that the price would fall because of a bountiful grain harvest, which would be sold abroad, bringing more gold into the United States. Some believed that gold would drop to $120, and if this happened, exporters would have to sell short to protect themselves against this bear market. Gould decided to buy gold in an effort to edge the price up, thereby forcing the short sellers to have to buy to cover their future promises. If Gould could create a bull market, he stood to profit handsomely, and this was an opportunity to gain the capital he needed to expand his railroad properties.

An estimated $15,000,000 in gold was available for trading in the open market in 1869, but the U.S. Treasury held an additional $100,000,000 in gold in its reserves. To create a bull market, Gould had to borrow enough money to buy the gold available in the market and keep the federal government from selling its gold on the market. For step one, Gould financed his purchases on margin, which at that time on the gold exchange was 10 percent. For every $1 of assets that Gould could pledge, he could borrow $9 to buy $10 worth of gold. He pledged his numerous shares of stock in the Erie Railroad as collateral; he also owned a controlling interest in the Tenth National Bank of New York and pledged a series of IOUs to his bank, which issued certified checks to add to Gould's collateral. Thus Gould had solved one part of his problem, raising the money to buy contracts for gold. The second problem, what the U.S. president and U.S. Treasury would do, was more complicated.

Abel Rathbone Corbin, whom Gould had known earlier, had married Virginia ("Jenny") Grant, the sister of General Ulysses Simpson Grant, hero of the War Between the States. When Grant was inaugurated as America's eighteenth President in 1869, Gould saw the Corbin-Grant connection and knew that Corbin had boasted that he had the "confidence" of his brother-in-law, now president. In this Gould saw a way to keep the Treasury's gold off the market, or, at the worst, a way to keep informed about President Grant's intentions regarding fiscal policy.

Gould approached Corbin with the idea that national prosperity would follow if gold prices rose: farmers would get more for their grain, the railroads would haul more grain, and the economy would be revitalized. On the other hand, Gould argued that a government sale of gold would lead to contrary results, causing a depression. Through his brokerage firm Gould then added another inducement: He bought $2,000,000 worth of gold in Corbin's name.

Corbin did not succeed immediately in convincing his brother-in-law, the president, that a bull market was the right policy. Gould recognized the need for a broader campaign, so he hired a financial journalist to write newspaper and magazine articles extolling Gould's position, and he employed numerous individuals to go to various social and political functions where President Grant was expected, again informing the president of their view that a surplus of gold would cause a depression.

Next Gould, through Corbin's influence on the president, had Daniel Butterfield appointed as assistant U.S. treasurer for New York. If the Treasury bought or sold gold, it would be through the New York subtreasury. To gain Butterfield's allegiance to Gould's plan, Gould bought $1,500,000 worth of gold for Butterfield's account. Gould, Corbin, and Butterfield would all benefit if the price of gold increased.

By July 1869 Gould felt he had all of his pawns in place, so he began to buy. Although others were playing a bear market, the market rose. Gould started buying at 135½ and acquired options to buy for some $60,000,000 in gold by the end of August. By that time, the price of gold had reached 140½. Gould used numerous brokers for his purchases, so it was not apparent that one person was driving the market.

As prices continued to rise, however, there were suspicions on the Street that something out of the ordinary was happening. To allay these fears, Gould had Corbin write an editorial for the *New York Times*. Appearing on August 26, 1869, the editorial carried no byline but was attributed to a person who had the "confidence" of President Grant. The editorial said that President Grant had not declared an "official" policy but from his actions it was "not likely [that] Treasury gold would be sold [on the exchange]."[5]

President Grant and his wife, Julia, visited Abel and Jenny Corbin in early September 1869. While there, the president wrote George S. Boutwell, secretary of the treasury, instructing him not to sell federal gold without a specific authorization from the president. Ten days later the president again wrote Boutwell to hold gold regardless of how high the price rose.

Meanwhile, Gould needed more financial support and brought his friend Jim Fisk into the plan. Fisk started buying gold and told others that the president, his family members, and certain members of Congress were all a part of the plan to maintain the bull market in gold. Fisk was also useful on the local political front, as he had connections with Tammany Hall, a social club that controlled the local Democratic party, and New York City as well, through William M. "Boss" Tweed.

But Gould had not counted on finding an honest person in the White House. Horace Porter, a West Point graduate and retired general, was personal secretary to President Grant and was responsible for handling all incoming and outgoing correspondence. Gould wished to be privy to what was happening in the office of the president, so he purchased $500,000 in gold for an account in Porter's name. When told of this, Porter refused and notified Gould that he would not accept this account.

Porter told the president, and it became more apparent that Gould and Corbin were in tandem. What followed was a unique sequence of events: President Grant told his wife about the apparent connection between Gould and Corbin; Julia Dent Grant then wrote Jenny Corbin, "Tell your husband that my husband is very much annoyed by your [Abel Corbin's] speculations. You must close them as quickly as you can."[6] Mrs. Corbin was very distressed to learn of her husband's apparent part in this. Confronted, Corbin agreed that he should withdraw from the plan. Corbin told Gould he was pulling out, but promised not to tell anyone else about the letter. Corbin closed his account with Gould and pocketed $100,000 in profits.

Gold was at $141 when Corbin withdrew. Gould sensed his position was in danger because the president could authorize a release of Treasury gold at any time. Gould started selling, using various brokerage houses to mask his actions. Publicly, Gould made it appear that he was buying. Jim Fisk, however, was still buying and telling others to buy. Gould used numerous brokers to sell his $60,000,000 in gold at prices from $140 to $144 but did not tell Fisk (or anyone else) that he was selling. When the gold exchange closed Thursday, September 23, 1869, gold was at $141.

The exchange opened Friday, September 24, to a rising market, and gold was at $150 by 10:00 A.M. By 11:00 A.M. gold had reached $164 and the floor trading was frantic. At 11:25 A.M. President Grant authorized Treasury Secretary Boutwell to tell Butterfield to sell $5,000,000 from the New York subtreasury. The market plummeted. By noon gold was 133½, and trading was suspended as the scramble to sell continued; this panic became known as "Black Friday."

Authorities disagree on how much Gould made from his sales.[7] His highest sale on Thursday was at $144, and he testified before a congressional investigating committee that he placed no buy or sell orders on Friday, when the panic occurred. He maintained that "I had no idea of cornering it [the gold market]. . . . The worst panics are bear panics. . . . The bears just marked [bid] it [gold] up themselves."

Butterfield sold his gold before the collapse, but Jim Fisk and numerous others were caught short and were unable to cover their contracts. Fisk, however, repudiated all of his contracts and had two Tweed ring judges, Albert Cardozo and George C. Barnard, issue twelve restraining injunctions in one day against those who tried to collect from Fisk. The judges placed the exchange in receivership and ordered that no accounts were to be paid without a court order.

A congressional investigation followed, but President Grant was not called to testify since the House of Representatives felt that it had no authority to summon his appearance. The President was innocent of any complicity, but some of those around him were not the sort of person that Diogenes would have admired.

Although the House committee passed resolutions calling for investigations of the use of certified checks as collateral, the possibility of taxing transactions on the exchange, and the need for legislation to "define and punish conspiracy against the credit of the United States," there were no legal actions taken against those involved.

In the course of events a public outcry led to the eventual downfall of some of those involved: Tweed lost office in the next election and was jailed for stealing public monies, Judge Barnard was impeached, and Judge Cardozo was forced to resign; as the result of a different set of events, Jim Fisk was shot and killed by his mistress's other lover.[8] Gould, apparently defeated, turned from the East to the West, but the odor of the Erie wars and Black Friday would follow him the rest of his days.

Tracks and Wires

Gould's lack of profits from gold in 1869 put him in a dire financial position, but once again he used the Erie to bail himself out. A falling-out with Henry Smith, his brokerage firm partner, moved Smith to ally himself with Daniel Drew, who still carried his Erie grudge against Gould. Smith and Drew began speculating in stock of the Chicago and Northwestern Railroad, selling it short. When Gould learned of this (no one ever knew how he found out about these things) he went long and Erie stock rose. Smith and Drew lost some $2,000,000 covering their shorts and vowed vengeance on Gould. Smith, using former partnership records, had Gould jailed on the complaint that he had charged some of his speculation losses to the Erie. Gould made the $1,000,000 bail and agreed to leave the Erie and reimbursed it with some real estate and stock allegedly valued at $2,500,000 in return for the charges being dropped. The Erie gave a sigh of relief at Gould's departure but would learn some years later that the true value of the exchange was only $200,000. Gould had taken the Erie for one last ride.

Gould began buying Union Pacific stock in 1873, again mostly on borrowed money. The Union Pacific was suffering the aftershocks of a congressional investigation into Credit Mobilier, the contracting company that built the Union Pacific and which, not by coincidence, also owned the railroad. Credit Mobilier had taken advantage of a corrupt political environment and had spread bribes around generously to members of Congress, to the Speaker of the House, a future vice president (Henry Wilson), and a future president (James A. Garfield). Through dummy construction companies that laundered the money from government subsidies into Credit Mobilier's pockets, $120,000,000 was spent to build a railroad that cost $58,000,000.

With Russell Sage and Sidney Dillon, Gould gained control of the Union Pacific at bargain prices and began buying connecting lines to increase through traffic. The Kansas Pacific (Kansas City to Denver), the Denver Pacific, the Texas and Pacific, the St. Louis Southwestern, and the International and Great Northern gave Gould control of over half of all track mileage in the southwestern United States. The Union Pacific also invested in the Utah Southern, which connected with numerous iron ore reduction furnaces in Utah as well as coal and mineral deposits. Of these lines, the Missouri Pacific prospered the most, but Jay Gould had shown that he could build prosperity into his ventures. His Southwest and mountain states lines provided competition that helped break a pooling arrangement between the Burlington and other lines and opened new mineral deposits and markets.

Despite the consolidation of various lines, Gould never overcame the Union Pacific's history of poor construction, the quarrels with Congress over previous scandals, and the fact that it was heavily capitalized. The Southern Pacific remained a nemesis in the South; the Central Pacific blocked his path to the Pacific; and the Burlington, Chicago and Northwestern and other members of the "Iowa Pool" continued to fight through rate wars. After Gould's death, Edward H. Harriman would provide the strategy that would turn the Union Pacific around.

Gould's moves made headlines, usually unfavorable ones, and he learned that virtuous conduct did not sell newspapers. He owned the *New York World* for four years, perhaps hoping for better press, but eventually sold it to Joseph Pulitzer, who would turn the *World* into a profitable enterprise.

The Western Union Telegraph Company was another of Jay Gould's ventures and a demonstration of how to play monopoly with real money. Western Union had created a powerful network of lines and offices, but the barriers to entry in the telegraph business were not too high for a speculator such as Gould. Cornelius Vanderbilt controlled Western Union; he was a formidable foe, one not easily fooled by Gould's intricate dealings. For example, Vanderbilt had stayed clear of the gold market in 1869 and used dropping stock prices to increase the number of railroad shares he owned.

Thomas Edison, always strapped for money, had invented a quadraplex system that enabled the sending of multiple messages over one wire. The patent rights had been sold to the Automatic Telegraph Company—or had they? Edison was also under contract to Western Union for such a device. From his position on the Union Pacific, Gould saw the importance of the telegraph to the railroads and to commerce and trade, including, of course, market speculation.

The Union Pacific, under Gould, canceled its contract with Western Union and turned to a small company that Gould controlled, the Atlantic and Pacific Telegraph Company. Gould also proceeded to buy the Automatic Telegraph Company and with it Edison's device. Western Union never had paid Edison for his work, but Gould offered him $30,000 and three thousand shares of the Atlantic and Pacific; Edison agreed.

A series of court battles followed. Western Union claimed the patent as one of its employees was allegedly the coinventor with Edison. The Atlantic and Pacific Telegraph Company claimed it had Edison and his patent. Meanwhile, Cornelius Vanderbilt had died and his son, William H. Vanderbilt, took up the Western Union fight. He saw Gould making contracts with other railroads for telegraph service and becoming more of a threat as long as the litigation continued. He bought Gould's interest in the Atlantic and Pacific Telegraph Company (at a substantial profit to Gould) and thought he had gotten rid of the pesky Gould.

The Western Union acquisition of the Atlantic and Pacific Telegraph Company had an unusual repercussion. While headed for lunch, Gould was accosted by A. A. Selover, described as a "brawny six-footer," who felt that he had been cheated of $15,000 by Gould in the Western Union deal. In retaliation, Selover "hoisted him [Gould] over the [sub-level] railing and let him dangle over an eight-foot drop"; he struck Gould repeatedly in the head, and finally dropped Gould into the basement area below.[9] Although the *New York Times* gleefully reported the event as something that should be done to Gould "from January to December," the *Chronicle* pointed out that there were winners and losers if one played the speculation game, and the practice of beating others was not a "satisfactory method of settlement." Thereafter, the frail Gould would be accompanied in all public places by a bodyguard.

Vanderbilt thought Gould had turned to other ventures, but the shrewd speculator had merely had his appetite sharpened by the possibilities of the telegraph. He formed the American Union Telegraph Company and gave it contracts for the railroads he owned. He formed a new telegraph alliance with the Baltimore and Ohio Railroad, purchased Dominion Telegraph of Canada, and announced his plans for building a new transatlantic cable.

After absorbing Atlantic and Pacific Telegraph, Western Union had seen its stock rise, and the shares remained high, paying substantial dividends. But when Gould posed his American Union Telegraph threat, Western Union shares dropped from $105 to $90, then to $82½, and eventually to $78. Gould's Union Pacific stock was strong after his consolidations had improved traffic and earnings. He began to sell his Union Pacific shares and by 1881 had sold all, using the proceeds to buy Western Union stock. Gould eventually acquired ninety-thousand shares, making him the largest Western Union shareholder.

Now Gould owned American Union and a large share of Western Union, whose board found Gould "all sweetness and amity." Rather than "being the chief enemy of the Western Union . . . [he] was now its chief proprietor."[10] An agreement was reached that Western Union would issue $15,000,000 of stock to pay for American Union—a sum about twice its original cost. Gould had delivered for his American Union shareholders, as he had for his Atlantic and Pacific share owners, and for himself. Jay Gould was now in control of one of the most profitable and influential companies in the United States.

How can we of this regulated and taxed age understand the complexities of a Jay Gould? His business was conducted against a background of few laws, rules, or regulations. America was in an age of transition from a self-governing agrarian society, with its Jeffersonian–Jacksonian ideal of economic egalitarianism, to an industrial one. The laws that did exist were for that earlier period, not for an age in which capital had to be provided for a growing economy and large-scale enterprise. The inheritance tax and the income tax that had been instituted as temporary revenue generators for the Civil War had expired; there was no corporate income tax; rules about trading on the New York Stock Exchange were few; and the Fourteenth Amendment to the Constitution provided that "no state shall make or enforce any law which shall abridge the privileges or immunities of citizens of the United States; nor . . . deprive any person of life, liberty, or property, without the due process of law; nor deny . . . the equal protection of the laws." Intended as a human and civil rights amendment, the U.S. Supreme Court interpreted it as affording protection to business as well. For example, seven of the first eight cases before the Supreme Court under the Sherman Anti-Trust Act were decided on the basis of the Fourteenth Amendment in favor of business and not the Department of Justice.

It was also an age of "yellow journalism," when New York City papers were locked in a circulation war and sensationalized headlines were intended to make sales, not report facts. In this climate, anything Gould did seemed to make good copy. When Gould bought the *New York World* it was interpreted as infringing upon the freedom of the press; when he won Western Union it was feared that he could tap the wires and take advantage of that information in his speculations.

Henry Adams described Gould as "small and slight in person, dark, sallow, reticent, and stealthy, with a trace of Jewish origin."[11] Others assumed that Gould was Jewish and tried to make him a Shylock of the nineteenth century. That myth arose because he was descended from Nathan Gold, who arrived in Connecticut in 1647 from England. The name *Gold* became *Gould*, but Jay was of Scotch-English descent and an unfortunate target of those of anti-Semitic beliefs.

Another factor in this period was political corruption. The U.S. Senate had twenty-five millionaires among its members in 1900, and it is not apparent that this came from their work; rather, it seems to have come from their influence. Legislators competed for bribes and held the power to grant or withhold public lands, subsidies, or favorable legislation. Municipal government, such as the Tweed group in New York City, was as corrupt as state and federal officials were. Not until President James A. Garfield, himself a taker of Credit Mobilier money, was assassinated by a disappointed office seeker did the "spoils system" of government begin to give way to reforms such as the Pendleton Act of 1883, which established the civil service system.

Jay Gould was no saint, and neither were those who were throwing the stones. His legend has had a long life, threatening to overshadow the lessons we can learn from this complex character. One Jay Gould was the loving family man of Fifth Avenue, the other the cunning speculator of Wall Street. He was secretive and devious, yet he had a loyal band of those who felt he was of good character—the builder Sidney Dillon, the financier Russell Sage, the railroad engineer Grenville Dodge, Cyrus Field of transatlantic cable fame, and even Collis P. Huntington, who had bumped heads more than once with Gould.

Gould had the Union Pacific on its feet, and it was not until after he sold his interests did it decline (later to be resurrected by Edward H. Harriman).

Gould manipulated Western Union until it provided a nationwide telegraph system—it could be called a monopoly, but that was not illegal until later. He reorganized the New York City transit system under the Manhattan Elevated Company, and he brought a system of railroads to the plains, deserts, and mountains of the Southwest. His legacy has often been interred with his bones while his legend lives on.

Frail at birth, sickly as a child, and typhoid fever as a youth yielded a life of discomfort and fatigue for Gould. He was diagnosed as having tuberculosis as early as 1888 yet he continued to maneuver and manipulate until his death December 2, 1892.

Gould named his yacht Atalanta, after the fleet-footed huntress of Greek mythology. Wooed by many, Atalanta agreed to marry any of them who could outrun her; but those who lost were to be put to death. Hippomenes won his race with Atalanta by dropping three golden apples given to him by Aphrodite, the goddess of love; Atalanta slowed and picked up the apples and lost the race. Gold—the Lorelei of myth and reality, of the past and the present.

J. PIERPONT MORGAN

Zsa Zsa Gabor has been quoted as saying that she never met an ugly rich man. She would have loved J. P. Morgan. Morgan's life was that of a person born to wealth and influence who was expected to do great things. His grandfather, Joseph Morgan, was a Connecticut farmer who demonstrated the Yankee drive to achieve by amassing wealth via a stagecoach line, hotels, and founding the Aetna Fire Insurance Company of Hartford. Joseph and Sarah Spencer's son, Junius Spencer Morgan, started as a dry-goods merchant in Boston and later became a partner in the London investment banking house of George Peabody, a fellow Yankee merchant who had settled in England to make his fortune in merchant banking.

Of Junius Spencer and Julia Pierpont Morgan's five children, John Pierpont Morgan, born in Hartford, Connecticut, on April 17, 1837, would become the most renowned. Junius Morgan moved his family to Boston when John was fourteen years old. The young Morgan received an exclusive education and graduated from Boston's English School at age seventeen. He was educated in the classics, French, German, arithmetic, and handwriting—the basic education expected in those days. Morgan became fluent in

French and German and would find those languages useful in his later life as an investment banker.

When Junius Morgan joined George Peabody and Company in London, the young Morgan attended a private school in Switzerland and then spent two years at the University of Göttingen where his mathematics skills were developed to such a level that he was encouraged to pursue graduate study and become a professor of mathematics. He declined and found other venues where he could use his knowledge of mathematics. He spent a year with his father in George Peabody's banking firm and was sent to New York to work for Duncan, Sherman, and Company, Peabody's U.S. representatives.

It was common for merchants to become bankers because of the need for credit, for discounting notes, and for the transfer of funds in commercial trade. Both Peabody and Junius Morgan began in that way, but the industrial development of the United States, especially the railroads, led to investment banking, an outgrowth of merchant banking. The expansion of the nation's railroad system from 52,000 miles in 1870 to 240,000 miles by 1910 and the increase in steel production from 200,000 long tons in 1870 to 31,000,000 long tons in 1913 were characteristic of the need for capital. The United States did not have enough money to finance this rapid growth and turned to international investment houses such as J. and W. Seligman, which had branches in London, Paris, and Frankfurt as well as its headquarters in New York. It was the task of Seligman and other banking houses to seek capital by selling securities abroad; as late as 1914 the United States was borrowing more from abroad than it could borrow domestically.[12] Investment bankers also sold government bonds as well as bonds of railroads, industrial enterprises, and utilities, and for private firms these banks could also provide means of placing initial public offerings and newly issued stock. As America developed its industrial base, investment bankers played a key role in providing the capital.

Mr. Morgan's Neighborhood

In 1860, the firm of J. Pierpont Morgan and Company was formed, mainly to represent Peabody's and the elder Morgan's interests in the United States. The young Morgan made some early mistakes, such as what became known as the "Hall carbine affair." The carbines were developed by Captain John H. Hall and manufactured by Simeon North. Five thousand carbines were sold to the U.S. government but by 1861 they were obsolete. The War Department then offered to sell them and they were purchased by Simon Stevens for $11.50 each.

After the Union Army's defeat at the Battle of Bull Run, Major General John Charles Fremont needed rifles, and Stevens borrowed $20,000 from Pierpont Morgan so the barrels could be "rifled" (given spiral grooves rather than a smooth bore) and the breeches enlarged to meet army standards. Stevens then sold the retooled rifles to the army for $22 apiece, and Morgan cleared nearly $6,500 for his financial assistance. He was criticized as a war profiteer, even though the following investigation revealed that he was unaware of how he had been manipulated by Stevens. Although guiltless, the transaction left a stain on Pierpont Morgan's reputation. The carbine affair and Morgan's payment to a volunteer to take his place in the Union Army during the Civil War led some to feel that Morgan was unpatriotic. Although paying a bounty to someone to serve one's turn in the army was a common practice, it was the belief that the poor fought the war while the rich stayed home to profit from it.

In London the elder Morgan was getting news of his son's activities and the criticism directed toward them, and he felt that the younger Morgan needed a tightening of the reins. Junius arranged for Charles H. Dabney, a partner at Duncan, Sherman, and Company and the man who had taught Pierpont Morgan how to interpret and keep accounts, to become a senior partner in J. P. Morgan and Company. When Dabney retired in 1871, Junius arranged for Pierpont to meet Anthony J. Drexel, a senior partner in a successful Philadelphia bank. The young Morgan was not elated at having his father arrange another partnership, but he and Tony Drexel agreed upon an arrangement that made Morgan a full partner in Drexel and Company of Philadelphia and gave each of the Drexels (Anthony, Francis, and Joseph) a partnership in the New York firm of Drexel, Morgan and Company.

Connecting with the Drexels would create in time one of the most successful international investment banking groups in the history of finance. It consisted of the Drexel interests of Philadelphia, J. P. Morgan of New York, J. S. Morgan of London (after Charles Peabody's retirement), and Drexel's Paris affiliate, Drexel, Harjes and Company. This international network enabled U.S. seekers of capital to find it quickly and discreetly in the United States as well as in London and Paris. J. P. Morgan would become the polestar of this network, and his company would eclipse other firms as an international investment banker. Rather than calling it the House of Morgan, a more fitting description would be Mr. Morgan's neighborhood.

Pierpont Morgan's health and personal life were not the same successes as his business. As a youth he was tall, gangly, and had rheumatic fever, which affected his walking. His tall, lanky look gave way in adulthood as he avoided exercise and became "a heavily built, broad chested man of some two hundred and ten pounds." Six feet tall, his physique emanated power, and he had "small, dark, piercing eyes" that a photographer compared to the "headlights of an express train." Most prominent of all his features was his nose, described as "huge, swollen [and] badly inflamed," which became increasingly distracting as he aged. He had inherited his skin condition (clinically, acne rosacea) from his maternal grandfather, and particularly during periods of stress his nose would become more inflamed. Morgan used his appearance, his size, and long periods of silence to intimidate those who opposed him, but among those who knew him well, he was "affable, friendly, and generous."[13]

Pierpont Morgan married Amelia Sturges, the daughter of a friend of Junius Morgan. Just before they were to be married, she developed a lung infection, diagnosed as bronchial pneumonia, and Pierpont carried her to the altar for their marriage in September 1861. For their honeymoon, they sailed to Algiers, where it was hoped the warmer climate would help in her recovery. Unfortunately, medical wisdom was in short supply—she had tuberculosis and died four months after their marriage. Pierpont was desolated but four years later he married Frances Tracy, the daughter of a prominent New York attorney, whom he had met through his attendance at St. George's Episcopal Church. J. P. and Frances Tracy Morgan took up residence at 219 Madison Avenue and they would have four children, a son and three daughters.

Acting as a Central Banker

It is difficult to imagine the power and wealth of a private banking firm that would bail the U.S. government out of financial trouble not once but twice. The first occasion followed a financial panic in 1893, when some 75 railroad companies became bankrupt or went into receivership. The stock market fell and other businesses encountered difficulties. During the administration of President Benjamin Harrison the Treasury had been spending gold to buy silver, as authorized by the Sherman Silver Purchase Act. Foreign investors, to protect their security investments, began exchanging them for gold, resulting in a gold outflow that drove Treasury gold reserves below their legal minimum level of $100,000,000. By 1894 the nation's gold reserve was $69,400,000 and drastic action was required.

The U.S. Congress stalled and President Grover Cleveland turned to private bankers for help. Four firms, each representing a syndicate of investors, were formed to offer a private sale of bonds that would replenish the nation's gold supply. In England, the syndicate heads were J. S. Morgan and Company and N. M. Rothchild and Sons; in the United States they were August Belmont and Company and J. P. Morgan and Company.

President Cleveland asked for a meeting with Morgan, and an agreement was reached that the syndicate would sell some $60,000,000 worth of bonds in Europe so the United States could replenish the Treasury's gold reserve and restore confidence in the Yankee dollar. The Morgan-Belmont syndicate for the United States consisted of some forty banks, trust companies, and two life insurance companies. In total, the syndicate sold $62,000,000 worth of U.S. thirty-year bonds at 4 percent, and the crisis ended. Although J. P. Morgan considered this one of his most notable accomplishments, he and the syndicate came under fire from the media. The *New York World*'s publisher, Joseph Pulitzer, called it a "Wall Street conspiracy" that had profited by $8,400,000 from the bond sale. In fact, J. P. Morgan and Company profited by only $295,000, and other syndicate members made little more. This was but one of the shots fired in the gold-silver, cheap-money-versus-dear-money controversy that would carry over to the "cross of gold" speech of William Jennings Bryan in the 1896 election campaign.

Morgan's role in the panic of 1907 was largely that of the central banker of the United States and demonstrated his prestige and influence. By 1907 there was still no central bank, but there were over eleven-thousand state-chartered banks, and a growing number of trust banks. If there was a single spark that ignited the panic, it was the trust banks. Trust banks had been founded to act as trustees for corporations and individuals but had expanded their role into corporate finance, and although they could not perform all of the functions of a bank, they were also free of the restrictions that state charters placed on banks. Trusts could buy stock or real estate and finance commercial loans but were not required to keep a cash reserve against deposits. Neither banks nor trusts kept all of their deposits on reserve; rather, they kept a fraction of them to cover demand withdrawals.

The 1907 crisis began with a small incident, but its effects would ripple throughout the financial system. Interest rates had climbed slightly, business activity had slowed, and stock prices were in a downswing in 1907. As stock prices fell, short sellers began to sell to cover their losses, money tightened, and interest rates increased more rapidly. Depositors at the Knickerbocker Trust wanted their money, but there was not enough ready cash to please all. As the news spread, other depositors became alarmed and started asking their trust or bank for their money — in short, a run developed. Of course, all of the money was not in the bank, and the waves of panic grew larger. There was no insurance guaranteeing deposits, nor was there any way to create money, such as a central bank could do.

The news reached Morgan when he was attending an Episcopal Church convention, and he hurried back to New York to assess the events. J. P. Morgan and Company was in excellent financial condition, as were George F. Baker's First National Bank and James Stillman's National City Bank, the bank to John D. Rockefeller. Morgan, then in his seventieth year, drew upon his knowledge of finance and his persuasive powers to assemble a group of bankers who agreed to fund a $50,000,000 pool that would enable others to satisfy their depositors and avoid Knickerbocker Trust's fate.

But that $50,000,000 finger did not plug the leak. Another pool had to be formed to save the Trust Company of America; then Morgan shook $10,000,000 out of the Rockefeller money tree to save the Union Trust Company. The Pittsburgh Stock Exchange closed its doors, and the New York Stock Exchange was also seeing a sell-off. The NYSE president approached Morgan to say that the exchange would have to be closed; "Morgan pointed his finger at the unhappy man and, emphasizing each word with a jab, ordered him to keep the Exchange open; Morgan would find money to lend the brokers."[14] Morgan called a meeting of clearing-bank presidents and pointed out the impending calamity; a pool of $27,000,000 was raised to lend to brokers at 10 percent instead of the going rate of 75 percent. When Morgan glowered, bankers cowered.

The most famous meeting occurred when Morgan called a group of bankers to meet in his library to save the brokerage house of Moore and Schley. Morgan put the commercial bank presidents in the East Room, the trust company presidents in the West Room, and he retired to the librarian's office to play solitaire (his favorite diversion in times of stress). The groups met through the night; when the bankers had an agreement, they tried to leave the room to report to Morgan, but the door was barred—Morgan had locked them in! Then, having their promises, he told the trust company presidents what their shares would be in the salvage operation. When Morgan unlocked the doors it was 4:45 A.M. on a Sunday.

J. P. Morgan's company was the closest thing in the U.S. to a central bank. He leveraged the funds to keep the stock exchange open, raised the money to keep all but one of the trust companies solvent, arranged a $30,000,000 loan so the city of New York could meet its standing and due obligations, and, with Stillman and Baker, issued clearinghouse certificates that could be used in lieu of legal tender to create money based on debt (a device that bears a substantial resemblance to how today's federal deficits are financed through the banking system).

The Great Consolidator

The panic of 1893 placed numerous railroads in bankruptcy or receivership, and it was apparent that some system building and consolidation could bring better coordination and efficiencies. Morgan knew a lot about America's biggest business and had bailed out William H. Vanderbilt and the New York Central Railroad in the late 1870s. Morgan was opposed to the Interstate Commerce Act of 1887 and instead sought to form an Interstate Commerce Railroad Association. Summoning railroad presidents and leading railroad bankers to his home in late 1888, he swore all to secrecy and tried—unsuccessfully—to sell his idea of railroad self-regulation.

Without any agreement on his plan, Morgan became a financial lever to make some railroad consolidations and reorganizations a reality. Among those that felt the Morgan touch were the Baltimore and Ohio, the New Haven, the Norfolk and Western, the Erie, the Southern, the Philadelphia and Reading, and the Northern Pacific. Of the major railroad groups in the United States, only the Harriman and Gould lines were independent of Morgan influence.

In previous pages we learned of the struggle between the Harriman-Schiff and the Hill-Morgan interests with regard to the Northern Pacific. The settlement was the formation of the Northern Securities Company, a voting trust of the sort that Morgan favored. To Morgan's dismay, President Theodore Roosevelt asked the attorney general, Philander C. Knox, to prosecute this arrangement under the Sherman Act. When he learned of the intention to prosecute, Morgan went to Washington to meet with Roosevelt and Knox. Under Morgan's rules of engagement, it was considered courteous for one party to let the other know of such intentions. When Morgan protested, President Roosevelt responded that they deliberately had not warned Morgan. Morgan persisted: "If we have done anything wrong, send your man [presumably Attorney General Knox] to see my man [a Morgan lawyer] and they can fix it up." To this Knox responded: "We don't want to fix it up, we want to stop it."[15] Morgan was angry but it was quite clear that a new watchdog was in Mr. Morgan's neighborhood.

In addition to the consolidation of numerous railroads, Morgan was also involved in some of the largest mergers of that period. Morgan referred to these combinations as "creating a community of interests," a euphemism for trust or monopoly, but his intention in consolidating was to diminish the chaos of competition. Among these combinations were the International Mercantile Marine Company, a merger of U.S. and British shipping firms to serve the heavy passenger and freight traffic of the North Atlantic; International Harvester, a merger of five firms including the nation's two top agricultural-equipment makers, the McCormick Harvesting Machine Company and the Deering Harvester Company; General Electric (cutting out "Edison" from its previous title); American Telephone and Telegraph; and the United States Steel Corporation. Of these communities of interests, only General Electric would survive intact to the present; the others were unable to hold their dominant position due to a decline in the agricultural sector (International Harvester), declining traffic in the northern Atlantic and the sinking of its flagship, *Titanic* (IMM), deregulation (AT&T), and proof that size alone was insufficient (U.S. Steel).

When Morgan was thirteen years old he learned a lesson in the value of money when he lost a small sum out of his pocket. Junius reprimanded him for being so careless and sent Pierpont one dollar with the advice not to spend it foolishly. Much of Pierpont's life was lived in the shadow of his father, who watched over his activities and rarely praised him. The shadow ended with the death of Junius Spencer Morgan in 1890. While Pierpont was financing railroads in the United States, Junius was driving a horse-drawn carriage an ocean away in France. Legend says that Junius's horse bolted at the sound of a train's whistle, throwing Junius from the carriage, and that his death followed from those injuries. It was not a happy family occasion, but J. P. Morgan, now fifty-three years of age, began to spend his money more freely.

His first yacht he named *Corsair*—the name on Wall Street for Jay Gould—and, after the death of Junius, Pierpont commissioned *Corsair II*, an even more luxurious yacht. He visited Europe frequently, buying art, books, manuscripts, and statuary, and was a discerning collector. He almost rivaled Napoleon in the items he brought out of Egypt. The results of his hobby of collecting would be given to the Metropolitan Museum of Art, in New York, and other gifts would benefit the American Museum of Natural History, also in New York.

In 1912 it was alleged that there was a "money trust" and that the head of this conspiracy was J. P. Morgan. A House of Representatives inquiry, headed by Arsène Pujo, a Louisiana lawyer and chair of the House Banking and Currency Committee, began its hearings in May of that year. Chief counsel for the committee was Samuel Untermyer, a multimillionaire lawyer who had changed his views in his late years about the evils of money. Morgan gave two days of testimony and the following excerpts give some idea of Morgan face to face with Untermyer.

- On competition:

Untermyer: You are an advocate of combination and cooperation as against competition, are you not?

Morgan: Yes, cooperation I should favor.

Untermyer: Combination as against competition?

Morgan: I do not object to competition, either. I like a little competition. . . .

Untermyer: Now, suppose you owned all the banks and trust companies, or controlled them. . . . And somebody wanted to start up in the steel business, you understand, against the United States Steel Corporation. . . . You would be under a duty, would you not, to the United States Steel Corporation, to see that it was not subjected to ruinous competition?

Morgan: No, sir; it has nothing to do with it. . . .

Untermyer: You would welcome competition?

Morgan: I would welcome competition.

Untermyer: The more of it the better?

Morgan: Yes.

- Regarding power:

Untermyer: Your idea is that when a man has got a vast power, such as you have—you admit you have, do you not?

Morgan: I do not think I have.

Untermyer: You do not feel it at all?

Morgan: No; I do not feel it at all. . . .

Untermyer: Your idea is that when a man abuses it, he loses it?

Morgan: Yes; and he never gets it back again, either.

- On borrowing:

Untermyer: Is not commercial credit based primarily upon money, or property?

Morgan: No, sir; the first thing is character.

Untermyer: Before money or property?

Morgan: Before money or anything else. Money cannot buy it. . . .

Untermyer: If that is the rule of business, Mr. Morgan, why do the banks demand, the first thing they ask, a statement of what the man has got, before they extend him credit? . . . He does not get it on his face or character?

Morgan: Yes; he gets it on his character. . . . Because a man I do not trust could not get money from me on all the bonds in Christendom.[16]

The Pujo hearings were more a political harangue than an impartial investigation, and both sides remained convinced that their position was correct. The committee disclosed that Morgan and the company partners held seventy-two directorships in 112 of the nation's largest corporations. While the committee saw this as a conspiracy that tended to restrain trade, Morgan's position was that none of these directorships held a majority position and therefore could not control any board's actions. But surely Morgan would have to admit that when approached for a loan, the first thing a banker wants to see is the applicant's business plan, not the character references.

Although the Pujo committee recommended closer scrutiny of the stock exchanges, competitive bidding for securities, a breakup of financial power, and improved banking laws, it would be some years before any of these recommendations would come to fruition. The Federal Reserve (Glass-Owen) Act of 1913 was triggered more by the money panic of 1907 than by the Pujo hearings, and securities exchange oversight and reporting legislation would come much later.

The hearings had left J. P. Morgan despondent and he headed to Europe in the hope of putting all of this behind. He died in Rome on March 31, 1913, shortly before his seventy-sixth birthday. The autopsy revealed that "there was nothing organically wrong with Morgan, only a melancholy and the loss of his will to live."[17] Perhaps he wrote an epitaph for himself and for Jay Gould when, after the Pujo inquiry, he was heard to say: "American business must henceforth be done in glass pockets." The death of John Pierpont Morgan ended an era in American financial history.

Part II

ORGANIZING AND MANAGING THE BUSINESS ENTERPRISE

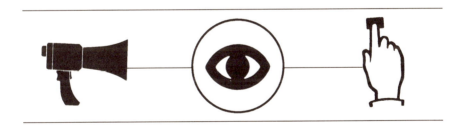

7

WORKING SMARTER

The latter part of the nineteenth century in the United States was characterized by national economic expansion and rapid technological growth in
manufacturing, transportation, and communication, fostering the growth of
enterprise. As firms grew, their size exceeded the grasp of the family management practices of the past, and finding managers for these firms was no
easy task. America's first successful school of business, the Wharton School
of Finance and Economy, founded in 1881 at the University of Pennsylvania,
did not offer a course in management. Where could managers be found for
this burgeoning economic system? Some came from law and were steeped
in the legal tradition, while others came from financial institutions and were
schooled in accounting and banking.

Engineers, who had played a large role in building canals and railroads
and in designing and installing the equipment for manufacturing organizations, also became managers because of their technical skills. The individuals selected here represent the efforts of these engineers to move beyond
strictly engineering matters to the question of the best use of the firm's
resources. Frederick W. Taylor, Frank B. Gilbreth, and Lillian M. Gilbreth
promoted the idea of systematic management and the importance of the
human factor in production. In Japan, Yoichi Ueno would bring East and
West closer together by extending the influence of Taylor and the Gilbreths
across national boundaries.

FREDERICK W. TAYLOR

A widely read U.S. business journal recently reported that the late Frederick W. Taylor was micromanaging a gift of $10,000,000 to the Stevens Institute of Technology in Hoboken, New Jersey.[1] According to this article, Taylor provided in his will for how this endowment was to be invested and how the funds could be spent. In this way Taylor was allegedly exerting control over his money long after his death, some eighty years earlier. The article was entirely false, except for spelling Taylor's name correctly and providing the correct $10,000,000 figure. Taylor's will (he died in 1915) and the will of his widow, Louise Taylor (who died in 1949), mentioned no gift to Stevens. The idea that Taylor was managing from his grave will add to the myths about Taylor but do nothing to provide an accurate portrayal of him.

The reality was that Stevens had received a gift of $10,000,000 from Robert P. A. Taylor in memory of his father, Frederick W. Taylor. Fred and Louise Taylor had adopted three children who were orphaned by a tragedy that took the lives of both their parents. One of them, Robert Taylor, became an extremely successful investment broker and, upon his death in 1993, made the gift to his father's alma mater; the specific instructions on managing the money came from Robert, not from Frederick W. Taylor. Why does Taylor continue to exert a grip on modern minds so long after his death?

Frederick Winslow Taylor lived in relative luxury from birth until death. The Taylor family had a cook, maid, and coachman at their house on Ross Street in the Germantown section of Philadelphia, where Fred was born on March 20, 1856. His father, Franklin, a Quaker and a lawyer who practiced but briefly, had inherited great wealth, and more wealth came from their ownership of a large number of farms and other properties in Bucks County, Pennsylvania. Fred's mother, Emily Winslow Taylor, was of the Delano family, as was Franklin Delano Roosevelt. Emily traced her Puritan roots to a Plymouth, Massachusetts ancestor, who arrived in 1629. She was an ardent feminist and had been called "anti-American" before the Civil War because she attended a world antislavery conference in London.

Emily's method of child rearing was based on "work, drill, and discipline," and she believed in "definite instructions" for young Fred. This insistence on preciseness perhaps led to Fred's love of mathematics, mechanical inventions, and trying to find better ways of doing things. Even games were serious matters, and as a boy he saw croquet as an opportunity to work out carefully the angles of the various strokes, the force of the impact, and the advantages and disadvantages of the understroke and the overstrike.

Fred attended a prep school, Phillips Exeter Academy in New Hampshire, and his parents wanted him to become a lawyer and his brother Edward to become a physician. Edward fulfilled his parents' ambitions, earning a medical degree from the University of Pennsylvania. He met one patient, then "retired" to the life of a gentleman, as family lore has it.

It was Fred who broke with his parents' plan. At Phillips Exeter he excelled in scholastics and athletics as a gymnast, a member of the boat crew, a skater, and captain of the baseball team. He left Exeter in 1874 after passing the entrance exams for Harvard with honors. He began having headaches and vision problems, however, and his family feared that he might go blind if he were to enter the rigors of the study of law at Harvard. Perhaps it was to society's betterment that a lawyer was lost but an engineer was gained.

Rather than entering the gentlemanly life of retirement, as his brother Edward had, Fred sought a job as a worker. He used family friends to land a job at the Enterprise Hydraulic Works of Philadelphia as an apprentice pattern maker and machinist. These tasks required good vision, but that difficulty was solved with corrective eyeglasses. During his apprenticeship, Taylor lived a rare social life for a worker: belonging to Philadelphia's most exclusive social club and teaming with his brother-in-law, Clarence M. Clark, in 1881 to win the first U.S. Lawn Tennis Association doubles championship in Newport, Rhode Island.

Taylor took another job at Midvale Steel, again with the aid of family friends. He began as a common laborer but gained rapid promotions until he eventually became chief engineer. During this time Taylor enrolled in a home-study course through the Stevens Institute of Technology in Hoboken, New Jersey. He never attended classes, except to take examinations, yet he joined a fraternity, Theta Xi, Gamma chapter. His name does not appear on any of the official class lists at Stevens and he clearly caught the faculty by surprise when his name appeared on the 1883 graduation list, printed in pencil.[2]

What Is a "Fair Day's Work"?

As a worker, Taylor learned to curse, a habit that he often used on the wrong occasion. He admired his coworkers for their pride of workmanship, but he felt that management did not create the appropriate work environment. Workers restricted output, a practice called "soldiering," because they believed there was only a limited amount of work to be done and a more rapid work-pace would put them out of a job. Managers placed the burden of finding proper work methods on the workers in the hope that they would work harder to get their rewards. The quality of supervision was uneven, but was usually poor, creating a lack of harmony between workers and managers.

In his working experience Taylor had observed that there was no clear idea of how much work a person *should* be expected to do. That is, what is a fair day's work? The performance standard depended largely upon past production records. Taylor did not like this rule-of-thumb approach and suspected this was the primary cause of the restriction of output. Work methods and tools varied greatly and managers had no idea of what would be a fair amount of work to be accomplished in a given time period. The practice of setting performance standards based on past experience left it up to the worker to meet that standard, and all management could do was cut the rate if it was felt that the workers earned too much.

Taylor began to use a stopwatch to study jobs to see what motions the worker made and how long they took, and to determine if these movements were necessary or if they were they fatiguing and/or wasted. Taylor did not invent time study, nor was he the first to study workers' motions, but he was the first to try to discover whether a worker's motions were necessary or not. Taylor tried to find how long a job *should* take when done with the proper methods, motions, and tools. Where others were content with the total time a job took, Taylor broke the job into its component parts, analyzed each part, and reconstructed the job as it *should* be done, more efficiently and with less fatigue.

Pay, People, and Performance

Pay for performance is an old idea, but Taylor gave it a new twist, determining how much work should be done in order to earn the highest pay. He also observed that *quality* of work had to be stressed before striving for an increased quantity of work. He did not like profit sharing because all shared regardless of contribution and because the reward typically came much later than the performance; nor did he like gain sharing because the workers had to share the results of their efforts with management and the efforts of those who worked diligently could be offset by others who soldiered. He felt people should be paid for their performance, not for their attendance on the job.

Piece-rate payment plans, which paid according to output, were in use as economic incentive systems long before Frederick Taylor, but he is often criticized as relying solely on money to motivate people. This "economic man" assumption was not developed by Taylor but rather had been clearly articulated by Adam Smith over a century before. The problem of incentives, in Taylor's view, was not in the payment plan one could use but in the inexactness of the performance standards. To Taylor, determining the proper standard must come first and should be accompanied by selecting and training those who would be doing the work. All of this should be done before incentive payment plans were implemented.

It is a myth that Taylor provided for only economic incentives. Taylor made the case that more than money can be used to provide an incentive, such as the hope of rapid promotion or advancement, shorter hours of work, better surroundings and working conditions, and the supervisor's "personal consideration for, and friendly contact with, workmen which comes only from a genuine and kindly interest in the welfare of those under him."[3]

Taylor made at least two contributions that have influenced modern thinking about motivation. One concerned the importance of worker beliefs about if and how much they will be rewarded. In the past, when they worked harder they saw management cut the rate, and the expectation developed that their effort would not be rewarded. In modern expectancy theory, employees must feel that effort leads to output and that this performance will be rewarded. Second, Taylor advocated setting specific work goals or targets for employees to accomplish. The more specific the goal, the better: difficult goals are better than easy ones and the goal should challenge (but not exceed) the individual's abilities. Employees also need to be able to keep track of their performance by receiving regular feedback about results. Without a knowledge of results, employees could not gauge the relationship between their actual performance and the expected performance.

Incentives (both financial and nonfinancial) are also necessary to reward the meeting of the goals. The parallels between Taylor's ideas and goal setting, a widely accepted modern notion of motivation, is apparent: challenging but attainable goals by individuals who are properly selected and trained; specific tasks; feedback of results about a person's progress toward the goal (Taylor advocated daily feedback); and money, with other nonfinancial incentives, as the reward for task accomplishment.

The typical factory at the turn of the twentieth century placed responsibility for the selection, training, and retention of employees in the hands of the line manager, usually the first-line supervisor. Taylor felt that specialized knowledge was needed and described the duties of a "shop disciplinarian" (not the most appropriate title) as selecting and discharging employees, keeping performance records, handling disciplinary problems, administering wage payments, and serving as a peacemaker. In recognizing the need for an employment specialist, Taylor prepared the way for the emergence of human resource management.

Taylor's idea inspired Hugo Münsterberg to create the discipline of industrial psychology. Münsterberg established a laboratory at Harvard for the study of the psychology of work. Münsterberg considered Taylor the "brilliant originator" of scientific management and sought to put science into the study of human behavior by studying the demands jobs make on people and the necessity of selecting those people whose mental qualities make them best fitted for the work they had to do; determining the psychological conditions under which the greatest and most satisfactory output can be obtained from every person; and producing the influences on human needs that are desirable for the interests of the business.

Taylor's Legacy

It would be difficult to chronicle all of Taylor's ideas that influenced modern managerial thinking and practice. Some proposals were handed off to others to make advancements, as with his ideas about human resource management, personnel testing, and industrial psychology. One lofty goal, Taylor's call for a "mental revolution" that would permit labor and management to abandon adversarial positions and to work together to create a larger pie instead of fighting over how to slice it, has seldom been attained.

Many of his notions provided foundations for current practice. Examples include setting standards for evaluating performance and for product quality, and an "exception principle," under which managers look for both good and bad exceptions to standards so corrective action, such as quality control, can be taken. What is today called Japanese-style management is an outgrowth of Taylor's ideas, which were introduced into Japan in the early 1910s. The Japanese liked Taylor's emphasis on mutual interests, cooperation, and harmony.

His Quaker-Puritan family life instilled in him beliefs and attitudes that shaped his view of work and management. He had a strong work ethic, a belief that a person must earn what he got—no entitlements permitted. Even though he was born into wealth, he started as an apprenticed worker. He earned approximately $50,000 per year from 1900 to 1911 from consulting ($35 per day plus expenses), invention, and investments. In 1910, he refused his share of his father's $900,000 estate; yet when Taylor died, his own estate was estimated at $700,000.[4] At Taylor's home, called Boxly, in the Chestnut Hill region of Philadelphia, there were three maids, an estate superintendent, a cook, a coachman, and yard laborers who looked after the estate and its tennis court.

He did not drink, he would not permit alcohol to be served in his home, he did not take such stimulants as tea or coffee, and he did not use tobacco. Yet one personality trait that distinguished him for the rest of his life, which he picked up while serving his apprenticeship, was a habit of swearing. His swearing was indeed unique. He did not swear when most individuals would, but he did swear when most would not dream of it. It is claimed he never swore on the golf course, but did while lecturing at Harvard University.

He loved being onstage and engaging in competitive sports. He played cricket, sang as a tenor in the choral society, and was frequently in amateur theatricals. He was not a large man, perhaps 5'8" or 5'9", but he was an athlete. Beyond his U.S. lawn tennis championship, he skated in the winter and played golf frequently. He developed new mixtures for soils for better golf greens, thoroughly investigated the best grasses for them, and set out to design some new concepts in golf clubs. He developed a putter with a Y shaft, experimented with lengths and thicknesses of shafts, and spent a great deal of time in practice on the links, which he jokingly referred to as scientific inquiry. He had taken up golf at the age of forty and his skills developed rapidly, as he carried a handicap of eight when he won the handicap championships at the Philadelphia Country Club in 1902, 1903, and 1905. A plaque bearing evidence of these victories still hangs in the Philadelphia Country Club.

Before a House of Representatives committee, Taylor testified that, "scientific management is a scheme for greatly increasing the output of the man without materially increasing his effort," and that is what has happened. As Peter Drucker has pointed out:

> The most important step toward [a] "knowledge economy" was, however, scientific management—that is, the systematic application of analysis and study to manual work, first pioneered by Frederick W. Taylor. . . . Before, work had always been taken for granted . . . and that the only way to produce more was to work more and work harder. Taylor saw that this was false. The

key to producing more was to "work smarter." The key to productivity was knowledge, not sweat. . . . [Systematic work study] is the only basic American idea that has had worldwide acceptance and impact. Wherever it has been applied, it has raised the productivity and with it the earnings of the manual worker, and especially of the laborer, while greatly reducing his physical efforts and his hours of work.[5]

Unfortunately, Taylor often presented his ideas to the industrial world as a medicine instead of a candy—he may not have been the best salesperson for his philosophy. He was often arrogant, somewhat caustic, and inflexible in how his system should be implemented. These characteristics neither endeared him to the critics nor helped him successfully promote his thoughts.

Despite his wealth and growing fame, the last five years of his life were difficult. His wife, Louise, exhibited symptoms of involutional depression that often incapacitated her. Because of this, Fred ceased writing, became abrupt and antagonistic, and had less contact with his followers, except for his closest disciples. In February and early March 1915, as Taylor was on a lecture tour in Cleveland and Youngstown, he caught a cold. His cold grew worse and on March 12 he went to the hospital in Philadelphia. On March 21, 1915, one day after his fifty-ninth birthday, he suddenly died. His gravestone reads as he instructed: "Frederick Winslow Taylor, 1856–1915, 'Father of Scientific Management.'"

LILLIAN AND FRANK GILBRETH

The bricklayer's apprentice was puzzled: His observations of his coworkers showed there were three different ways to lay bricks, so how was he to learn the one best way? One set of motions was used for working fast, another for a slower pace, and yet another for teaching the apprentice how to do the job. Though bricklaying was one of the world's oldest occupations, the young apprentice, Frank Gilbreth, set out to find the best way of laying bricks, handling materials, rigging scaffolding, and training others.

Frank Bunker Gilbreth was born on July 7, 1868, in Fairfield, Maine. When he was three, his father died and the family moved to Boston, where he was educated at Andover and the Rice Grammar School. He prepped for the Massachusetts Institute of Technology, passed the qualifying exams, but decided not to become a financial burden on his family by attending college. His Sunday school teacher was in the construction business and helped Frank get started as an apprentice bricklayer. He worked his way up in the construction business until he had his own firm.

Far across America another individual was preparing for a meeting that would change numerous lives and the course of systematic management. Lillian Moller was born on May 24, 1878, the daughter of a German-born sugar refiner, and spent her early years in Oakland, California. She was an exceptionally bright student, receiving her bachelor's and master's degrees in English from the University of California at Berkeley. She earned a Phi Beta Kappa key for her scholarship at Berkeley, but her name was omitted from the list of recipients (she later was given the key she had earned). She was the first woman asked to speak at the commencement exercises; she was told by university president Wheeler to dress like a woman in a soft dress beneath her graduation gown, and his advice for delivering her speech was: "Don't scream. Don't give an oration. Read what you have to say, and from small sheets of paper. Don't imitate a man. Look and speak like a woman."[6]

Lillian's speech, "Life—A Means or an End," was met with applause, and she was recognized by the San Francisco and the Oakland papers for her commencement address. After her baccalaureate degree, she set out to tour Europe; her guide was Minnie Bunker, a cousin of Frank B. Gilbreth. In Boston she met Frank Gilbreth, already the successful owner of a construction company. A year of coast-to-coast letter writing followed before their marriage, on October 19, 1904.

Cheaper by the Dozen, the story of the Gilbreth family written by Ernestine Gilbreth Carey and Frank B. Gilbreth Jr., recounts how Frank and Lillian agreed to have a dozen children. After their marriage in Oakland, California, they took a train for San Francisco, where the bridal suite of the St. Francis Hotel awaited them. The following summarizes their decision:

> *Frank:* We're going to have a wonderful life, Lillie. A wonderful life and a wonderful family. A great big family . . .
> *Lillian:* How many would you say we should have, just an estimate? . . .
> *Frank:* We'll sell out for an even dozen. . . . What do you say to that? . . .
> *Lillian:* A dozen would be just right . . .
> *Frank:* Boys or girls? . . .
> *Lillian:* I'd like to have half boys and half girls . . . .
> *Frank:* We'll plan it that way [and in his memorandum book he wrote] don't forget to have six boys and six girls.[7]

Over the next eighteen years they would have twelve children: Anne, Mary (who died of diphtheria at age five), Ernestine, Martha, Frank Jr., William, Lillian, Fred, Daniel, John (called Jack), Robert, and Jane. *Cheaper by the Dozen* became a best-seller and a movie, and other books about the Gilbreth family abound. The family story is but one part, however, of a marriage partnership that influenced scientific management, workplace safety, industrial engineering, vocational rehabilitation, and work simplification, and made other contributions that persist to the present.

Motion Study

Before meeting Frederick Taylor or reading of Taylor's ideas, Frank Gilbreth had developed motion study by studying bricklaying and realized, as Taylor had, that wasted motion increased worker fatigue. Improved jobs increased efficiency and benefited the worker. In numerous books and articles Gilbreth wrote about estimating costs for bids, cost keeping, and rules such as no smoking on the job. He established a suggestion system, including a $10 prize each month for the best idea on how to improve work, give better service to customers, or secure additional construction jobs. He recommended photographing working conditions at the time of any accident for evidence in case of subsequent lawsuits or other claims. He devised a "white list" card, an early appraisal form for workers, to be filled out by the supervisor.

Though his advice was quite detailed and applicable to construction, it indicated Gilbreth's desire to improve the workplace in general. The results of his extensive analysis of bricklaying showed that motions could be reduced from eighteen to six and that workers could increase their output from a thousand to twenty-seven hundred bricks laid per day with no greater effort and less fatigue. Gilbreth concluded that there was indeed "one best way," and this became his slogan.

Taylor and Gilbreth met in 1907 and for a while had a mutual admiration society. Gilbreth installed selected parts of the Taylor system on some of his jobs (usually an incentive wage and a planning department), and Taylor devoted eight pages of *Principles of Scientific Management* to Gilbreth's motion studies of bricklayers. Taylor selected Gilbreth to represent him at the New York Civic Forum and again at the meetings of the Western Economic Society. Taylor asked Gilbreth to write responses to all the letters he received after the publication of *Principles of Scientific Management*, and Gilbreth's answers were published as *Primer of Scientific Management* in 1912.

During 1911, a number of members of the American Society of Mechanical Engineers were finding it difficult to get papers on management recognized by that organization. Gilbreth led the formation of a separate organization, first called the Society to Promote the Science of Management, then (after Taylor's death), the Taylor Society, which would eventually become part of the American Management Association. Gilbreth also participated in coining the phrase "scientific management" and named the largest room in his sister Anne's music school Taylor Hall.

Taylor called his work "time study" and Gilbreth called his "motion study." Gilbreth maintained that the stopwatch was not an essential ingredient to his system, and his bricklaying studies were of motions only. After he came into contact with Taylor, he developed more and more uses for the time dimensions of work. In one of the many amusing anecdotes about the Gilbreths in *Cheaper by the Dozen*, Frank was described as the "efficiency expert" at home and on the job. He buttoned his vest from the bottom up instead of from the top down, because the former took only three seconds and the latter took seven. He used two shaving brushes to lather his face and found that he could reduce shaving time by seventeen seconds. He tried shaving with two razors and found that he could reduce the total shaving time by forty-four seconds, but abandoned this scheme because it took two minutes to apply bandages to all the cuts. His biographers suggested that it was the two lost minutes that bothered him and not the cuts.

Gilbreth found it difficult for the human eye to follow human motions, and he developed two techniques to overcome this problem. One was a list of seventeen basic motions, each called a *therblig* (Gilbreth spelled backward with the *t* and *h* transposed), such as "search," "select," "position," "hold," and so on. These motions could not be further subdivided and gave Gilbreth a more precise way of analyzing the exact elements of any worker movement. The second technique used the infant technology of the motion picture camera. Gilbreth placed a large-faced clock, calibrated in fractions of minutes, in the camera's field of vision of the person being studied. Gilbreth thought the camera was better than a stopwatch because the film enabled multiple viewings and constituted proof to the worker, while the stopwatch depended on the dexterity of the observer and could not be easily replicated. This was the beginning of what Gilbreth called "micromotion" study.

Numerous applications of this type of study can be found in films Gilbreth made to study the work of nurses, surgeons, industrial workers, golfers, and baseball players. For example, he filmed a pitcher and catcher at the Polo Grounds in a May 13, 1913, baseball game between the New York Giants and the Philadelphia Phillies. His measurements showed that it took .3 seconds for the pitcher's throw to reach the plate. In cases where a base runner on first tried to steal second base, Gilbreth's time showed 1.5 seconds elapsed while the ball moved from pitcher to catcher to second baseman. Frank concluded that, with an eight-foot lead off first, the base runner would have to be a world-class sprinter to reach second base safely. It was a time before radar guns and more precise measuring devices, but Frank was interested in the motions as well as time and would later use this baseball study to train soldiers to throw hand grenades.

Gilbreth left the construction trade in 1912 to become a consultant, making him a potential competitor of Fred Taylor and his associates. The first inkling of a spat occurred after Gilbreth's first job at the New England Butt Company of Providence, Rhode Island, a manufacturer of machines for making braided materials, such as trimmings for clothes, shoes, and so on. Frank felt this work went smoothly and was finished ahead of schedule. He thought he should be greatly admired by Taylor for this, but Taylor was led to believe that the success was not attributable to Gilbreth but mostly to his assistants.

A second incident began when Milton Hermann visited Taylor to complain that Gilbreth had overcharged and done poor work for his firm, the Hermann Aukam Company, a handkerchief manufacturer. Taylor met with the Gilbreths in Providence and Frank claimed that he had, with the use of micromotion studies, reduced the number of motions required to fold handkerchiefs from 150 to 16 and that the disagreement concerned Hermann's "hogging" all of the profits that were due to Gilbreth's work.

Taylor came away unconvinced that Gilbreth was in the right. He had an associate named King Hathaway assume the work with Hermann Aukam, thinking that Gilbreth had canceled his contract, which Gilbreth denied. Once at Hermann Aukam, Hathaway reported to Taylor that Gilbreth's work had brought about a confused state of affairs at the company. Gilbreth was bitter over the statements by Taylor and Hathaway and became instead a vocal critic of Taylor and his associates.

After Taylor's death in 1915, all was quiet until 1920, when the Gilbreths attacked Taylor's followers (Carl Barth, Dwight Merrick, and Sanford Thompson) for continuing to promote stopwatch study because of their interests in selling timing devices, forms, and books about time study. The mutual distrust would continue even after Frank's death in 1924—few of the Gilbreth offspring have kind words for Taylor even to this day.

After the deaths of Fred Taylor and Frank Gilbreth, their search for improved job design, better work methods, and reduced fatigue would be carried on in texts, conferences, colleges of business, and departments of industrial engineering. Lillian Gilbreth tried to pour oil on the troubled waters in a 1927 *American Machinist* article that argued there was room for both motion *and* time study in scientific management. Today, we hear the phrase "working smarter, not harder," not realizing that it was coined by a Gilbreth follower and work simplification pioneer, Allan H. Mogensen. Quoted by numerous others, this phrase aptly describes Taylor and Gilbreth's work.

The First Lady of Management

Frank and Lillian Gilbreth gave new meaning to the idea of teamwork. After their marriage, Lillian decided to change her academic interests to psychology, for she thought that this field would best complement the work her husband was doing. Her study was to be under the guidance of Edward Lee Thorndike, a pioneer in the psychology of learning. Lillian combined marriage and family with research on her doctoral thesis, "The Psychology of Management," which she submitted in 1912. The University of California at Berkeley informed her that the thesis was acceptable but that she would have to return to campus for a year of residency. Lillian had been led to believe that this requirement would be waived in her case, but the university officials were steadfast.

Frank was furious and began shopping around for a publisher. Her dissertation did appear in book form, but the publisher insisted that the author be listed as "L. M. Gilbreth" with no mention of her being a woman. When a colleague asked Frank if he was related to this "L.M. Gilbreth," he responded, "Only by marriage."

Eventually the University authorities agreed that she could spend her residency in any college that gave an advanced degree in industrial psychology or management. These were scarce at that time, but Frank discovered that Brown University was planning to offer a Ph.D. program in applied management and moved the family and his work to Providence, Rhode Island. At Brown, Lillian wrote a new dissertation, "Some Aspects of Eliminating Waste in Teaching," finally completing her Ph.D. degree requirements in 1915. During the oral defense of her dissertation, one of the examiners barked, "So you have become a behaviorist, have you?" suggesting a low esteem for the behavioral sciences at that time. She survived the defense successfully, and her graduation gown provided adequate maternity wear for commencement—she was nine months pregnant with the Gilbreths' sixth child, William, who was born three days later.

Lillian's book *The Psychology of Management* stressed that management must be more of the person than of the work and that effective industrial training and education would help the workers make better use of their abilities. The book compared the attributes of scientific management to conditions that existed previously under "traditional management." Lillian expounded the virtues of scientific management in motivating the worker and emphasized the importance of the human element in its application. A strong psychological thread ran through all of her writings, and she made contributions: the application of management and motion study techniques to the home, to the rehabilitation of the handicapped, to workplace safety and health, to the elimination of fatigue, and to the use of leisure time, which she called "happiness minutes" gained by more efficient management.

When Frank was called to duty as an army major during World War I, he and Lillian became interested in how to use motion study to design jobs to retrain soldiers, especially amputees, so they could resume a productive life after the war. They developed devices to assist the disabled, such as a typewriter for a one-armed person, and Lillian worked with the General Electric Company to redesign home appliances for disabled homemakers. The Gilbreths were among those who lobbied Congress to pass the War Risk Insurance Act after World War I to provide vocational rehabilitation for disabled soldiers. Later, this act would form the basis for legislation to assist others who were not war casualties but needed vocational rehabilitation.

Frank's military duties at Fort Sill, Oklahoma, were to make training films using motion economy on such topics as throwing grenades and disassembling and reassembling weapons. There he became grievously ill with a heart condition and, due to a lack of specialist physicians, was sent to Walter Reed General Hospital for treatment. His medical records never arrived, however, and hospital officials asked Fort Sill authorities why. The response was that Gilbreth's records had been sent to storage with the notation that Gilbreth had died. History does not record what Frank said about military efficiency, perhaps because the words were not printable. Frank received a medical discharge and resumed their busy joint career, but his illness foreshadowed a new burden for Lillian.

The years that remained to them after the war were increasingly involved with motion study, work with the handicapped, devising methods to improve on-the-job safety, consulting, and delivering seminars for people from industry and colleges across the country. After the war was over, the family moved to Montclair, New Jersey, near where many of their scientific management associates lived.

Lillian was now doing an incredible amount of the actual work. While Frank was away on trips, she spent more and more time taking care of matters at home, writing, reading, and managing much of the business. Their family increased almost yearly until 1922, when their twelfth child and sixth daughter, Jane, arrived to fulfill their plans of having them come "cheaper by the dozen"; the eldest child was seventeen at the time.

The early summer of 1924 held bright hopes for the family. Frank was scheduled to speak and preside at meetings in London and Prague, with Lillian accompanying him, while the children were to stay at Nantucket Island. On June 14, 1924, however, the day after Ernestine's high-school graduation, Frank died suddenly of his heart condition.

Immediately following Frank Gilbreth's death, Lillian Gilbreth was faced with perhaps her most important decision. She was a widow with eleven children, the family funds had largely been spent on developing the family business, and she had lost her partner for life. What was she to do?

Three days after Frank's funeral services she sailed from New York on the S.S. *Scythia*, presented the two papers that Frank was scheduled to give at the World Power Congress in London, and proceeded to Prague to preside at the American delegates' portion of the First International Management Congress. When she returned to the United States, however, she found that virtually every client of Gilbreth, Inc., had given notice that they would not renew their contracts.

She did not surrender but continued the motion study seminars for managers, engineers, and educators, and she relied upon friends such as Wallace Clark to provide entrées for consulting jobs. Women were rarely found in engineering and management, and her presence at conferences was newsworthy: *Business Week* ran a photo of Lillian in her coat and cloche hat in their January 1930 issue. She was noteworthy as "the only woman delegate to the World's Engineering Congress" in Tokyo.

Her success prompted her to write an article for the *North American Review* entitled "Why Women Succeed in Business." She outlined some steps for success: feel that work is worthwhile; study jobs and assess your abilities; feel that you can make a quality contribution; feel that you can "extend your personality"; and accept your limitations. Women should seek careers, but not as a means to escape from home and children, because if one is irritated by children at home, one will probably be irritated by the "childlike minds" in industry and business. Women who succeed will do so not because they are women but because they are "trained, adequate, understanding human beings."[8] If someone could write of how to be successful, it was Lillian Gilbreth.

The "firsts" that can be ascribed to Lillian Gilbreth are astounding. She became the first woman member of the Society of Industrial Engineers in 1921; the first woman member of the American Society of Mechanical Engineers; the first woman to receive an honorary master of engineering degree at the University of Michigan; the first woman professor of management at an engineering school (at Purdue University in 1935); and the first woman professor of management at Newark College of Engineering. The Gilbreth Medal, named for both Frank and Lillian, was awarded to Lillian in 1931, and she is the only woman recipient to date; she also is the only woman to receive the coveted Gantt Gold Medal and the only woman to be awarded the prestigious International Committee of Scientific Management (CIOS) gold medal. There can be no doubt about why she has been called the "First Lady of Management."

YOICHI UENO

The Industrial Revolution arrived in Japan later than it came to economically developing nations in the West. In the early 1600s Tokugawa Ieyasu conquered all rivals and established a centralized government that was distrustful of all outsiders. Some three hundred lords ran the country, each controlling a feudal fiefdom and each pledging undying loyalty to the central government. Society was divided into rigidly defined classes: the emperor and his lords at the top; followed in status by the *samurai* warriors; the farmers upon whose produce this island kingdom depended; the artisans; and, at the lowest rung of the ladder, the merchants. Within each social group, each person knew exactly his or her standing relative to the caste hierarchy.

Confucianism, the official belief system, served as a prop for the rigid social system because of its emphasis on this world rather than heaven or hell and its cultural standards of benevolence, wisdom, proper behavior, and obedience. There were no absolute standards of "good" and "bad"; rather, these virtues depended upon the approval or disapproval of others. To maintain the status quo, the Tokugawa shogunates banned contact and trade with other nations, except for trade with China. From its Tokugawa feudal past Japan would retain its emphasis on family ties and affection, respect and loyalty between servant and master, harmony in marriage, precedence to be given to elders, and trust in relationships among friends.

From 1603 to 1867, under the Tokugawa shogunates, feudalism prevailed in Japan while the rest of the world was changing. Merchants were the first to break with the ban on economic intercourse with other nations and, since they were members of a common caste, they began to develop more intricate ways of trading that protected them and their relationships with other members of society. With peace ensured by the government and the *samurai*, commercial activities expanded and Japan's excellent ports hosted the ships of other nations. Commerce began to open the door of a closed society. With their prosperity and strong class ties, the merchants developed their own rules and gained power—a phenomenon that did not fit into the idea of being a lower caste. The central government regulated commercial activities and often looked the other way when trade brought contacts and Western wealth to Japan. From its Tokugawa heritage, two important developments would carry Japan into its next age: one, a close tie between government and trade; and two, a strong merchant class that had devised a meticulous code of behavior for themselves based on trust and the building of mutual relationships.

The Meiji restoration in 1868 was a return to Japan's past of direct rule by the emperor. The new regime placed high priority on building a strong military and on industrialization as a national goal. To speed progress, the government decided to sell its state enterprises in textiles, metals, and chemicals to a small number of wealthy families. When we think of privatization today, we should remember its use over a century ago to spur economic progress in Japan. The families who took over the ownership (usually paying a small percentage of what would have been the market value), the employees, and the management of these businesses developed them into financial and industrial combinations more commonly known as *zaibatsu*. While these were nominally private, the Meiji government remained the dominant partner and used the *zaibatsu* to promote national goals.

Wakon yosai (meaning "Japanese spirit and Western technology") became the guiding slogan of the Meiji.[9] Being closed to Western ideas and technology for such a lengthy period meant that Japan had to jump-start its economic motor with what had been previously considered forbidden. Catching the west would not be easy: in 1870, more than 80 percent of Japan's population was engaged in agriculture and less than 5 percent in manufacturing; even by 1930, only 50 percent of the population was employed in manufacturing.[10] The manufacturing firms were family-owned and -controlled, were generally backward in technology, and lacked any knowledge of management methods that were being developed elsewhere. Japan needed both an industrial revolution and a managerial one—and for these it looked westward.

Efficiency as Management

Ideas about Western management appear to have first filtered into Japan as the result of the visit of Yokinori Hoshino, director of Japan's Kajima Bank, to the United States in 1911. Frederick Taylor's *Principles of Scientific Management* was published that year, and Hoshino's contact with Taylor's writings provided him with the most advanced thinking of that time. Taylor was at the peak of his influence as a result of the Eastern Rate Case before the Interstate Commerce Commission. Hoshino obtained permission to translate Taylor's book into Japanese, and the translation was published in Japan in 1912.[11]

Landing in fertile soil, the ideas of scientific management would spread rapidly and form the cornerstone of Japan's transition from feudalism to the modern age. One of the leading influences in bringing systematic management ideas to the attention of scholars and practicing managers was Yoichi Ueno. Ueno was born in Tokyo on October 28, 1883, was educated in a Nagasaki mission school, where he apparently learned English and became interested in Western culture, and graduated from Tokyo University in 1908 with a degree in psychology. His interest in psychology led him to translate John Dewey's *The School and Society* and Alfred Binet's writings on measuring intelligence in children, and he introduced Japan to the ideas of Sigmund Freud.

Hoshino's translation of Taylor's book brought Ueno to scientific management, and in 1912 he published a paper, "On the Efficiency" (early Japanese writers found no closely parallel word in their language for *management* and instead substituted *efficiency*), that described the ideas and accomplishments of Taylor and Frank Gilbreth, whom Taylor had praised in his book.

Ueno launched and edited a monthly psychology journal, *Shinri Kenkyo*, to publicize scientific management writers as well as the work of the pioneer industrial psychologist, Hugo Münsterberg. Ueno followed that with a best-selling introductory psychology text (*Shinrigaku Tsugi*) that gave him a national reputation and would serve as a springboard for his consulting practice. As he studied the work of Taylor, Gilbreth, Münsterberg, and others he was able to appreciate the psychological foundation upon which their philosophies were based. The scientific management ideas of harmony, cooperation, mutual interests, and a mental revolution between labor and management fit very well the Japanese culture. For Ueno, efficiency served both the employee and the employer.

Ueno's interest in the psychology of scientific management aroused his interest in how Taylor and Gilbreth had used motion and time studies to redesign jobs to make them less fatiguing and more rewarding. Taylor died in 1915, so Ueno began corresponding with Frank Gilbreth sometime in 1917, as he recalled:

> One day, I came upon an article of photographing a physical motion in an American magazine and wanted to know the detailed methods. So, I wrote a letter to the writer asking how it was done. It happened to be that the writer was Mr. Frank B. Gilbreth, the pioneer of motion study.
>
> A letter from an unknown Japanese youth seemed to have aroused an interest in Mr. Gilbreth. He told me later that he had pleasant chats over the letter with his wife, Dr. Lillian M. Gilbreth. Various materials about the problem were kindly sent to me, in 1919. I wrote a book *"On Psychology of Efficiency of Individuals and Business"* (*Hito Oyobi Jigyo Nohritso No Shinri*), using these materials in which I devoted a chapter introducing his methods. This book was so popular that edition after edition were sold out.[12]

After one of his lectures, Ueno was invited to study the operations at the Lion Tooth-Powder Company. His first study of factory work was of a labor-intensive task and seems incongruous in terms of modern methods:

> I first picked up the packing operation of tooth powder. After mixing of materials, a certain amount of powder was put in a paper bag with a small shovel by hand, the mouth of it was turned down. Then the bag was put in a outer paper bag and sealed. Half a dozen of them [were] placed in a carton and tied crosswise with a string. These were again placed in a wooden box. These packing operations were done all by hand at that time.
>
> The time and motion study was tried by me at the first time in my life, as exactly as it was explained in textbooks of Scientific Management. Side by side with female workers, I myself tried the operation among a pretty cloud of the

powder for some time. A plan of improvement hit upon me I asked the plant manager to lend me 15 of the female workers to see how this plan would work. This was consented. I remember that I could hardly sleep the night before the improved operation would be put into practice, lest I should find what I had studied might prove an academic theory impracticable in factory.[13]

The next day Ueno's fears were overcome as the employees quickly learned the new method and improved productivity from sixty-two dozen to seventy-nine dozen packages per day. As a result, the workers were permitted fifteen-minute breaks in the morning and in the afternoon, and management was able to reduce the length of the workday one hour with no decrease in output. Since productivity had increased, Ueno proposed to management that they share the savings with the employees and reduce the price to the consumer. His idea was rejected, and he felt the sting that many consultants have experienced when good ideas are not compatible with management's goals. Ueno was paid a consulting fee, however, and, as far as we know, he became the first Japanese management consultant.

Watch on the West

Ueno's success as a consultant in cosmetic firms, textile mills, and manufacturing plants provided a step toward another role in his career. The president of Kyoto Imperial University, Masataro Sawayanagi, held small seminars in which the participants had to talk about what each was studying. Sawayanagi was so impressed by Ueno's research that he introduced Ueno to the Kyochokai (Society for the Promotion of Coordination of Capital and Labor). The Kyochokai officials were also impressed by Ueno's work and, sensing the possibilities of scientific management, sent Ueno to America and Europe to learn all he could.

In America Ueno called on his pen pal Frank Gilbreth and became the first Asian student to attend the Gilbreth school in Montclair, New Jersey. In the United States he met a number of scientific management authorities, some of them the proclaimed disciples of Frederick Taylor. Ueno invited Carl Barth, Wallace Clark, Dwight Merrick, Morris Cooke, H. King Hathaway, and others to visit Japan. When he returned home, Ueno helped organize the National Japan Federation of Efficiency Engineers, which immediately began publishing a monthly magazine, *Sangyo Noritsu* (which could be translated as *Industrial Efficiency* or *Industrial Management*).

Carl Barth, considered by Taylor as one of his anointed, appears to be the first "efficiency expert" to visit Japan. Barth lectured on efficiency to Japanese audiences in 1924 and paved the way for others to bring their ideas to Japan. Following Barth's visit, Ueno organized the Japanese branch of the Taylor Society and served as its president for over a decade. Ueno's work took him to Paris in 1929 for the fourth International Congress of Scientific Management, where he reported that he was honored to meet Taylor's widow, Louise S. Taylor. He presented her with a "Map of Management History," a nearly two-by-three-foot portrayal of the streams of management thought beginning with a Taylor "river" and his followers as its "tributaries"; the other "river" was that of Harrington Emerson, fed by the Louis Brandeis "tributary." The map is preserved in the Frederick Taylor Collection at the Stevens Institute of Technology in Hoboken, New Jersey.

The international exchanges between East and West continued, and Ueno was a prime mover in these conferences. Following Paris, Japan hosted the World Engineering Congress in 1930; the American participants included Lillian Gilbreth, H. King Hathaway, and Harrington Emerson, all of whom were considered world-class authorities on efficiency. Ueno served as interpreter for the U.S. participants. In her report on the congress, Lillian Gilbreth told of overflow attendance at all of the American seminars because of the "live interest in scientific management in Japan."[14] After touring numerous plants, Lillian Gilbreth concluded that while many plants were well managed, others had much to learn about production and its human component. Japan was watching the West, but had not yet caught up in its progress toward industrialization.

When we think of Japanese consumer products before World War II, the term shoddy comes to mind. Because the Japanese were not known then for quality products, one might suspect that the lessons of the efficiency experts failed to gain an enduring place in the minds of Japan's managers. Such a conclusion would be in error, however, as we tend to forget that Japan under the emperor had expansionist goals in mind and the purpose of industry was to ally itself with the military. *Shoddy* would not be an appropriate term to describe Japan's military matériel in World War II. For example, Mitsubishi's Zero fighter plane performed well in combat.[15] The lessons of quality and efficiency were learned, but in imperial Japan they were not applied to consumer goods.

What we call Japanese-style management is not a postwar phenomenon; it was started by Yoichi Ueno and other scholars and practitioners who learned from the West. Ueno was one representative of those eager to learn how to modernize their factories and produce more efficiently. Ueno's travels and activities were sorely curtailed by the war, but afterward he helped rebuild Japan's civil government. He reopened his Efficiency School after the war and continued to teach until his death on October 15, 1957.

Biographers who knew him well say that "he derived his greatest pleasure from teaching students . . . [and] his followers knew him best as the witty, kind-hearted good old professor."[16] He followed the spiritual discipline of Zen Buddhism and constantly sought to downplay racial and cultural differences between nations. As prewar tensions between the United States and Japan elevated, H. King Hathaway wrote Ueno that if they had been in charge, the "bitterness between the two nations would never have been possible."

Yoichi Ueno's desire to have his son follow in his path became a reality—Ichiro Ueno became an advocate of value analysis in manufacturing and a well-known name to those who study quality management. Yoichi Ueno's Efficiency School became the SANNO Institute of Business Administration, and Ichiro Ueno succeeded his father as president.

When the Industrial Revolution came to Japan, that country needed technology as well as revised notions about how to manage a growing manufacturing sector. Yoichi Ueno served to bring the ideas of scientific management to Japan and provided for a cultural exchange of knowledge by encouraging Japanese scholars and practitioners to visit the United States and vice versa. His contribution was to open Japan to Western ideas about managing, enabling the economy to develop by working smarter, not harder. The rising sun of management thought for Japan was found in the words of Frederick Taylor, Frank and Lillian Gilbreth, and their followers.

8

ORGANIZERS

Teamwork is a frequently used word, but in practice the goal often falls short of achievement. Getting people to work together in pursuit of a common end is an ancient problem in military, religious, governmental, and economic endeavors. Economic enterprises are different from other kinds of undertakings: They cannot rely upon the rigorous training and discipline of the military, nor upon the possibilities of hell and heaven and the devotion of the faithful found in the church. Nor can they pass laws and use taxes, as governments can. While leadership is critical to goal attainment, it typically occurs within some organizational setting.

Early economic organizations were largely family-owned and -managed. Cyrus McCormick, for example, placed his brothers in charge of production, sales, and other activities and later passed the helm of the firm to his son. America's first big businesses, the railroads, were also the first enterprises to move away from this model, splitting themselves into departments for traffic operations, maintenance and repairs, ticket and freight sales, legal matters, accounting, and so on. Here we begin to see a further division, between line responsibilities for traffic operations and staff duties for advising line managers. A hierarchy of authority was established, in which supervisors were held accountable for results and channels developed for providing information to those who had to make operational decisions.

Those selected to represent the organizers, William C. Durant, Alfred P. Sloan Jr., and Chester Barnard, exemplify different ideas about how to proceed in organizing and managing large-scale organizations (and how not to). Durant represents the visionary builder who could never effectively connect the parts to serve a common purpose. Sloan inherited a second-place automotive company that was in organizational shambles and created new ideas about multiple-product firms. Barnard was not an organization chart fanatic but suggested a different idea of authority, seeing the need to create a cooperative system of people who were willing to work toward a common purpose. The ideas of these organizers illustrate the need for an organizational framework upon which effective teamwork depends.

WILLIAM C. DURANT

William Crapo Durant was a Flint, Michigan, maker of horse-drawn wagons and carriages who saw possibilities in attaching an internal combustion engine to his vehicles. In 1904 Durant bought the failing motor car company of David Dunbar Buick, and in that year twenty-eight Buicks were made and sold. By 1908 Durant's Buick led U.S. auto makers in unit sales: 8,484 Buicks were sold, compared to 6,181 Fords, and 2,380 Cadillacs. Durant dreamed of creating a larger company and used Buick's profits to acquire Weston-Mott, a maker of wheels and hubs, Albert Champion's Ignition Company (which became AC Spark Plug), Oldsmobile from Ransom Olds, the Oakland Motor Car Company, and Cadillac (one of Henry Ford's early ventures). He also approached Henry Ford and the owners of the Reo and the Maxwell-Briscoe about a merger. Henry Ford was willing but wanted cash only, no stock, in exchange for his company. Durant was financing his acquisitions through the exchange of stock (he was always short of cash), so Ford was left out of the deal that led to the creation of the General Motors Corporation (GM) in 1908, capitalized at $10,000,000. Through one acquisition after another GM became a loosely coupled firm of some twenty-five companies manufacturing automobiles, accessories, and parts, each maintaining its own identity and operations.

Dream Maker

Durant was a visionary leader who could create, but he had shortcomings in organizational and financial matters. While Henry Ford scorned Wall Street, integrated his firm, and centralized decision making, Durant carried decentralization at GM to the brink of anarchy. He had borrowed heavily, and a financial crisis in 1910 saw the price of GM's shares drop from $100 to $25. Durant was told by his bankers, "We are not sure that the automobile business is sound or here to stay. Your loans must be paid at maturity."[1] Durant could not raise the money, so the bankers took over. For five years GM did not have Billy Durant at the helm, though he was able to pick Charles W. Nash to become president.

Durant was not idle, however; when Louis Chevrolet retired, he bought into that company and capitalized it at $20,000,000. As the economy returned to more prosperous times the Chevrolet Company profited, and Durant used as much of those profits as he could to buy stock in GM. By 1915, Chevrolet and Durant held 450,000 of GM's 825,589 shares of common stock. The bankers could have chosen a proxy fight but decided instead to compromise with Durant: They would dissolve the voting trust on the condition that Pierre S. du Pont, who was widely respected for his organizing and managerial talents at the DuPont Powder Company, was made chairman of the board of GM. Pierre felt that GM could develop a better organization, such as DuPont had, that would bring some order out of the chaos that Durant had created. Pierre held nearly 25 percent of GM's shares, and the bankers thought that this would be the force needed to counter the seemingly immovable Durant. They were wrong—Durant used his Chevrolet/GM shares to win control without Pierre's support, refused to work with GM's board of directors, and rejected the DuPont Company's functional, centralized, structure and executive committee controls. The bankers and Pierre du Pont underestimated Durant—Billy was back in charge.

Durant's next step was to create United Motors in 1916 to acquire the Hyatt Roller Bearing Company, Dayton Engineering Labs, Remy Electric, Perlman Rim, and Harrison Radiator, parts and accessory makers. Included in the deal were people such as Charles F. Kettering and Alfred P. Sloan Jr., whom Durant named president of United Motors. If *Fortune* magazine had existed in 1917, its Fortune 500 would have included three companies that were put together by Durant: GM, ranked number thirty; Chevrolet, number fifty-one; and United Motors, number eighty-nine. In contrast, Ford was number sixteen.[2] In 1918 Durant folded Chevrolet and United Motors into GM and launched another acquisitions binge: Guardian Refrigerators (with its Frigidaire brand); Samson Tractor Company; Sunnyhome (to manufacture home appliances and portable electric generators); and Modern Housing Corporation (to build homes for GM employees).

A short, steep depression in the fall of 1920 and extending into 1921 created another financial crisis for GM, the auto industry, and the economy. The auto market fell, as did the stock market, and Billy Durant started buying GM shares on margin, perhaps to take advantage of the bargain or to bolster the price. While Durant was buying, Pierre and other du Ponts and J. P. Morgan and Company were trying to sell GM securities to prevent bankruptcy. The financial lunacy of this was apparent, as the outcome was that Durant lost his large personal fortune and wound up owing his brokers $30,000,000 million. Durant turned to the du Ponts in search of aid and Pierre, fearing that Durant would dump his shares and threaten GM's already shaky credit, worked with J. P. Morgan and Company to buy out Durant. Durant resigned, having lost the company he built, and Pierre du Pont came out of retirement to become president of GM.

Durant never stopped dreaming after he left GM at the age of sixty. He formed Durant Motors Incorporated, which made the Durant, the Star, the Flint, and the Locomobile, but this firm would succumb to the Great Depression. His genius was building, not organizing or managing, but he did have the ability to spot talent and some of the "Durant men" who would shape GM or the auto industry in later years were Sloan, Charles F. Kettering, Charles S. Mott, Charles W. Nash, and Walter P. Chrysler. The dreamer started with Buick in 1904 and by 1920 left GM with $350,000,000 in assets.

ALFRED P. SLOAN JR.

Chance and ability each play their role in our affairs, and had Billy Durant been a more effective organizer, Alfred P. Sloan Jr. might have spent his career as a refrigerator salesman rather than retiring as the architect of the world's largest corporation. When Pierre du Pont became the president of General Motors in 1920, he inherited a Massachusetts Institute of Technology–trained engineer, Alfred Pritchard Sloan Jr. Sloan was born in New Haven, Connecticut, on May 23, 1875, and from the age of ten grew up in Brooklyn, New York. His father was a coffee, tea, and cigar wholesaler who had invested $5,000 to buy the nearly bankrupt firm of John Wesley Hyatt in 1898. Hyatt's antifriction roller bearings were essential to bicycles, which had begun to enjoy wide popularity in the 1880s and 1890s, and to the automobile, which was slowly emerging from the horse-drawn wagon and carriage industry.

After his graduation from MIT, the young Sloan went to work for the Hyatt Roller Bearing Company, left the company for a short period to sell electric refrigerators, then returned to become Hyatt's general manager. When Durant bought Hyatt to add to his parts and accessory stable called United Motors, Sloan and his father sold their interest for $13.5 million, not a bad return on a $5,000 acquisition at a time when there was no tax on capital gains. Alfred Sloan Jr. became president of United Motors, which was later brought into the GM fold.

Organizing Billy's Dream Machine

Sloan had done an organization study for Durant while at United Motors on how to manage an organization of multiple divisions with different products being made by each. Sloan envisioned decentralized operations for the divisions but a single nationwide department to service the numerous small products made by the various divisions, since it was uneconomical for each division to have its own service department. Sloan implemented this concept for United Motors, but it was not adopted by Durant for GM.

Sloan sent a copy of this plan to Pierre du Pont when the latter became GM's president and was searching for answers to a multitude of GM problems. The Du Pont Company had been studying the problem of organizing and managing a multiproduct firm since it had lost its dominance in explosives due to an antitrust breakup in 1913, but it was at GM that the idea would be conceived and first implemented. Sloan's United Motors study was his springboard to GM's Executive Committee, along with Pierre and two Du Pont associates he had brought over, John J. Raskob and J. Amory Haskell. Together, this group would begin a plan to improve inventory control, forecast demand and coordinate inventory, sales, and production, improve cash management, and solve interdivisional problems. The solution to all of these, they felt, resided in the organization of GM.

Wisely, Pierre du Pont saw that the centralized, functional structure of the Du Pont Powder Company would not work at GM because of the nature of the competitive market and the diverse product line. Sloan's plan of organization, however, was unique and innovative and contrasted with the family management of firms such as McCormick's, the entrepreneurial leadership of firms such as Carnegie's, or the line-staff functional arrangement that existed at Du Pont. It is easy to underestimate the significance of Sloan's concept of organization because it is so commonplace today, yet for its time it was novel in how it solved the problem of organizing a large, multiproduct firm. Sloan's idea had three elements that would become the model for the modern firm: central committees for policy formulation and financial control; general staff officers to advise and assist as needed; and divisions (organized around products) for implementing policy and conducting operations. Sloan and GM began with establishing the product divisions.

Before reorganization, GM had five car divisions that competed with Buick in the midmarket: Chevrolet, Oakland, Oldsmobile, Sheridan, and Scripps-Booth. The lowest-priced car, Chevrolet, cost $300 more than Henry Ford's Model T. The product line was streamlined by eliminating one division, then repositioning the remaining ones in different price ranges that minimized head-to-head competition. The low price bracket belonged to Chevrolet (since the Sheridan and Scripps-Booth lines were discontinued), then ranged upward to Pontiac (which replaced the Oakland), Buick, Olds, and Cadillac. With the GM Truck Division, these comprised the car and truck group. In addition, there were groups for accessories and parts and an export division.

The division managers of these product groups had administrative control over their manufacturing, sales, dealer relations, and division-level staff for purchasing, personnel, finance and accounting, engineering, and styling (although styling would later become more centrally coordinated). Within corporate-level policy and forecasts, divisions could make decisions about production, inventory, employment, equipment, methods, and procedures. Exceptions to corporate forecasts, for example, could be made by a division if they could be justified to the central operations committee. With product divisions, GM intended to make "a car for every purse and purpose."

GM's product divisions resembled the assortment of companies that Durant had built, but Sloan's plan provided other elements that brought the parts into a whole: central committee management and general advisory staff. The Executive Committee was the ultimate authority in GM, and this select group set overall goals and policies, made major personnel decisions, kept the price brackets intact, and allocated resources to the divisions. Other central committees, such as the Operations Committee (comprising all product division heads), the Interdivisional Relations Committee, and the Finance Committee, were crucial to coordination. For example, under Durant, Buick was GM's "cash cow," but it hoarded its cash to a degree that prevented GM's desired expansion of other manufacturing operations.

Through the new Finance Committee all division revenues were to be credited to corporate accounts and would not be under division control unless otherwise authorized by central management. Through these central committees and central staff offices, GM achieved a level of coordination and control that had been the bane of Bill Durant.

An Essay in Federalism

The structure of product divisions, committees, and staff units was only the first step in Sloan's plan—but structure tells little about an organization if it does not explain relationships, authority, and responsibility. Sloan described the GM philosophy of organization as "decentralization with coordinated control." This philosophy is easier to explain than to practice because it requires a delicate balance between the autonomy of division managers to make decisions and the central policy and control framework within which the managers must operate—in short, choosing how to play the game but having to do so within the established boundaries and rules.

Durant had paid little attention to GM as a firm, instead keeping it as a loose bin of pieces, each doing its own thing: for example, Buick hoarded cash; other divisions purchased more materials than needed for final assembly; dealers' inventories were not coordinated with production; and so on. Sloan's plan provided divisions with more autonomy to develop younger managers, to adjust to market characteristics that were unique to their division, and to create more initiative and flexibility within the division.

The "coordinated control" of GM's philosophy involved top-level committees that made policy decisions about capital budget allocations, price brackets, and general forecasts, and held financial control. For example, the head of corporate staff for sales analysis and development was Norval H. Hawkins, who came over from the Ford organization. His general sales forecast was the starting point for division forecasts. The Finance Committee was in the hands of Donaldson Brown, who had been Du Pont's treasurer and was brought to GM to provide better financial information. At Du Pont, Brown developed the classic ROI (return on investment) formula: $R = T \times P$, where R represents the rate of return on capital invested in each division, T stands for the rate of turnover of invested capital, and P is for the percentage of profit on sales. This became the famous Du Pont chart system, which endures yet today and is used to portray the relative performance of various units, to forecast, and to control.

At GM Brown provided the key connection between delegated divisional operations and central control and coordination. Return on investment provided a means of measuring how effectively each division was using its resources, regardless of whether it produced automobiles, trucks, parts, accessories, or refrigerators. ROI enabled a comparision between apples and oranges because each was reduced to a common denominator, rate of return on investment. The best division was not necessarily the one with the highest ROI, but the one with the highest *attainable* return after considering market conditions.

Since the accessory and parts division sold both within GM and outside the company, they had to meet the market test of staying competitive. A division manager, for example, could (but rarely did) go outside GM for accessories and/or parts. Again, ROI was a measure of how well these units were operating. For GM, Brown's formula provided the means for central management to delegate authority because it now had a measure of how well that division was operating. "Coordinated control," in GM's philosophy, was based on information that compared performance.

Peter Drucker called this GM plan an "essay in federalism . . . [that] attempts to combine the greatest corporate unity with the greatest divisional autonomy and responsibility; and like every true federation, it aims at realizing unity through local self-government, and vice versa. This is the aim of General Motors' policy of decentralization."[3] The GM model distinguished policy formulation from day-to-day implementation of policy and provided for decentralized operations with coordinated control. For GM, for other firms, and for all organizations both public and private, decentralization with coordinated control is like a narrow tightrope; it requires a delicate balance to keep the one without destroying the other.

But Sloan knew that times change, and in his autobiography he provided a lesson that his successors at GM and all managers should heed:

> No company ever stops changing. Change will come for better or worse. I also hope I have not left an impression that the organization runs itself automatically. An organization does not make decisions; its function is to provide a framework, based upon established criteria, within which decisions can be fashioned in an orderly manner. Individuals make the decisions and take the responsibility for them. . . . The task of management is not to apply a formula but to decide issues on a case-by-case basis. No fixed, inflexible rule can ever be substituted for the exercise of sound business judgment in the decision-making process.[4]

Pierre du Pont passed the reins on to Alfred P. Sloan Jr. in 1923 and GM would remain under Sloan's leadership until he retired in 1946, at age seventy-one. When his reorganization plan was being first implemented in 1921, GM had 12.8 percent of the U.S. automobile and truck market and Ford had 55.7 percent. During Sloan's presidency GM passed Ford and became the world's largest corporation. Sloan's model for GM sustained the firm for half a century and provided the framework for other firms that followed a strategy of diversification and needed to manage a multidivisional organization. Billy Durant's dream was realized through the work of Alfred P. Sloan Jr.

CHESTER I. BARNARD

Chester Barnard did not have the entrepreneurial flair of an Andrew Carnegie, nor the confidence of wealth of a John Pierpont Morgan, nor the organizational transformation genius of an Alfred Sloan Jr., but he would earn seven honorary doctorates (with no bachelor's degree) and establish a reputation that extended beyond his time. Chester Irving Barnard was born on November 7, 1886, in Malden, Massachusetts. His father was a machinist, but Barnard's mother died when Chester was five years old, so he spent most of his childhood with his maternal grandparents, from whom he learned to love music and reading.

He apprenticed himself as a piano tuner and eventually became an accomplished pianist, a lover of the music of Johann Sebastian Bach. He attended the Mount Hermon School, a top-ranking prep school in Northfield, Massachusetts, and financed his education by working on the school's farm, plowing and pitching loads of hay. After Mount Hermon came admission to Harvard University, where his major was economics. He would have been a member of Harvard's class of 1910, but his work outside of class—conducting a dance orchestra and typing theses for other students—to pay for his education prevented him from meeting the science requirement for graduation. He left school in 1909 and is perhaps one of Harvard's most famous dropouts.

Making Connections

Without a degree or a job, Barnard asked his uncle, who worked for the Southwestern Bell Telephone Company in Dallas, Texas, for advice. His uncle put Barnard into contact with Walter S. Gifford, who had been recently named the chief statistician for AT&T. The role that fate plays in lives and careers is debatable, but there is no doubt that circumstances can create opportunities. This was the case for Barnard, who found an initial common ground with Gifford: both were born in Massachusetts, a mere ten miles apart, and Gifford entered Harvard in 1905 and graduated in 1909 with a degree in economics. This friendship grew over the years, and Barnard's career was helped as Gifford rapidly rose in the AT&T hierarchy. The Gifford-Barnard friendship deepened when Barnard married Grace Noera in 1911, for Grace's father had bought his building supplies from Gifford's father, who was a lumber dealer, and Grace had given a pony to Walter when she no longer wished to take care of it. Perhaps the moral of this story concerns fate, but Barnard was able to couple ability with chance and having a sponsor/mentor did not hurt his chances.

When Barnard joined AT&T the Bell System had approximately one million subscribers. The role of the statistics department was to study the rates and methods of other telephone companies in the United States and abroad, enabling corporate management to make their case(s) before various regulatory agencies. Barnard had studied German, Italian, and French at Harvard, and this plus his study of economics helped him in this job. Barnard's skills were rewarded with a promotion to the title of commercial engineer in 1915, and he traveled throughout the Bell System giving seminars on the economics of rate making. This brought him into contact with top-level people in AT&T as well as providing him with a view of the Bell System as the top-level executives saw it.

Walter Gifford became an AT&T vice president in 1916, an executive vice president in 1923, and president in 1925, where he served until 1948, the longest tenure of any AT&T CEO. Barnard had latched onto this rising star, belonging to the same social clubs as Gifford and participating in the same community activities, and moved up the Bell ladder as well: In 1922 he shifted from his staff work into Pennsylvania Bell, a subsidiary of some twenty-five thousand employees, and became vice president of that division in 1926. His task was to bring numerous smaller independent companies that operated in western Pennsylvania into the larger Pennsylvania Bell. This was done by acquisitions, all of which had to be justified in district courts, and Barnard noted that this experience taught him that building, rearranging, and consolidating different groups into one was an "endless job" of dealing with change and different personalities. In 1927, at age forty-one, he was promoted to the presidency of New Jersey Bell, where he was asked again to consolidate the southern part of the state, served by the Delaware and Atlantic Telephone and Telegraph Company, with northern New Jersey, then the territory of the New York Telephone Company. He found this task of "amalgamating two entirely different organizations" challenging because the southern portion was small-town and rural while the northern part was heavily urbanized, yielding two different company cultures.

These experiences as an executive responsible for instituting change in differing units undoubtedly influenced Barnard's thinking about the social and human processes of organizations. How can people with different training and outlooks be brought together to work as a group? Barnard served as president of New Jersey Bell until his retirement in 1948 and was familiar with the formal organization within the Bell System. It would be his interest in the less well known aspects of how to attain human cooperation, however, that would be his legacy. His work as a practicing executive would have been remembered by only a few persons if it had not been for his academic connections and the events that followed.

Barnard helped Harvard in raising money to endow professorships, and this led to his becoming a member of Harvard's visiting committee to advise on academic matters from an executive's viewpoint. He made numerous friends in the Harvard Graduate School of Business Administration and was invited by A. Lawrence Lowell, Harvard's president, to give a series of lectures before the Lowell Institute. Barnard recalled that attendance was low: "I don't believe there were more than fifty people ever in my audience and half of them were my friends and relatives."[5] The lectures would have disappeared into the ether if the editor of the Harvard University Press had not asked Barnard to convert them into a book. Barnard wanted to call it *The Sociology of Organizations*, which would have been a more descriptive title, but instead it became *The Functions of the Executive*, now a classic in understanding organizations.

The Social Process of Organizations

Barnard did not see organizations in terms of charts with lines and boxes that connected various activities. Instead, he thought of organizations as the social process through which social action is accomplished, and if any organization fails, it is because of a failure to provide an opportunity for human cooperation. Leaving aside the technologies of their respective fields, the clergy, military leaders, government officials, university administrators, and leaders in widely diversified businesses all face similar problems in getting people to work together toward a common purpose.

To compete effectively and survive, all enterprises need to maintain an internal harmony among physical, social, and human elements as well as to make adjustments to external forces that continuously fluctuate and affect the firm. Barnard rejected the traditional view of an organization as having boundaries and included in his framework investors, suppliers, customers, and others whose actions contribute to the firm even though they might not be considered members of the firm itself. He saw the firm as an open system subject to the actions of others, a view that did not become widely accepted in organizational thinking for some period of years.

Why do we have organizations? Barnard's answer was that organizations afford possibilities for expanding the powers of the group beyond what the individual can accomplish alone, for example, for national defense, making products, creating services, education, charity, and so on. Barnard defined an organization as "a system of consciously coordinated activities or forces of two or more persons." The late British management consultant Lyndall Urwick told us that this was a poor definition since "boy kisses girl" could also be considered an organization, using Barnard's definition. Validation of Urwick's observation can be found in Barnard's description of the common elements of all formal organizations:

- Willingness to cooperate
- Common purpose
- Communication

Securing the willingness to cooperate is no easy task, and Barnard suggested two approaches: offering objective incentives, and changing people's attitudes through persuasion. Objective incentives are material (such as money), nonmaterial (such as prestige, power, and so on), and associational (such as social compatibility, participation in decision making, and so on). Barnard never gave a clue as to what works best and suggested only that individual motives are highly subjective, saying that "you cannot deal effectively with people unless you get their point of view, which means know what influences their behavior."

Willingness to cooperate cannot be brought about unless employees know what effort is required of them and what satisfaction might accrue as a result of their cooperation. They need to know the purpose of the firm, their unit, and their own task. Since the purpose of the company and personal motives often differ, individuals contribute not because their goals are the same as the organization's, but because they feel that personal rewards will come from accomplishing the purpose of the organization.

All organizational activity involves communication, and Barnard stressed the importance of communication, which might well have been expected, considering his experience in the Bell system. He felt that channels of communication should be clearly defined and that the line of communication should be as direct as possible in order to reduce distortions caused by transmission through many offices or persons.

Barnard was also aware of the personal contacts and interactions that occur in the informal organization within every formal organization. Without structure, and often without conscious recognition of joint purpose, informal groupings arise out of job-related contacts and in turn establish certain attitudes, customs, and norms. The informal organization is an indispensable part of the formal organization, and Barnard believed that managers should recognize and accept it as a natural occurrence in the sociology of organizations.

In taking account of both formal and informal organizations, Barnard was clearly thinking about his earlier experiences of consolidating different companies into one. Before its breakup in recent years, the Bell System and each of its divisions probably represented the ultimate in organizational formality outside of federal and state bureaucracies (although whether they were actually outside governmental bureaucracies may be debatable, because AT&T and its regional divisions were considered public utilities and were heavily regulated). Barnard recognized this formal organization, but from the social and human facets of the organizations he also took into consideration the need to establish common purpose and willingness to serve.

The Authority of Leadership

One of Barnard's most striking ideas concerned the nature of authority. Before, the basis for a person's authority was considered either formal, that is, granted by the organization to the occupant of a position or rank, or informal, resting upon personal abilities such as gaining the respect of others, earning the trust of followers, and so forth. Barnard gave these ideas a new twist. For Barnard, individuals need to accept authority and will do so if four conditions are met:

- They understand what needs to be done.
- They believe that the request is consistent with the purpose of the organization at the time of their decision.
- They believe that the request is compatible with their personal interests as a whole.
- They are mentally and physically able to comply.[6]

To explain in terms of such a unique idea how an organization can function, Barnard developed the concept of a "zone of indifference" for each individual, within which orders are accepted without questioning authority. The zone of indifference might be narrow or wide, depending on the degree to which the incentives outweigh the burdens and sacrifices for the individual. If an employee thinks a request runs counter to a personal moral code, for instance, then the advantages of staying employed have to be weighed against that personal value system. Not all cases are this clear-cut, and Barnard admitted to many borderline possibilities; however, compliance or noncompliance is always up to the individual. From Barnard's idea we can better understand whistle blowing and similar phenomena.

Barnard did not reject traditional ideas of authority entirely. In some cases, a request might be accepted because the employee feels that making the request is a legitimate part of the manager's job; this is formal authority, or the authority of position. In another instance, the request might be accepted because the employee has respect for and confidence in the individual's personal ability and not because of rank or position; Barnard called this the "authority of leadership."

When the authority of leadership is combined with the authority of position, the zone of indifference becomes exceedingly broad. Nevertheless, Barnard stressed that the determination of authority remains with the individual. In a free society, individuals always have the choice either to go along with the costs and benefits of directives or not. As long as labor is not conscripted, the acceptance theory is valid. What appears so striking in Barnard's theory is simply another way of stating that all organizations depend on leadership that can develop the capacity and willingness of members to cooperate.

An organization without people is a shell, and the moving force in an organization is what Barnard called "moral leadership." Leaders have to hold some moral code, demonstrate a high capacity for responsibility, and be able to create a moral faculty in others. He observed that "the endurance of an organization depends upon the quality of leadership; and that quality derives from the breadth of the morality upon which it rests. . . . A low morality will not sustain leadership long, its influence quickly vanishes."[7] Barnard's words ring as true today as they did some sixty years ago.

Barnard worked in organizations as well as writing about them. He was active in various community organizations, for example: community chest fund-raising drives; the New Jersey Emergency Relief Administration, during the Depression; and the New Jersey Reformatory Commission. During World War II he was president of the United Service Organization (USO), which had a small paid staff but over three thousand clubs and six hundred thousand volunteers. He stated that this was the toughest job he ever held since it involved "responsibility without authority." He also served as a member of David Lilienthal and Dean Atcheson's Committee on the Control of Atomic Energy. He retired from New Jersey Bell in 1948, at age sixty-two, and spent the next thirteen years of his life as president of the Rockefeller Foundation, chairman of the National Science Board of the National Science Foundation, president of the Bach Society of New Jersey, and in many other such positions.

Barnard, the organizer, saw people in action, not charts and hierarchical pyramids. He drew upon his experiences in business and other endeavors as a participant and as an observer to add the social and human factor to our understanding of organizations. He enriched our understanding of the need to define the purpose of enterprises, to elicit cooperation, and to recognize that managers in all organizations must use their communication and leadership skills to build teamwork and cooperation.

9

MOTIVATORS

Human motivation has been problematic since the first human wondered why her or his fellow humans did what they did. Some, such as Peter Drucker, suggest, "We know nothing about motivation. All we can do is write books about it." Is Drucker right? Or can we learn from others and understand better this puzzling question? The word *motivation* comes from the Latin *movere*, "to move"; from that root comes *motive*, why someone does something, and *motivation*, what impels, incites, or induces people to act as they do.

The ancient Greek philosophy of hedonism first articulated the enduring belief that people seek pleasurable experiences and act to avoid painful ones. For example, the tale of the donkey driver who uses both a carrot and a stick provides an easy way of saying people can be pulled by rewards or pushed by punishments. But the medieval philosopher Jean Buridan suggested a more difficult problem, that of the donkey who starves while standing halfway between two equally attractive bales of hay. This analogy further complicates our understanding of the process of human choice.

Some people argue that fear is the greatest motivator, while others say that the hungry person makes the most reliable, diligent employee. It was this thinking that led people to label economics as the "dismal science." Counter to the idea of keeping employees at the subsistence level was Adam

Smith, the eighteenth-century liberal economist, who argued that "where wages are high, accordingly we shall always find the workmen more active, diligent, and expeditious than where they are low."

Smith's position was reflected in the use of economic incentive systems in the emerging British factory and in America, giving rise to the notion of "economic man." Frederick W. Taylor, for example, engaged in work improvement techniques to find better ways to do jobs, to set performance standards, and to reward employees for meeting or exceeding the standards. While engineers dominated the systematic-management period of pay for performance, others were beginning to question "economic man" assumptions.

The figures we have chosen as motivators were social and behavioral scientists whose philosophies extend our understanding of motivation. Elton Mayo emphasized the social aspects of work and the type of supervisor needed to stimulate both improved morale and better performance; Abraham Maslow wrote of human needs and their role in why we work; and Frederick Herzberg felt that fulfilling work would eliminate the need for the carrot and the stick.

ELTON MAYO

The General Electric Company wanted to sell more light bulbs—how many psychologists, engineers, and social scientists would it take to do this? Electric lighting had not been fully installed in offices and factories in the early twentieth century, so GE sponsored research into the question of whether or not improved lighting led to improved performance. An early researcher was a psychologist, Hugo Münsterberg, but his results did not fully support a relationship between illumination and productivity. Rather than surrendering, GE sponsored other research that produced more satisfying results, indicating that better lighting led to increases in employee productivity.

Concerned that its sponsorship of this research might lead to questions about the validity of the findings, GE provided the money for an impartial group, the National Research Council, to conduct another study. The place chosen for study was the Hawthorne plant of the Western Electric Company, the equipment supply arm of AT&T. The research group consisted of electrical engineers from the Massachusetts Institute of Technology, and they began their work in 1924. They observed existing lighting conditions and performance records in Western Electric's punch press, coil winding, and relay assembly departments to establish a baseline for the level of worker performance. The level of lighting was then varied in all groups with the result that output "bobbed up and down" without any relation to illumination.

Forging ahead, they selected two groups of coil-winding operators, equal in experience and performance, and designated one the experimental group (that is, the level of lighting was to be varied), and one the control group (no changes in lighting were to be made). The groups were placed in different buildings, separate from the other employees. In a suprising finding, output went up in *both* groups. In another attempt, productivity was maintained even under conditions of insufficient lighting. In one instance, the lighting was gradually lowered down to the level of moonlight; again, output went up.

The Relay Assembly Test Room

In 1927 the electrical engineers gave up, but some Western Electric managers recognized that *something* other than lighting was improving performance, and that if an answer could be found it would be important. GE and the National Research Council dropped their support, but Western Electric continued by having one of the relay assemblers select four other employees to form a new group for study. A layout operator was appointed to make sure the parts supply was accurate and adequate, and one of the company supervisors was chosen to observe—and to try not to be a "boss" but to be supportive of the assemblers.

The relay assembly group was placed in a separate room, the plan of the study was explained, and, to ensure that no one was hurt financially by the change, they were put on a small group incentive plan that gave them the opportunity to earn more money if they assembled more relays. Over a period of time, the overall trend was a dramatic improvement in output. But what was responsible for the reduced absences, higher morale, and increased output?

Rest pauses had been introduced, but these did not appear to reduce fatigue, so that was not the answer. The smaller size of the group was considered; one assembler reported the group "was just family, you know, real friendly." Also, the test room observer-supervisor was in dramatic contrast to the regular supervisor, Frank Platenka. As one of the operators, Theresa

Layman, explained, "We were more relaxed. We didn't see the boss [Platenka], didn't hear him. . . . he was mean. He died; I didn't even go to see him."[1] Western Electric reported that the employees were more "content" due to the "pleasanter, freer, and happier working conditions" caused by the "considerate supervision."

The opportunity to make more money was also considered as a possible factor. On the shop floor there were more than a hundred assemblers paid on a large group rate and each could do little to increase his or her pay, but in the test room those operators on a small group rate were able to increase their "earnings . . . significantly above the [Illinois] state average [for electrical apparatus workers] and, even more dramatically, above the regular department pay the workers recall receiving before the test."[2] Their average wage before going into the test room was $16 per week, but in the test room they averaged from $28 to $50 per week; when one of the operators was asked what they liked about the test room, the response was "We made more money in the test room." Western Electric's personnel manager, Mark Putnam, told *Business Week* that pay was the number-one concern expressed by employees when they were interviewed in 1930.

Another possibility was the attention they were receiving from their observer-supervisor. But when asked, the operators said that they did not act differently because they were being watched by this "friendly supervisor": "No, we kept working. It didn't matter who watched us or who talked to us." Another added that the workers "got relaxed" as the study went on.[3]

The Social Person

The "official" explanation of what happened to cause the increased productivity came from a mild-mannered professor of philosophy and psychology from Australia. George Elton Mayo was born December 26, 1880, in Adelaide. He was educated in logic and philosophy at the University of Adelaide, taught at Queensland University, and would later study medicine in Edinburgh, Scotland. His family wanted him to become a doctor of medicine, but Mayo failed an examination and that terminated his opportunity for a career in medicine.

From medicine Mayo turned to physiology, psychiatry, and psychology as it applied to the workplace. He was able to emigrate to the United States in 1923 and found a six-month research appointment with the Wharton School of Finance and Economy at the University of Pennsylvania. Mayo's research with various firms in the Philadelphia area concerned how a person's past experiences, home life, and working conditions led to obsessional reveries, which in turn became emotional maladies that led to higher employee turnover, low productivity, and radical views of society. These issues were of widespread concern among academics and businesspeople, and numerous lectures by Mayo attracted a broader audience and an invitation to join the Harvard University Graduate School of Business Administration.

Arriving at Harvard in 1926, Mayo was to devote all of his time to research, and his only contact with students in those early years were three lectures per academic year concerning his research findings. Mayo's research was far-ranging, as evidenced by J. Edgar Hoover's invitation to talk to Federal Bureau of Investigation instructors about interviewing techniques. Mayo became an adviser to the movie industry and, as a frequent film fan, he "recognized how movies could broaden and enrich life. . . . He concluded that in Hollywood there was a systematic attempt to destroy the social order. . . . [Mayo] provided guides for selecting film plots—the story must relate to 'contemporary circumstances'; plots should not abandon their social message nor be too 'sentimental or nonsensical'; [and] the story should not be secondary to sex—love, yes, but not mere sex—because it cannot sustain interest for two hours.' "[4] Hollywood never accepted Mayo's ideas and the industry's wayward ways continued, in Mayo's opinion, to destroy the social fabric.

Mayo's classroom style was relaxed; he chose to sit on a table close to the students rather than using the lectern, as most instructors did. He wished to create an air of informality to encourage discussion, and he would sit cross-legged on the table; as students soon learned, his socks often failed to match, and they began the practice of guessing what the colors of Mayo's socks would be that day.

Although Mayo appeared relaxed and informal, his biographer noted that "to some people he seemed arrogant." Whether to students or to prospective faculty members, Mayo's remarks could be cutting, as the following incident illustrates. In 1942, early in his career, Peter Drucker interviewed for a faculty position at Harvard. In the discussion following a presentation by Mayo, Drucker took issue with Mayo's view of authority: that cooperation required the consent of subordinates and could not be imposed on them by a domineering executive. Drucker felt that human relations could be used by supervisors to manipulate employees. Mayo, upset by this view, stood and poked fun at Drucker's position: "To show what a subordinate thinks about a manipulative boss, Mayo put his thumb to his nose and, looking at Drucker asked: 'You know what this means?' Drucker did not. 'Then you should,' replied Mayo." It was apparent to those in attendance that Mayo's thumbing his nose meant not only "the attitude of a subordinate who was unwilling to consent to directives from a domineering boss but also Mayo's view of the ideas that Drucker had expressed."[5]

Drucker did not get an offer from Harvard, and he eventually joined the faculty at Bennington College in Vermont. Mayo and Drucker exchanged apologies, but Drucker apparently was still carrying some of that baggage in later years when he expressed his feeling that Harvard's goal was "to become education's highest quality delicatessen store."[6] We will never know whether or not there would have been enough space in Morgan Hall to contain both Elton Mayo and Peter Drucker. Instead, each would go his way, each leaving an indelible mark in management history.

If Hollywood would not help mend a shredding social fabric, perhaps Mayo could find another avenue. Although many of the studies had been done when Mayo arrived, he took Hawthorne as a means of interpreting what future managers should do—human relations. In 1931, at the height of the Great Depression, employees at the usually job-secure Western Electric Company were being laid off, and the studies of employee behavior at the Hawthorne plant were creeping to a halt. In a speech that same year, Mayo acknowledged these difficult times, praising earlier forms of community life in which work was part of a collective social fabric that provided solidarity and belonging. With the Depression, this communal oneness was neglected and had to be restored in the workplace in order to provide cooperation and social collaboration.

When Mayo wrote of the relay assembly test room at the Hawthorne plant, he attributed the group's ability to maintain a higher level of performance to the strong social ties that had been built among the employees, including the sympathetic test room observer. According to Mayo, the key factor explaining the motivation of the relay assemblers was that they became a social unit, enjoyed the added freedoms granted by the friendly observer, and developed a sense of participation because they were consulted before changes were introduced. The group was able to build an internal equilibrium that enabled it to produce more despite the manipulations of rest pauses, length of work day, payment schemes, and so on.

Mayo felt that the advances of a technologically oriented society places too much emphasis on engineering and efficiency, pushing the social needs of individuals into the background and thereby reducing people's capacity for collaboration in work. Managerial emphasis on efficiency stifles the individual's desire for the group approval, social satisfaction, and social purpose that had previously been gained through communal life.

A human-relations manager needs training in the human and social aspects of organization, in developing listening and counseling skills, and in recognizing and understanding the nonlogical side of people. Under a human-relations-oriented manager, employees would obtain the recognition, security, and satisfaction that make them willing to cooperate and contribute their efforts toward accomplishing the organization's goals. The motivation, then, comes from meeting these social, "belonging" needs of people.

Was Mayo's interpretation of human motivation based on what had been found at Hawthorne? There is substantial evidence that Mayo's personal beliefs shaded the official account of the Hawthorne studies, which was written by Fritz Roethlisberger, a Harvard colleague, and William J. Dickson, chief of Western Electric's employee relations department.[7] Mayo changed his interpretation of the Hawthorne studies before they published their book. The major difference was in the emphasis on social needs rather than on financial incentives in the relay assembly test room. The employees said they liked the test room because they made more money; Mark Putnam, the personnel manager, told *Business Week* that money was the number-one factor; and a 1930 memo to Mayo said that "economic and financial factors are of considerable importance in the test room. The employees are anxious for high earnings."[8] There was evidence that pay for performance had contributed to the relay assemblers' increased output, but Mayo used the Hawthorne results to support his belief that the need for efficiency had led to a neglect of people's social needs.

What can we conclude? Elton Mayo and his human-relations followers challenged the primacy of financial incentives, emphasizing instead human relations and employee feelings. Although we now know that Mayo should not have downplayed financial incentives and neglected an essential part of why performance increased in the relay assembly test room, social scientists such as Mayo have enlarged our understanding of social and group needs, working conditions, and supervision. Human relations was an idea whose time had arrived. The "social person" concept added to, but did not take the place of, the "economic man" concept in our understanding of human motives; it prepared the way for a broader consideration of human needs. Then, as now, the question is not whether to reward performance, but which performance to reward and how to reward it.

ABRAHAM H. MASLOW

The idea that human beings have certain needs that they try to satisfy is one of the oldest notions in our understanding of motivation. The philosophy of hedonism, for example, was based on the need to savor pleasurable events while fleeing from unpleasurable ones; economists developed consumption and utility theories around human needs.

Modern need theories, however, have revolved primarily around the ideas of Abraham Harold Maslow, born on April 1, 1908, in Brooklyn, New York, to Jewish immigrant parents. When it came time for college, Maslow headed for the University of Wisconsin, where John B. Watson was a member of the psychology faculty. Maslow had read Watson's work on behaviorism, the idea that psychology was the science of human behavior, which could be studied under controlled laboratory conditions, like animal behavior. Watson believed that all behavior was a response to certain stimuli and that these responses could be conditioned. For example, a classic study of Watson's was the conditioning of eleven-month-old boy to fear white rats and other furry objects. (Only recently did the use of human subjects for experiments come under closer ethical scrutiny.) When Maslow arrived in Madison in 1926, he found that Watson had left to join the J. Walter Thompson Company, one of the largest advertising agencies in the United States. (So if those commercials provide stimuli to condition and reinforce your buying habits, blame it on John B. Watson.)

With Watson gone, Maslow turned to Harry Harlow, a rising young psychologist who was becoming famous for his studies of the social behavior of monkeys. His more widely known research concerned the bonds of affection between a mother and her offspring and the finding that infant females who had been deprived of this bond with their mothers did not develop maternal instincts when they became adults. Further, Harlow discovered that monkeys raised in isolation did not get along well with other monkeys in later life. Maslow used monkey subjects in his doctoral dissertation under Harlow's direction and found that dominance was related to sex and to maleness,

> but somebody [else] discovered that two months before me. . . . One day, it suddenly dawned on me that I knew as much about sex as any man living—in the intellectual sense. I knew everything that had been written. . . . Then I suddenly burst into laughter. Here was I, the great sexologist, and I had never seen an erect penis except one, and that was from my own bird's-eye view. That humbled me considerably.[9]

Doctorate in hand, Maslow taught at Brooklyn College and later at Brandeis University, where his research was concerned with primates. But one event, the birth of Abraham and Bertha Maslow's first child, became one of those "peak experiences" in life: "When my first baby was born, that was the thunderclap that settled things. I looked at this tiny, mysterious thing and felt so stupid. I felt small, weak, and feeble. I'd say that anyone who's had a baby couldn't be a behaviorist." Maslow had been a behaviorist, but that would soon be over.

The Third Force

The two most widely accepted views of psychology in the mid-1900s were behaviorism and psychoanalysis. As Maslow moved along in his career, he became disenchanted with the behaviorist view of stimulus and conditioned response. The dominant thinker in psychoanalysis was Sigmund Freud, but there Maslow saw an emphasis on the study of neurotics, or worse. Maslow saw shortcomings in basing psychology on the emotionally disturbed or on the study of monkeys and rats.

Maslow proposed that psychology should be a study of the *whole* person, not limiting the field to the evil and ugly, but expanding our human understanding to include those values and choices that people make that can be good, honorable, creative, heroic, and so on. Maslow's "humanistic psychology" was a revolt against behaviorism and psychoanalysis, creating what became known in psychology as the Third Force. The Third Force gathered momentum as other prominent psychologists agreed that previous thinking had omitted the majority of people who were well-adjusted and leading productive, rewarding lives.

The most notable work of Abraham Maslow was published in 1943 concerning his theory of human motivation. Rarely have so many enduring ideas been developed in only twenty-six pages of text; his insights have been reprinted hundreds of times in other works. Here are some prose bites:

Typically an act [behavior] has *more* than one motivation. . . .

Human needs arrange themselves in hierarchies of pre-potency. That is to say, the appearance of one need usually rests on the prior satisfaction of another, pre-potent need. . . .

Man is a perpetually wanting animal. . . .

No need or drive can be treated as if it were isolated or discrete [from other needs or drives]. . . .

Motivation theory should be human-centered rather than animal centered. . . .

While behavior is almost always motivated, it is also almost always biologically, culturally, and situationally determined as well.[10]

In these premises, Maslow provided the basis for humanistic psychology.

Maslow identified five categories of human needs: physiological, safety, love, esteem, and self-actualization. The most basic needs are physiological, such as hunger, sex, and thirst. If a person is hungry, *truly* hungry, utopia is a cafeteria. But: "It is quite true that man lives by bread alone—when there is no bread. . . . A want that is satisfied is no longer a want." When physiological needs are relatively well satisfied, safety needs emerge. These needs are broadly drawn to include protection from temperature extremes, safety from criminal assaults, having a savings account, having health insurance, and others.

Love needs are for affection, belonging, acceptance in a group, and so on. Maslow emphasized that the need for love is "not synonymous with sex . . . a purely physiological need." Esteem is also a multifaceted need—for achievement, recognition, confidence, independence, freedom, appreciation, prestige, and others.

Self-actualization is the highest-order need and emerges only after the other needs have been satisfied: "A musician must make music, an artist must paint. . . . What a man *can* be, he must be . . . to become more and more what one is, to become everything that one is capable of becoming." Paths to self-actualization vary greatly among individuals and could take such forms as being an ideal parent, being an athlete, inventing, creating, or whatever it takes to reach one's potential.

The need hierarchy, as Maslow concluded, is not rigid or fixed in the sense that each is a step that must be achieved before another can be taken. For example, some individuals place a greater importance on self-esteem than on love; creative people might forsake as many basic needs as possible in order to carry out their creative impulses; some people's level of aspiration may have been lowered or deadened to such an extent that higher needs may be abandoned. Further, one need does not require 100 percent satisfaction before another can emerge; instead, Maslow said, it would be more realistic to describe the hierarchy "in terms of decreasing percentages as we go up the hierarchy of pre-potency. For instance . . . 85 percent in his physiological needs, 70 percent in his safety needs . . . 10 percent in his self-actualization needs."

For Maslow, humans act as if they are unfilled cups, and all needs are never really fully gratified. The uniqueness of his notions is that they address human needs, and with that Maslow changed the course of psychology in his time.

Motives for Leaders

Far less well known than his hierarchy of human needs is the work of Maslow's later years, which brought a richness of insights into the motives of leaders/managers in business organizations. In the summer of 1962 Maslow became a visiting fellow at Non-Linear Systems, Inc., of Del Mar, California, at the request of Andrew Kay, the firm's president. This was Maslow's first contact with industry, and Kay, as owner and president, was applying ideas gathered from Douglas McGregor's *Human Side of Enterprise* and Peter Drucker's *The Practice of Management*: using participative management; eliminating the assembly line and organizing work around teams of six or seven employees; eliminating time cards and placing all employees on salary; making departments autonomous and having them keep their own records; and eliminating quality inspectors.

Maslow's ideas provided the point of departure for some of McGregor's and Drucker's work, so the summer at Non-Linear Systems was an opportunity for Maslow to see management and behavioral ideas in practice. He kept journals that summer and later published these in book form as *Eupsychian Management*. *Eupsychian* was a neologism, a new word, and meant "moving toward psychological health." Coupled with the word *management*, the phrase meant management by competent, mentally healthy, self-actualizing individuals. Maslow felt that one way to improve the mental health of all people would be to begin at the workplace and its management since most people were employed.

Another selection of prose bites illustrates Maslow's thinking:

The only happy people I know are the ones who are working well at
something they consider important. . . .

[Some see] self-actualization as a kind of lightning stroke which will hit them on the head suddenly without their doing anything about it. . . .

Too much responsibility can crush the person just as too little responsibility can make him flabby. . . .

[Peter] Drucker . . . neglects the presence of evil, of psychopathology, of general nastiness in some people. . . .

The best managers under the American research conditions seem to be psychologically healthier people than the poorer managers in the same researches. This is easily enough supported by the data from [Rensis] Likert. . . .

The best managers increase the health of the workers whom they manage. . . .

The correct thing to do with authoritarians is to take them realistically for the bastards they are and then behave toward them as if they were bastards. . . .

I am dissatisfied with the material on leadership in the management literature . . . there's some tendency, as in McGregor, to be pious about the democratic dogma. . . .

The person who seeks for power is the one who is just exactly likely to be the one who shouldn't have it. . . .

The safest person to give power to is the one who doesn't enjoy power. . . .

The more grown [mature] people are, the worse authoritarian management will work. . . .

People who have experienced freedom can never really be content again with slavery. . . .[11]

In the early 1970s the aerospace industry went into a tailspin, taking Kay's firm with it. His reaction was to return to more traditional management practices, such as tightening financial controls, reducing the workforce, paying more attention to day-to-day operations, and changing production line techniques. Although some people believed that this cast doubts on the efficacy of McGregor's Theory Y, others felt that the Non-Linear Systems experience was not a true test of McGregor's and Drucker's ideas. Maslow noted, "These principles [i.e., McGregor's and Drucker's] hold primarily for good conditions, rather than for stormy weather." Just as individual's reaction to a personal crisis that threatened the normal striving for growth and self-actualization would be to move to lower-order needs, become defensive, or use other adaptive mechanisms, an organization would also revert to previous coping mechanisms.

Despite this, Maslow still had his doubts about the validity of Theory Y: "A good deal of the evidence upon which [McGregor] bases his conclusions comes from my researches. . . . But I of all people should know just how shaky this foundation is. . . . My work on motivations came from the clinic, from a study of neurotic people. . . . I would like to see a lot more studies of this kind before feeling finally convinced that this carry-over from the study of neurosis to the study of labor in factories is legitimate."

The tragedy of Maslow's life was that he was never on the faculty of a major research university, nor fully accepted into the psychology fraternity, because his work was considered nonscientific and not grounded on extensive research. Maslow suffered a near-fatal heart attack in 1967, did "psychic housekeeping" in what he called his "post-mortem" years, and died on June 8, 1970. One of his final journal entries represented the essence of his humanist psychology: "Every baby born is capable, in principle, of self-actualization. You should never give up on anyone, ever. Man has an instinctoid higher nature. It's possible to grow this or to stunt it. Society can do either."

Maslow's Third Force provided a significant opportunity for changing managerial thinking about people. He did not discover human needs, nor was he the first to put them in a hierarchy of strength, but his observations made us more aware of the potential within each of us.

FREDERICK HERZBERG

Janus-like, work appears throughout history both as an irksome duty and as a way to fulfillment. The question of why we work probably arises more frequently on Mondays and Fridays than on other days, though most of us will find our way to work regardless of grumbling because we have somehow, in some way, found value in that activity. Work is often seen as a punishment, such as in the Old Testament story of Adam and Eve, where Adam is admonished: "Because you have listened to the voice of your wife, and have eaten of the tree of which I commanded you, 'You shall not eat of it,' cursed is the ground because of you; in toil you shall eat of it all the days of your life. . . . In the sweat of your face you shall eat bread till you return to the ground, for out of it you were taken; you are dust, and to dust you shall return" (*Genesis* 3:17–19). This punishment seems rather severe for a few apples and fig leaves. Yet this passage characterizes work as a punishment by God for a sin by humankind.

The New Testament does not offer much relief and makes work a moral duty: "If anyone will not work, let him not eat. For we hear that some of you are living in idleness, mere busybodies, not doing any work. Now such persons we command and exhort in the Lord Jesus Christ to do their work in quietness and to earn their own living" (2 Thessalonians 3:10–12).

The morality of working is not limited to Judeo-Christian values, for we find it also in the words of the prophet Mohammed: "[He] who is able and fit and doth not work for himself, or for others, God is not gracious to him. . . . God is gracious to him that earneth his living by his own labour, and not by begging."[12] These teachings provided a basis for interpreting work as a punishment, an irksome heritage of times long ago, and for the view that idleness is bad. In different languages this negativism continues: the Greeks used *ponos*, meaning "sorrow" or "burden," for work; the Latin *laborare* ("burdensome") was opposed to *facere* ("easy"), a more positive word; and in English we get the word *travail*, meaning "hard, troubling times," from the French *travailler*, "to work." Frederick Herzberg put a positive spin on work, however, and represents another of our motivators. His own motive for a different interpretation of work came out of a wartime experience.

Does a KITA Work?

Near the end of World War II a young infantry sergeant was told to:

> drive some half-tracks down the autobahn as quickly as possible and help at the liberation of Dachau Concentration Camp near Munich, Germany. The first thing we saw as we entered were the rows of railroad cars filled with lime-covered corpses; the next, as we broke into the guards' houses, were the housefraus [sic] packing up china and other loot. . . .
>
> I had just turned 22. Nothing in my education in history or psychology had prepared me for this experience. The shock has influenced all my thinking. There are always around 15 percent nuts in any society. But a whole society had gone insane. . . . How could apparently normal people do such terrible things? I concluded that the most important role of a psychologist was to help the sane from going insane.[13]

Frederick Herzberg was born on April 18, 1923, in Lynn, Massachusetts, where his father, Lewis, was a foreman of shoe lasters in a factory. Frederick studied history and psychology at the City College of New York, but enlisted in the army before finishing his degree. After his war experiences, he finished his bachelor's degree and became interested in mental as well as physical health. The problem that attracted him was that we know when people were unhealthy, but know very little about what makes people healthy. His Ph.D. from the University of Pittsburgh focused on psychology, and he began to study job attitudes. His findings were contradictory, in that it was possible to find support in them for any point you wished to argue. More important, Herzberg observed that there was a pattern in the research results suggesting that job dissatisfaction and job satisfaction were caused by different factors.

Herzberg extended his studies and asked workers to respond to this question: "Think of a time when you felt exceptionally good or exceptionally bad about your job, either your present job or any other job you have had. . . . Tell me what happened." From the responses to this question and a series of follow-up questions, Herzberg set out to discover what things people reported made them satisfied or dissatisfied on their jobs. From people's responses he was able to isolate two different kinds of needs that appeared to be independent.

When people reported job dissatisfaction, they attributed those feelings to their job environment, or the job *context*. Herzberg called these "hygiene" factors, "for they act in a manner analogous to the principles of medical hygiene. Hygiene operates to remove health hazards from the environment of man. It is not curative: it is, rather, a preventive."[14] The hygiene factors include supervision, interpersonal relations, physical working conditions, salaries, company policies and administrative practices, benefits, and job security. When these factors deteriorate below what the worker considers an acceptable level, job dissatisfaction is the result. When the job context is considered optimal by the worker, dissatisfaction is removed. This does not lead to positive attitudes, however, but to some sort of a neutral state of neither satisfaction nor dissatisfaction.

The factors that lead to positive attitudes and satisfaction are called the "motivators," or things in the job *content*. The motivators are such factors as achievement, recognition for accomplishment, challenging work, increased job responsibility, and opportunities for growth and development. If present, these factors lead to higher motivation. In this sense, Herzberg was saying that traditional assumptions about motivating factors such as wage incentives, improving interpersonal relations, and establishing proper working conditions were incorrect; these things do not lead to higher motivation. They remove dissatisfaction and act to prevent problems, but once these traditional motivators are optimal, they do not lead to positive motivation. According to Herzberg, management should recognize that hygiene is necessary, but that neutralizing dissatisfaction does not lead to positive results. Only the motivators lead people to superior performance.

Herzberg felt that traditional ideas about motivation involved KITA (a kick in the ass). This could be a positive KITA, the "carrot," or a negative KITA, the "stick." In either case, the result would be only a short-term movement in a person's behavior. In the conditions surrounding the job, people need to avoid pain; but in the nature of the job itself, people can be motivated into growth and creativity, which are long-term behaviors.

To help managers understand how the attributes of healthy and unhealthy relate to motivation and hygiene, Herzberg applied some catchy phrases:

- "The Best of All Possible Worlds," for those whose hygiene needs have been met and whose satisfaction (motivation) is high
- "I'm All Right, Jack," for those who are not healthy (perhaps bored) but not unhealthy (suffering little or no pain)
- "The Starving Artist," for those who are motivated but whose dissatisfiers are poor
- "Down and Out," for individuals who have neither the motivators nor the hygiene factors

Herzberg is credited with coining the phrase "job enrichment," but an earlier idea of "job enlargement" was also alleged to enrich the job. Herzberg made a distinction by observing that job enlargement consisted of rotating jobs or combining two or more jobs into one. This extended the tasks in the work cycle, what Herzberg called "horizontally loading" a job, but did not necessarily add meaning to what was being done. He advocated job enrichment (sometimes referred to as "vertical loading") because it added depth, not breadth, to a job. Enrichment pushed responsibility downward (he never used the word *empowerment*, but the ideas are very similar) by giving an employee responsibility for an area or group of clients, creating a sense of accountability for results, encouraging helping behaviors, and giving the employee control of the resources to do the job.

Herzberg developed some principles of how to implement job enrichment:

- To increase a person's sense of responsibility and achievement, increase their accountability for their work; give them a complete natural unit of work.
- To enhance an individual's achievement and recognition, grant additional authority to employees in their work activity; provide more job freedom; make periodic reports of how well they are doing directly available to the employees.
- To promote growth and learning, assign tasks that develop an employee's expertise; introduce new and more challenging tasks not previously assigned.[15]

He recognized that implementation is not always easy and that efforts to enrich jobs need to be continuous, not a one-shot, one-size-fits-all endeavor. He did not use the term "continuous improvement" (*kaizen*), as later writers did, but his ideas clearly reflect that concept.

Herzberg's list of clients, such as AT&T, Texas Instruments, Alcoa, Imperial Chemical Industries (Great Britain), and Cummins Engine grew and grew as job enrichment became one of those practices that managers felt would improve productivity and create motivated employees. Not everyone accepted the motivation-hygiene theory, and some questioned Herzberg's methods—for example, if people are asked what work experience leads to satisfaction, they are more likely to attribute it to something they do on the job; conversely, it is typical to blame others in the job environment if things do not go well. Herzberg said money motivates only if given to reward achievement, growth, and responsibility. However, money is a hygiene factor if it is given regardless of merit in an across-the-board-manner. Nevertheless, Herzberg has been heard to say that money cannot buy happiness, but it can relieve a great deal of unhappiness.

In *Work and the Nature of Man*, Herzberg used the Old Testament's Adam as being an example of the pain-avoidance person, while Abraham provided an illustration of the growth-seeking person.[16] Perhaps it was sheer coincidence, but Herzberg agreed with Abraham Maslow with respect to humans seeking self-actualization through the motivators. Herzberg did not, however, agree with Maslow that self-actualization depends on the prior satisfaction of lower-order needs; rather, Herzberg felt that self-actualization operates independently and can be achieved through meaningful work.

We know that motivation is an elusive subject because of individual differences. Some people value work more highly in their life than others; work is a means for some people, not an end. Therefore one employee might respond to job enrichment while another may prefer to be told what to do. Extensions of Herzberg's ideas have explained these individual differences as being dependent upon an individual's "growth-need strength." Certain job characteristics such as the significance of the task, the variety of skills needed, knowledge of results (feedback), and autonomy appear to be important in achieving meaningful work. If these characteristics can be enhanced, for example by increasing the variety of skills used or by providing information about how well a person is performing, then the employee will experience more "meaningfulness" on the job. If a person already feels sufficiently challenged and experienced the job as meaningful, growth-need strength will be low and further efforts to improve the job will be less effective.[17] Some individuals seek more challenge, others do not; further, some jobs can be made more meaningful, others cannot. The key is to provide a closer match between job characteristics and employee needs.

Are you "Adam," the pain avoider, or "Abraham," the growth seeker? Jobs, seen as clusters of tasks, come and go; as a result of technological advances, we no longer need the ancient trades of cork cutters, button makers, and chandlers. But *work* is a different story, and our views about the meaning of work are central to a future of economic well-being, social wellness, and individual self-esteem. Frederick Herzberg called our attention to the importance of work, not as a punishment nor a moral duty, but as a way to achieve self-actualization.

Is Drucker Correct?

Earlier Peter Drucker was quoted to the effect that all we do is write books about motivation, but really we know nothing about the subject. It is true that the path to a *definite* conclusion about human motivation is littered with the debris of discarded notions. Specific theories may explain a few individuals but may fall short of being able to generalize about others. General theories obscure individual differences and are handicapped in that regard. Human need theories seem the most widely accepted, yet there are other ideas that are useful. Expectancy theory, for example, explains motivation as a process of choosing what to do based on our anticipation of obtaining pleasurable outcomes. What is the value of a particular reward to a person? Do we expect that the effort expended will lead to performance? Do we expect that if the job is done, the performance will be rewarded? The value of the reward could be positive (something highly desired) or negative (something to be avoided) and could vary in strength of the drive.[18] Richer, perhaps, but still resting on the pleasure/pain notion of hedonism.

Equity theory is not new and has its origins in the observations of Whiting Williams, an industrial executive who quit his job to find out "what's on the worker's mind." Williams argued that pay is relative from the worker's point of view; that is, what is important is not the absolute pay a person receives but the amount relative to what others receive.[19] Modern equity theory says that a person's perception of his or her rewards is based on at least two ratios: the person's pay relative to the pay of others, and the person's "inputs" (that is, effort expended, education, skill level, training, experience) relative to the person's "outcomes" (rewards). For example, a worker might be dissatisfied with his or her salary if the worker perceives that another person doing the same job is paid more; hence the cries of "equal pay for equal work" from those who feel discrimination in terms of salary. The source of dissatisfaction may not necessarily be the absolute amount of salary but the salary in relation to others and in relation to inputs and outcomes.

Goal-setting theory is based to a large extent on the earlier ideas of Frederick Taylor and Frank Gilbreth. The idea is to develop and set specific work goals or targets for employees to accomplish. The more specific the goal, the better: "Produce 100 units that will pass the quality inspection" rather than "Do the best you can today." Further, difficult goals are better than easy ones—the goal should challenge (but not exceed) the individual's abilities, rather than asking the employee to spread a four-hour job over an eight-hour day. Employees also need to be able to keep track of their performance by receiving regular feedback about results. Without a knowledge of results, employees cannot gauge the relationship between their performance and the expected performance. Incentives (both financial and nonfinancial) are also necessary to reward goals met.[20] Goal-setting theory has been successful and of more value to practicing managers than most previous theories. But goal setting is not a cure-all and works only with the exercise of good managerial judgment.

So Peter Drucker is partially correct—much more has been written about motivation than has been added to our understanding of it. Yet there are some factors that seem to have stood the test of time: people have differing needs and aspirations; work can be a positive force in our lives if we have realistic, challenging jobs matched to our abilities; growth is preferred over pain avoidance; the opportunity to grow and be recognized for that development is needed; information about how well we are doing is necessary; if a job is done well, it is essential that this be rewarded; and rewards must be equitably distributed based on performance.

We harvest the ideas of philosophers such as Mayo, Maslow, and Herzberg, study emerging ideas, and press on to better understand our fellow beings. It is in the crucible of everyday practice that we test the mettle of these philosophies.

10

LEADERS

William Shakespeare wrote, "Some are born great, some achieve greatness, and some have greatness thrust upon them" (*Twelfth Night*, act II, scene 5). These notions reflect commonly held explanations of what happens on the way to being a leader. Being "born great" suggests some natural set of qualities, abilities, or traits that distinguishes leaders from nonleaders. Over the years this list grew longer and longer: courage, sense of humor, judgment, health and fitness, intelligence, moral rectitude, an interest in people, imagination, initiative, decisiveness, and so on, but no clear sense of agreement about leader traits has ever been achieved.

The idea that it is possible to "achieve greatness" reflects a long-standing and widely published view of a success ethic—you can become a leader by reading certain books, by finding the right mentor, through education and/or experience, or by taking other actions to develop your leadership skills and abilities. Horatio Alger's stories brought the dreams of success to American readers for over half a century and set the stage for the enduring ideas of Dale Carnegie's 1936 book *How to Win Friends and Influence People*. Carnegie's personal-magnetism ethic advised that the path to success resided in making others feel important through a sincere appreciation of their efforts; making a good first impression; winning people to one's way of thinking by letting others do the talking and being sympathetic; and changing people by praising good traits and by giving the offender the opportunity to save face. This advice has withstood the test of time, and a person could do worse than follow Carnegie's formula of how to win the cooperation of others.

Having greatness "thrust" upon someone suggests that circumstances play a large part in who is chosen to lead. Chance, fortune, or being in the right place at the right time provide opportunities for some to ascend to a leadership role. Winston Churchill comes to mind, but there are undoubtedly countless others. Churchill, out of power and out of favor in Britain before World War II, became prime minister for wartime duties, then fell back out of power after the crisis ended. Another example, perhaps more difficult to justify, was Moses, who was empowered by a higher authority to lead the Israelites out of their bondage in Egypt. But was he a great leader? Divine intervention was required to part the Red Sea for the exodus, and afterward the Israelites wandered in the desert for forty years. If there are lessons of history in these examples, they suggest that some are chosen only as long as the crisis endures and that it is often difficult to follow the supreme efforts of an exemplary leader.

Despite years of study and a mountain of books, the qualities of a leader remain elusive, suggesting that leadership is very much an art. The philosophers selected for this section do not offer any one best way to lead but rather challenge our thinking about power, conflict, and human nature. Nicolò Machiavelli provides one view of people and the nature and use of power. Mary Parker Follett provides a counterpoint to Machiavelli about power and the role of the leader. Douglas McGregor urges that we examine our assumptions about human nature and how these guide our behavior. Together, these philosophers do not provide all of the answers, instead offering insights to stimulate our thinking about ourselves and others as leaders.

NICOLÒ MACHIAVELLI

Playwright, diplomat, soldier, and historian, Nicolò Machiavelli (1469–1527) is best remembered as an observer of power and its uses. The son of a Florentine lawyer, Machiavelli held a governmental office in republican Florence, wrote plays, and served as a soldier in a war between Florence and its nearby longtime enemy, Pisa. When the Florentine republic fell in 1512 to the Medicis, Machiavelli was arrested and tortured by four turns of the rack, but was finally acquitted and banished from the city. He had a country place near Florence, where he endured the sweat and mud, longing for a return to Florence and a more favorable life. For his return ticket he wrote *The Prince*, dedicated to Lorenzo di Piero de' Medici, hoping that this historical analysis of politics and power would regain him his former status. Written in 1513, *The Prince* became one of only a few books to be printed again and again over the centuries. The fawning Machiavelli never regained the position he sought, but his book did give him literary immortality and preserves his name in an adjective for describing a style of leadership.

Machiavelli did not seek to reform tyrants but to describe them as they were, "for how we live is so far removed from how we ought to live, that he who abandons what is done for what ought to be done, will rather learn to bring about his own ruin than his preservation." Machiavelli's times were part of the Italian Renaissance, and among his contemporaries were Leonardo da Vinci and Michelangelo. While others sought enlightenment in art and literature, Machiavelli described the forces of power at work, and he became as well known, perhaps more widely recognized by some, than the great leaders of the cultural rebirth of that period.

What is it about *The Prince* that explains its remarkable longevity? His assumptions about human nature seem out of step with contemporary beliefs—but are they? "Whoever desires to found a state and give it laws, must start with the assumption that all men are bad and ever ready to display their vicious nature, whenever they may find occasion for it. . . . It may be said of men in general that they are ungrateful, voluble, dissemblers, anxious to avoid danger, and covetous of gain; as long as you benefit them, they are entirely yours."[1] Some other observations also seem to be appropriate to modern times:

- On image management: "Everybody sees what you appear to be, few feel what you are, and those few will not dare to oppose themselves to the many. . . . In the actions of men . . . the end justifies the means."
- On fear and love: "[There] arises the question whether it is better to be loved more than feared, or feared more than loved. The reply is, that one ought to be both feared and loved, but as it is difficult for the two to go together, it is much safer to be feared than loved, if one of the two has to be wanting. . . . Still, a prince should make himself feared in such a way that if he does not gain love, he at any rate avoids hatred; for fear and the absence of hatred may go well together."

- Delegating the dirty work: "Princes should let the carrying out of unpopular duties devolve on others, and bestow favors themselves."
- Making changes: "It must be considered that there is nothing more difficult to carry out, nor more doubtful of success, nor more dangerous to handle, than to initiate a new order of things. For the reformer has enemies in all those who profit by the old order, and only lukewarm defenders in all those who would profit by the new order."
- Covering your backside: "A prince being thus obliged to know well how to act as a beast must imitate the fox and the lion, for the lion cannot protect himself from traps, and the fox cannot defend himself from wolves. One must therefore be a fox to recognize traps, and a lion to fight wolves. Those that wish to be only lions do not understand this."
- Human nature: "If men were all good, this precept would not be a good one; but as they are bad, and would not observe their faith in you, so you are not bound to keep faith with them. . . . It is necessary to disguise this character well, and to be a great feigner and dissembler; and men are so simple and so ready to obey present necessities, that one who deceives will always find those who allow themselves to be deceived."[2]

Machiavelli identified three ways to the top: fortune, ability, and villainy. Those who rose through their good fortune had little trouble in getting to the top spot, but had difficulty maintaining it because they must depend on the goodwill of others and were indebted entirely to those who elevated them. Those who gained the crest by ability endured a thousand difficulties getting there, but would be able to maintain their position more easily. Villainy, an oft-chosen path in Machiavelli's Florence, used methods that would gain power but not glory; afterward the crown would always rest uneasily as they awaited the next villain or revolt.

We need to see Machiavelli in his times and consider his motives. What we call Italy today was then a group of city-states, often at war with their neighbors; the Catholic Church and papal states were at odds with the remnants of the Holy Roman Empire; and power, intrigue, and villainy were the way things were. *The Prince* focused on how the top spot could be gained (by ability, fortune, or villainy) and how to stay on top (through deceit, treachery, and being a lion and a fox). Machiavelli wrote of the ruler, but not of the ruled; of power, but not of rights; of ends, but not of means. Machiavelli fed the ideas of Lord Acton about power corrupting, and absolute power corrupting absolutely. *Machiavellian* became an adjective to describe those who were unscrupulous, crafty, and cunning.

Can this enduring fascination with Machiavelli, despite such criticisms, be explained? Is it because he describes power and striving for power so well that he brings us face-to-face with the moral use of power? Does he awaken in us primitive urgings, stripping away the veneer of civility? Or, by posing the evils, does he make us contemplate what could happen?

MARY PARKER FOLLETT

W. L. Gore and Associates, J. C. Penney, and Wal-Mart share a number of characteristics: They are profitable firms as well as among those considered outstanding to work for. These firms deemphasize the hierarchy of authority, stress employee involvement and a "family" atmosphere, encourage employee stock ownership; display leadership styles that stress human relationships, and echo the technique of a management philosopher who was putting her ideas into print some six to seven decades ago. Each company bears the imprint of its founder's philosophy, but the rationale for how these companies operate is the product of the thoughts of Mary Parker Follett.

Born in Boston on September 3, 1868, and aided by a respectable inheritance from her grandfather and father, Mary Follett received her college education at the Annexe (later named Radcliffe College) at Harvard University and at Newnham College, Cambridge University, England. She was called home because of her mother's illness and did not finish her A.B. degree until 1898, shortly before attaining the age of thirty. By this time, however, she had already published a political science book that received very favorable reviews. Rather than pursuing an academic life, she spent most of her early years working in various community-service groups that sought to provide vocational guidance, education, recreation, and job placement activities for some of the less fortunate among Boston's youth. In these largely volunteer organizations, operating with little or no authority, she realized that there was a need to rethink previously held concepts of authority, leadership, and conflict resolution. In observing and working with these groups, she gained firsthand experience in the dynamics of groups and the need for teamwork.

Managing Conflict

One commonly observed problem that leaders encounter in working with groups is conflict—differences of opinion or fact or interests that are seen by each side as legitimate but which often lead to frustration and hostility rather than cooperation. Differences could be expected, but how can leaders redirect these to progress rather than conflict? Typically, she observed, one group or individual will surrender, or there will be a struggle and the victory of one side over the other. In both cases there is a win-lose result. Another common outcome is compromise, which Follett saw as on the same level as fighting because neither side achieves what he or she truly seeks and, as with fighting, the conflict goes away briefly, only to arise later in a nastier form. She used union-management relations as an example of the futility of compromise. Collective bargaining rests on the relative balance of power, creates an adversarial relationship, ignores the mutual interests of labor and management, and inevitably leads to a compromise that postpones, but does not resolve the problem.

Follett advocated *integration*—thinking creatively to find a solution that satisfies both sides without domination, surrender, or compromise. In her approach, the leader(s) work to make both sides rethink the issues and their total relationship. They are asked to share information openly, avoid win-lose quick fixes, be creative in examining the problem from different angles, and see the problem as "ours" and not "yours." Conflict, to be constructive, requires respect, understanding, talking it through, and creating win-win solutions.

Although Follett advocated integration, she was realistic enough to recognize that it might not be possible in every case, but suggested that it is possible in more cases than we realize. Without trying to achieve integration, we certainly will not succeed, but the important thing is to work for something better in each situation and improve our chances of success. And perhaps if it is not possible now, it will be later if we try.

The path to integration could be smoothed if people begin by recognizing their common purpose, that is, why they are working together. Labor and management tend to lose sight of what they have in common. In taking sides, for example, prolabor or promanagement positions solidify and the parties fail to see the business as a shared effort for which they have joint responsibilities. This responsibility begins at the departmental level, where employees are to be given group responsibilities to create a feeling of mutual interests: "When you have made your employees feel that they are in some sense partners in the business, they do not improve the quality of their work, save waste in time and material, because of the Golden Rule, but because their interests are the same as yours."

In Follett's view, this is not a reciprocal back-scratching arrangement, but a true feeling on the part of both labor and management that they serve a common purpose. People assume there is a line between those who manage and those who are managed, but there is no line, and all members of the organization who accept responsibility for work at any level contribute to the whole: "Labor and capital can never be reconciled as long as labor persists in thinking that there is a capitalist point of view and capitalists that there is a labor point of view. There is not. These are imaginary wholes which must be broken up before capital and labor can co-operate." Integration as a means of resolving conflict begins by recognizing the mutual interest of those in the enterprise as they work toward a common goal.

Leaders and Authority

A number of firms, including J. C. Penney, Wal-Mart, and others, refer to employees as *associates*. This term was based on the ideas of Mary Follett, who suggested that *boss* and *subordinate* are emotionally loaded words that create the feeling of "me" and "you," not "we." These notions of superior and subordinate work against creating the feeling of a shared purpose and commonality of interests. Follett suggested that we avoid having an order giver and an order taker by obeying what she called the "law of the situation": "One person should not give orders to another person, but both should agree to take their orders from the situation. If orders are simply part of the situation, the question of someone giving and someone receiving does not come up." The "situation" she referred to is what is necessary to do the job in accordance with the goals of the work unit and the firm. It is defined by the task, not by the authority of a person. Follett's law of the situation preceded by some years the similar concept of management by objectives of Peter Drucker.

Follett felt that obeying the law of the situation creates a different concept of authority by emphasizing working *with* someone rather than working *under* someone. This jointly exercised power is coactive, not coercive, and reflects the more modern use of the term *associate* instead of a hierarchy of authority. Decades ago she offered some phrases about leadership that still ring true:

- Team building: "The leader then is one who can organize the experience of the group—and thus get the full power of the group. The leader makes the team. This is pre-eminently the leadership quality—the ability to organise all the forces there are in an enterprise and make them serve a common purpose. Men with this ability create a group power rather than express a personal power."
- Transforming: "When leadership rises to genius it has the power of transforming, of transforming experience into power. And that is what experience is for, to be made into power. The great leader creates as well as directs power."
- Visionary: "The ablest administrators have a vision of the future. . . . The leader must see all the future trends and unite them. Business is always developing. Decisions have to anticipate the development."
- Followers: "Their part is not merely to follow, they have a very active part to play and that is to keep the leader in control of a situation. Let us not think that we are either leaders or—nothing of much importance. As one of those led we have a part in leadership. . . . Leader and followers are both following the invisible leader—the common purpose."
- Developing others: "A leader is not one who wishes to do people's thinking for them, but one who trains them to think for themselves. Indeed the best leaders try to train their followers themselves to become leaders. A second-rate executive will often try to suppress leadership because he fears it may rival his own."
- Purpose: "[A leader] should make his co-workers see that it is not his purpose which is to be achieved, but a common purpose, born of the desires and the activities of the group. The best leader does not ask people to serve him, but the common end. The best leader has not followers, but men and women working with him."
- Power: "Our task is not to learn where to place power; it is how to develop power. . . . Genuine power can only be grown, it will slip from every arbitrary hand that grasps it; for genuine power is not coercive control, but coactive control. Coercive power is the curse of the universe; coactive power, the enrichment and advancement of every human soul."[3]

Mary Follett was never a practicing manager but learned her lessons by observing groups at work. Her writings were read by business leaders of the 1920s and 1930s, and she lectured in Britain and often spoke to professional groups such as the New York city's Bureau of Personnel Administration.

After her death on December 18, 1933, many of her speeches were published, but time passed and many forgot the lessons she provided. A most modern expert of leadership, Warren Bennis, acknowledges her as a pioneer:

> Just about everything written today about leadership and organizations comes from Mary Parker Follett's writings and lectures. They are dispiritingly identical—or if not identical, they certainly rhyme—with the most contemporary of writings. . . . Follett was there first. It makes you wince when you sincerely believe, as I do, that what you have written about leadership was already literally bespoken by another 40 years before your precious and "prescient" sentences saw the light of day.[4]

Mary Parker Follett deserves a renaissance as a philosopher of leadership.

DOUGLAS M. MCGREGOR

Douglas McGregor's ancestors would have agreed with Nicolò Machiavelli's conclusion that human nature is essentially evil. These ancestors included a Scotch Presbyterian minister, a lay minister, and Doug's father, a biblical scholar who argued in lifelong correspondence with his son that humankind was sinful from the time of Adam and Eve. From this family tree would emerge a philosopher who challenged our assumptions about people.

Douglas Murray McGregor was born in Detroit, Michigan, on September 16, 1906, the son of Murray James and Jessie Adelia McGregor. As a youth, he worked in a shelter for homeless workers, played piano to accompany his mother, who sang for those transients, and later enrolled at Oberlin College intending to become a minister. Perhaps it was the rebelliousness of youth, but he dropped out of school to work, returning later to college to study psychology. He received his Ph.D. in psychology from Harvard University in 1935; his dissertation was entitled on "The Sensitivity of the Eye to the Saturation of Colors," an appropriate inquiry since McGregor himself was color-blind.

He taught at Harvard briefly, then joined the psychology faculty at the Massachusetts Institute of Technology, where he would be promoted through the ranks and eventually become the chair of the Industrial Relations Section. The peak experience that changed his life, however, was leaving MIT in 1948 to become president of Antioch College. On the eve of his retirement after six years as Antioch's president, he wrote of his experience:

It took the direct experience of becoming a line executive and meeting personally the problems involved to teach me what no amount of observation of other people could have taught.

I believed, for example that a leader could operate successfully as a kind of adviser to his organization. I thought I could avoid being a "boss." Unconsciously, I suspect, I hoped to duck the unpleasant necessity of making difficult decisions, of taking the responsibility for one course of action among many uncertain alternatives, of making mistakes and taking the consequences. I thought that maybe I could operate so that everyone would like me—that "good human relations" would eliminate all discord and disagreement.

I couldn't have been more wrong. It took a couple of years, but I finally began to realize that a leader cannot avoid the exercise of authority any more than he can avoid responsibility for what happens to his organization.[5]

After Antioch, McGregor found the human-relations model inadequate for coping with the realities of managing an organization, and he began a search to expand his understanding.

With his MIT colleague Joseph Scanlon, he began to study cases where labor and management were working together successfully. Scanlon, a former prize fighter, cost accountant, steelworker, and local union president, had been hired in the Industrial Relations Section and had a significant impact on McGregor's thinking about employee participation in decision making. The Scanlon Plan began in the 1930s yet endures today as a model for union-management cooperation and employee sharing in the benefits of reducing costs. In working with Scanlon, McGregor began to write about his evolving view of human nature: "A manager who believes that people in general are lazy, untrustworthy, and antagonistic toward him will make very different decisions [from] a manager who regards people generally as cooperative and friendly." McGregor also agreed with Mary Follett that collective bargaining is competitive and adversarial and prevents cooperation and mutual understanding. These were only the preliminary steps in McGregor's effort to find a new leadership philosophy.

Alfred P. Sloan Jr. was a member of MIT's board of advisors, and McGregor heard him raise the question of whether leaders were born or made— for if we had "born leaders," who needed a school of management? With a grant from the Sloan Foundation, McGregor began to try to answer Sloan's question, and in the process emerged with four major variables involved in leadership: the personality and ability characteristics of the leader; the attitudes, needs, and other characteristics of the followers; the nature of the organization, such as its structure and its mission; and the social, economic, and political environment of the enterprise. To McGregor this meant that leadership is not a property of the individual, but a complex interaction among these variables. The old argument over whether the leader makes history or history makes the leader is resolved by this conception. Both assertions are true within limits. Leaders are not born, but are created within a complex situation.

Assumptions About People

If leaders are not born but created, what circumstances guide that develop-ment? McGregor's answer returned to his long difference of opinion with his father about human nature. Leadership and motivation are insepara-ble—one has to be motivated to lead and followers have to be motivated as well. Without motivation one cannot have leadership, for leadership requires followership. Maslow's writings ended McGregor's search for a leadership philosophy based on the hierarchy-of-needs theory of motiva-tion. Maslow's humanistic psychology is growth-oriented, as individuals seek to satisfy higher and higher levels of needs. To McGregor, this meant that how leaders operate depends upon their assumptions about the needs of their followers. If it is assumed that lower-order needs are sought, a per-son will lead one way; if the leader assumes that higher-order needs are the goal, he or she will operate another way. Behind every action or decision by a leader are the assumptions he or she makes about human behavior and human nature.

McGregor called one set of assumptions about people Theory X and lumped into it all that his ancestors had said about human nature:

1. The average human being has an inherent dislike of work and will avoid it if he can. . . .
2. Because of this human characteristic of dislike of work, most people must be coerced, controlled, directed, threatened with punishment to get them to put forth adequate effort toward the achievement of organizational objectives. . . .
3. The average human being prefers to be directed, wishes to avoid responsi-bility, has relatively little ambition, wants security above all.[6]

Theory X reflects the punishment of Adam and Eve for their sinfulness in the Garden of Eden, consigning them to a life of labor by the sweat of their brow. Since work is distasteful, carrots and sticks must be used to prod people to put forth effort at work. Lower-order needs, such as physiological and safety needs, dominate as leaders seek to appeal to their employees.

McGregor's Theory Y put a more positive spin on human nature:

1. The expenditure of physical and mental effort in work is as natural as play or rest. . . .
2. External control and the threat of punishment are not the only means for bringing about effort toward organizational objectives. Man will exercise self-direction and self-control in the service of objectives to which he is committed.
3. Commitment to objectives is a function of the rewards associated with their achievement. . . .
4. The average human being learns, under proper conditions, not only to accept but to seek responsibility. . . .
5. The capacity to exercise a relatively high degree of imagination, ingenuity, and creativity in the solution of organizational problems is widely, not narrowly, distributed in the population. . . .
6. Under the conditions of modern industrial life, the intellectual potentialities of the average human being are only partially utilized.[7]

This theory is directed toward higher-order needs of work as a means to self-actualization and of self-direction and self-control. Out with KITA! People are basically good by nature and desire growth and development. Any limits to human efforts are not in the nature of people but in how they are nurtured by the organization. In Theory X the obstacle to performance is human nature; in Theory Y the only barrier is how people are nurtured.

Why are assumptions about people so important? According to McGregor, managers organize, lead, control, and motivate people in different ways depending on these assumptions. Those who accept the Y image of human nature will not structure, control, or closely supervise the work environment. Instead, they will attempt to aid the maturation of subordinates by giving them wider latitude in their work, encouraging creativity, using less external control, encouraging self-control, and motivating through the satisfaction that comes from the challenge of work itself. The use of external controls will be replaced by getting people *committed* to organizational goals because they perceive that this is the best way to achieve their own goals. A perfect integration is not possible, but McGregor hoped that the adoption of Y assumptions by managers would improve existing practices.

To McGregor, how people are treated is largely a self-fulfilling prophecy. If it is assumed that people are lazy, and if they are treated as though they are, then they *will* be lazy. On the other hand, if it is assumed that people desire challenging work and increased individual discretion, they will respond by seeking more and more responsibility.

The Best of All Possible Worlds?

Douglas McGregor died on October 13, 1964, leaving a legacy that has influenced generations of those who think about leadership. Yet his X and Y theories are often misunderstood as opposites, when they are merely different ends of a continuum of looking at the world. At Non-Linear Systems, for example, some felt that Theory Y had failed in Kay's grand experiment to run his company when turbulent times came. It was not a failure of Theory Y, however, and Kay admitted that the efforts at Non-Linear Systems caused their managers to take their eyes off the daily operations, thereby losing sight of the purpose of the business.

Is Theory Y "soft" on people? As Drucker commented: "Theory Y is not permissive . . . it's far more demanding than Theory X, it does not allow people to do their own thing, but demands self-discipline of them. It's a very hard taskmaster, so it will only work if you start out with high performance goals and performance standards and don't tolerate anything else."[8] Is Theory Y a one-size-fits-all scheme? Maslow pointed out that Theory Y will not work in some cases:

> It's become more & more clear to me that my theory of evil is needed to combat the perfectionism & impatience & unrealism, mostly of the young, but also the "inexperienced" intellectual . . . and "idealist." . . . Just as in McGregor's stuff, there's no systematic place in Theory Y for bastards & sick people & for just plain normal human foolishness, mistakes, stupidity, dopiness, cowardliness, laziness, etc.[9]

McGregor's essay about the Scanlon Plan could also be applicable to his view of Theory Y, in that he cautioned us about expecting quick fixes:

> It is simply this: we cannot learn to run until we have learned to walk. It takes time and lots of mistakes before we can grow from the pattern that we may be accustomed to, of treating people like children and having them respond like children, to the pattern of having them react like adults. . . . If you adopt

a way of life that is built on a genuine belief that people can grow, can learn together, and can solve their mutual problems together, you must still expect the process to take some time. . . . This [is a] natural but difficult process of growth and development that goes on when one attempts to practice a new managerial philosophy.[10]

Douglas McGregor challenged Machiavelli's assumptions about human nature and extended Follett's belief in the possibilities of human collaboration. He left us with the philosophy that what leaders are able to accomplish is influenced largely by the assumptions they make about others. McGregor did not create a perfect world, but he pushed us a step closer by asking us to question our assumptions about people and how they influence the way we practice the ancient art of leadership.

11

QUALITY SEEKERS

The importance of product quality is not a new idea. It began at least as early as the medieval period, when craft guilds developed the practice of placing a mark on the product (a hallmark) so that customers could connect quality with the maker of the item. In some guild halls it was the practice to work by an open window where passersby could see the worker and the work. Andrew Carnegie considered quality the bedrock of his enterprise: "There lies still at the root of business success the much more important factor of quality. . . . After that, and a long way after, comes cost." In *Shop Management* Frederick W. Taylor also emphasized quality; one of his "functional foremen" was an inspector whose job was to insure that a system of inspection was in place and smoothly operating "before any steps are taken toward stimulating the men to a larger output; otherwise an increase in quantity will probably be accompanied by a falling off in quality." Quality, in both process and product, is essential if a firm is to remain competitive, and our representative of those who sought improvements are W. Edwards Deming, Joseph M. Juran, and Taiichi Ochno.

W. EDWARDS DEMING

Viewers of NBC's June 24, 1980, program entitled *If Japan Can . . . Why Can't We?* could not have envisioned the revolution that was in the making.

NBC producer Clare Crawford-Mason had discovered that the Japanese award for quality production was named after an American, William Edwards Deming. The ninety-minute special was narrated by Lloyd Dobyns, and the last fifteen minutes were devoted to an interview with Deming, then a seventy-nine-year-old statistician unknown to all but a few Americans. The timing was perfect: U.S. manufacturers were losing market share to higher-quality Japanese products in the electronics and automobile industries, to name the more prominent examples. For Deming, however, the recognition was late: He had been preaching the quality gospel for over four decades, but few had listened except for the Japanese. Even Japan would have never heard of Deming except for a coincidence of events and a decision by General Douglas MacArthur.

William Edwards Deming was born on October 14, 1900, in Sioux City, Iowa, the eldest son of William Albert and Pluma Irene Edwards Deming. His father was a country lawyer who moved the family to Cody, Wyoming, in 1907. The Demings lived in a four-room tarpaper shack, and the young Deming remembered the cold, the cracks in the walls, and praying for food. Horatio Alger could not have created a more humble beginning for our hero. Young Deming started working at age eight, carrying coal, tending the boiler, and emptying washbasins in a hotel. His salary was $1.25 a week, but he recalled these were "gold dollars."

He attended a one-room country school after the family moved to Powell, Wyoming. Influenced by his father's love of knowledge, Deming gained the nickname "Professor." His mother had studied at Oberlin College's Conservatory of Music and from her he derived his love for and hobby of composing music. His education in Powell's only school completed, he took his savings and entered the University of Wyoming in Laramie. He studied engineering, working his way through college, and went on to the University of Colorado, where he received his master's degree in mathematics and physics. In Colorado he met and married Agnes Bell, a schoolteacher, and they adopted a daughter, Dorothy. Deming moved the family in order to seek his doctorate at Yale University. He worked the summers of 1925 and 1926 at the Western Electric Company to help finance his education. He worked on transmitters for this equipment supply arm of AT&T and heard others talk of the pioneering work of a Bell Labs statistician, Walter A. Shewhart.

Deming was awarded his Ph.D. in mathematical physics in 1928, and his first employment was with the U.S. Department of Agriculture. His task was to study the effects of nitrogen on crop growth. Deming said that he was attracted to this job because of the "great men" in the department doing research. There was also a great woman there, Lola E. Shupe, his research assistant; after his first wife died in 1930, he married her in 1932. They shared fifty-four years of marriage and had two daughters, Diana and Linda.

Statistical Quality Control

The agricultural research of Deming and others was made more difficult by the fact that a researcher had to wait until the crop matured before any evidence could be collected. One possible solution to this was through crop sampling, and Deming recalled the work of the statistician Shewhart. They met in 1927, and Shewhart shaped Deming's career and thinking from that time onward.

Walter Shewhart began working on industrial quality-control problems at Western Electric in the early 1920s with the goal of replacing the phrase "as alike as two peas in a pod" with "as alike as two telephones." Industrial production, the contrast to agricultural output, ran on a constant basis, and quality could be measured more frequently. Shewhart took samples of the work done and applied statistical analysis to identify variations in performance. Shewhart devised a control chart to define the acceptable limits of random variation in any worker's task so that any output outside those limits could be detected and studied to determine what caused the unacceptable variation.

To illustrate his point, Shewhart used different-colored chips drawn from a bowl to show that there were always differences in the number of chips of any given color drawn by one person compared with the number drawn by any other person. Thus, there was always some random variation in industrial production over which the worker had no control. But over numerous trials there would be some limits to this random variation. In industrial production, what happened outside these limits could be examined with an eye toward corrective action.

Deming felt that Shewhart's greatest contribution was identifying when to make corrections and when to leave the work process alone. From Shewhart's chips, Deming would get the idea for his bead experiments, where red beads, representing defects, were mixed with a larger quantity of white ones, representing acceptable quality. Drawn randomly, some red beads would always appear, indicating that it was highly unlikely to find acceptable parts all of the time. He used this illustration frequently in his lectures to distinguish a production process that is "in control" from one "out of control." If the process is out of control, the rate of defects is too high and the cause can be traced and reduced. The purpose is to constantly work toward reducing the variations in quality by removing the causes of nonrandom defects.

Deming applied Shewhart's ideas of sampling for statistical quality control in the U.S. Department of Agriculture, and later as an employee of the U.S. Census Bureau. His reputation as an expert on statistical sampling led to his employment during World War II to teach engineers and technicians how to use these techniques in the production of war materials. He became a charter member of the American Society for Quality Control, formed in 1946, and later received the society's Shewhart Medal for his contributions. However, national interest in product quality declined after the war, as consumers would buy any product that had been denied them during the austerity of wartime. Deming found himself out of step with this lack of interest in quality in the United States.

General MacArthur Makes the Decision

World War II left Japan in rubble and its industrial capacity in ashes. Quick to forgive, the United States named General Douglas MacArthur as the supreme commander of the U.S. occupation forces, and his job was to rebuild Japan. One of his goals was to establish a nationwide communications network that could reach into every village to inform, educate, and reassure the Japanese citizens. To do this, he needed someone who could teach the Japanese how to mass-produce radios and to rebuild the telecommunications network. The search led to Homer M. Sarasohn, who had worked as a radio development engineer with the Crosley Corporation and with Raytheon, and who was identified as one of the bright young telecommunications engineers in the United States

Sarasohn found the task formidable: The Japanese knew a great deal about electronics, but seemed to know nothing about management and production. He observed that their attitude about quality was "making half of your products okay and throwing out the other half." Sarasohn gained an ally in Charles Protzman, a Western Electric Company engineer who also became a member of General MacArthur's Civil Communications Section in 1948. Together they wrote a text for production management; the fundamentals were the same as those being taught at that time in the United

States. Sarasohn and Protzman's pupils were to become a who's who of Japan's electronics industry, including the leaders of firms such as Matsushita, Mitsubishi, Fujitsu, Sumitomo, and Sony.

Sarasohn and Protzman were meeting resistance, however. Those in the occupation force's Economics and Social Section objected to the policy of rebuilding Japan so rapidly, thus possibly enabling the country to become once more an international power economically and technologically. The disagreement went up the hierarchy to General MacArthur, who allowed each section twenty minutes to make its case.

Japan's fate hung in the balance. After the presentations, Sarasohn recalls, "General MacArthur stood up from his desk chair and started walking toward the door. . . . Just one step before the door, he turned around suddenly and gazed straight into my eyes and said, 'Go do it.' Then he disappeared from the room."[1] The Civil Communications Section had won—the Japanese telecommunications industry would be rebuilt and taught U.S. production know-how. Did MacArthur make the correct decision? Sarasohn would answer yes—the events that followed forced the United States to relearn some lessons it had forgotten.

After his stint during World War II teaching engineers and others about statistical quality control, Deming joined the faculty at New York University's Graduate School of Business Administration. In 1947 he went to Japan to help the U.S. occupation authorities prepare for a 1951 census of Japan and was shocked by the devastation, poverty, and industrial shambles he found there. He was fascinated by Japanese culture, frequently attending Kabuki theater and Noh plays, visiting temples and shrines, and delighted in invitations to socialize with his Japanese hosts.

He was pleased when Kenichi Koyanagi, managing director of the Union of Japanese Scientists and Engineers (JUSE), invited him in 1950 to present some lectures on statistical quality control. Koyanagi and his colleagues had continued their study of U.S. manufacturing methods after Sarasohn and Protzman returned to the United States in 1950. They had read Walter Shewhart's classic on production quality control and Shewhart's lectures, edited by Deming, on statistical quality control. As a follower of Shewhart, Deming was the logical choice to teach Japan's industrialists about these techniques.

Deming's first lectures were in Tokyo in the summer of 1950, followed by lectures in Osaka, Nagoya, and Hakata. The subject was the elementary principles of statistical quality control, essentially the same message he had provided U.S. technicians and engineers during World War II. There were eight day-long lectures, each to a standing-room-only crowd. Arrangements were made for Deming to meet with the Keidanren (Federated Economic Societies), an association of Japanese CEOs, to tell them of the importance of quality and of the need for top-level support if quality manufacturing was to succeed.

The U.S. occupation authorities paid Deming's expenses and salary, so he refused payment for his lectures and permitted JUSE to translate and publish them without a payment of royalties. The lectures sold well and JUSE used the proceeds to establish the Deming Prize in 1951—a silver medal engraved with Deming's profile. The coveted Deming Prize is still given annually in Japan during a nationally broadcast ceremony. Ten years after his lectures began, Deming became the first American to be awarded Japan's Second Order of the Sacred Treasure, a gold medal. Deming recalled: "I can say that nothing ever pleased me so much as this recognition." The United States remained largely unaware of Deming's ideas, but he was Japan's treasure because of his philosophy of how to manufacture quality products.

Deming's Philosophy of Management

At the time of the NBC program in 1980, Deming had one U.S. client, the Nashua Corporation (a maker of coated paper products), and that came about because of a referral from a Japanese firm, Ricoh. After *If Japan Can . . . Why Can't We?* Deming's longtime secretary and biographer, Cecelia Kilian, reported: "Our phones rang off the hook. . . . Dr. Deming's mail quadrupled, and beyond."[2] Ford Motor Company was the first caller, and then firms such as General Motors, Dow Chemical, Vernay Laboratories, Hughes Aircraft, Florida Power and Light, and others became interested in his work.

Deming was critical of U.S. management, perhaps because he had been ignored for so long, but more probably because U.S. firms were losing market share to more quality-oriented competitors. He blamed U.S. management because the wealth of a nation did not depend on its natural resources but on its people, management, and government: "The problem is where to find good management. It would be a mistake to export American management to a friendly country."

Dr. Deming identified seven deadly diseases that caused the decline of U.S. industry:

- A lack of constancy of purpose toward improvement of products and services

- An emphasis on short-term profits
- Merit rating or other evaluations of individual performance
- Job hopping by managers
- Managing by the numbers without considering figures that are unknown or unknowable
- Excessive medical costs (a factor peculiar to the United States)
- The litigious nature of the U.S. citizenry, causing excessive costs of liability that increased as lawyers worked on contingency fees

He called for a transformation of American industry built around fourteen points to overcome these deadly diseases:

- Create constancy of purpose toward improvement of product and service, with the aim of becoming competitive, staying in business, and providing jobs.
- Adopt a new philosophy. Western management must awaken to the challenge, learn their responsibilities, and provide leadership to change the situation.
- Eliminate the need for inspection on a mass basis by building quality into the product in the first place.
- End the practice of awarding contracts to the lowest bidder. Move toward a single supplier for any one item and build on a long-term relationship of loyalty and trust. Cheaper is not always better.
- Constantly improve quality and productivity in order to constantly decrease costs.
- Institute training on the job.
- Institute leadership. Supervision should help people and machines do a better job. Supervision of management is in need of overhaul, as well as supervision of production workers.
- Drive out fear, so that everyone may work effectively for the company.
- Break down barriers between departments. People in research, design, sales, and production must work as a team. (This is an insight into what was later called "reengineering.")
- Eliminate slogans, exhortations, and targets for the workforce such as asking for zero defects. Such exhortations only create adversarial relationships, since most of the causes of low quality and low productivity are in the system and are beyond the control of the workforce.

- Eliminate work standards (quotas) on the factory floor; and eliminate management by objectives. Eliminate management by the numbers and numerical goals. Substitute leadership.
- Remove barriers that rob employees of their right to pride of workmanship. The responsibility of supervisors must be changed from sheer numbers to quality. For example, abolish annual or merit rating of performance.
- Institute a vigorous program of education and self-improvement.
- Put everybody in the company to work to accomplish the transformation—through quality control circles, for example.

Deming stated that "such a system formed the basis for top management in Japan in 1950 and subsequent years." He warned, however, that it was not possible for the United States simply to copy these Japanese practices. American management at the highest levels had to become personally involved in the study of their firms to discover how to improve quality. Deming felt that U.S. managers looked for a quick fix, a lazy way to appear to be up-to-date, rather than true employee involvement in making improvements.

Some of Deming's points were debatable. For example, "drive out fear" might make a good slogan but, as Joseph Juran observed, "fear can bring out the best in people." We must assume that Juran did not imply constant fear, and Deming's catchy slogan does not seem to apply to his style of lecturing, which has been described as abrasive and intimidating. Consistency may be the hobgoblin of small minds, and Deming and Juran are to be permitted their differences on this point.

The idea of eliminating slogans, work quotas, annual merit reviews, management by objectives, management by walking around, and other such techniques placed Deming's points counter to much conventional wisdom about managing. The most widely supported modern motivation theory holds that people work best when they have specific, doable, challenging goals; when performance feedback is provided regularly; and when their efforts are rewarded. Management by objectives (MBO) is widely practiced (sometimes implemented poorly, however) and raises the question of what managers are supposed to work toward if they do not have objectives. Performance reviews or appraisals serve as feedback on how well a person is doing, provide for rewards, and could help to keep the firm out of court if differences arose about promotions, hiring, and other personnel matters.

Deming attributed 95 percent of all errors to the systems under which people worked, not the people themselves. Quality management began at the top of the organization, not with the employee. The goal was the reduction of variation through continuous improvement, discovering what was out of control as a result of special causes. Deming proposed a "Shewhart cycle" whose four steps are summarized in the acronym PDSA: Plan the improvement change; Do it; Study the results; Act. If improvement occurs, proceed; if not, try again. (Some call this the "Deming cycle" instead and use the acronym PDCA, substituting "check" for "study.")

After these problems were detected and eliminated, the system would be in control and stable. As noted, this did not mean zero defects. He used his bead experiment, borrowed from Shewhart's chips, to demonstrate that some red ("defective") beads would always be drawn, and it was foolish to ask the worker to stop drawing these. It was the task of management to make it possible for people to draw more white (acceptable) beads and fewer red ones.

Deming's last book, *The New Economics*, emphasized a philosophy of change more than the previous emphasis on statistics. In Deming's view, management still needs to be transformed, and this "requires profound knowledge . . . a new map of theory by which to optimize and understand the organizations that we work in."[3] Deming's idea of "profound knowledge" consisted of four interrelated parts:

1. Appreciation for a system. The best way to optimize an organization is by cooperating rather than by setting up competing departments or profit centers, which would inevitably lead to suboptimization.
2. Knowledge about variation. Variance in people, performance, and quality is to be expected, and management needs to make attempts to reduce it if possible.
3. Theory of knowledge. Management is prediction and requires theory so that experience can be tested, studied, and revised to build better knowledge.
4. Psychology. To transform an organization, a leader must understand the psychology of individuals, groups, society, and change.

The New Economics is chock-full of anecdotes from Deming's and his colleagues' fifty-plus years of experience. Highly readable, and more portable than his previous books, Deming demonstrated his constancy of purpose and continual improvement in his last work, published shortly before his death.

W. Edwards Deming held the spotlight during a time when U.S. managers were being told by others how to build an excellent company, how to do it in one minute, to practice *kanban* as the Japanese did, to manage by walking around (Deming felt that managers rarely knew the right questions to ask nor did they stop long enough to get an answer), to change inventory practices to just-in-time, and to implement numerous other quick fixes as a response to global competition. Deming's lectures appealed to the masochistic streak in U.S. managers, who paid big bucks to be told what a lousy job they were doing and who relieved themselves of more money by hiring consultants to tell them how to remedy their shortcomings. Deming was described by observers as brutal, surly, impatient, intimidating, and a curmudgeon, but he always spoke to a full house of well-paying listeners.

Deming was critical of the Baldrige Award, America's belated (1987) response to Japan's Deming Prize. The Malcolm Baldrige National Quality Award was named for a U.S. commerce secretary who died in a rodeo accident while the enabling legislation was being debated. It is ironic, perhaps even prophetic, that the U.S. award is given in the name of a government bureaucrat, while Japan's is awarded in honor of the founder of modern quality control. A further irony is that U.S. officials got their idea for an American award from a Japanese quality expert, Kaoru Ishikawa.

Deming retained his love for learning and work to the end. Despite a continual loss of hearing, phlebitis, and prostate cancer, he continued his seminars. In early December of 1993, he gave his last seminar from a wheelchair while connected to an oxygen tank. He died on December 20, 1993, at the age of ninety-three, finally recognized as a philosopher of quality improvement in his native country.

JOSEPH MOSES JURAN

The slight man in the tweed jacket and his trademark black bow tie took the podium and began the slide show. The conference room was packed with people who had paid $395 each to hear "The Last Word," the lessons of this well-known octogenarian's lifetime. Participants could also buy mementos of this management legend's final tour on the speakers circuit—for example, $50 for a Lucite black bow tie paperweight keepsake. Like Deming,

Joseph M. Juran had been preaching the gospel of quality for four decades and was making his last rounds before retiring to write his memoirs.

Juran was born on December 24, 1904, in Romania, the son of a shoe-maker who moved his family to the United States in 1912. Juran soon excelled in the Minneapolis public schools but, being small and slightly built, he recalled that he "got beat up quite a bit . . . [and] I had a pretty sharp tongue, and that didn't help matters." He became more bookish, was four years ahead of his class, and entered college early. Juran received an engi-neering degree at the University of Minnesota and went to work in the inspection department of the Western Electric Company's Hawthorne plant in 1924. Deming was also at the Hawthorne works in the summers of 1925 and 1926, but there is no evidence that they met at that time, although it is possible that Juran might have inspected some of the transmitters that Dem-ing's department was producing.

Juran was also inoculated with the statistical quality-control ideas of Wal-ter Shewhart, whose influence was felt throughout the Bell System at this time. Juran questioned, however, that quality was solely a matter of statis-tics and traced the beginning of a separate quality-inspection responsibility to the writings of Frederick W. Taylor.

Juran worked for AT&T's Western Electric Company from 1924 to 1941, acquired a law degree (J.D.) from Chicago's Loyola University in 1935, and rose to the position of chief of inspection for Western Electric. World War II intervened, however, creating for Juran a more expansive notion of qual-ity management.

Quality as a Company-Wide Responsibility

Juran was an administrator in the U.S. Office of Lend-Lease Administration from 1942 until the war ended in 1945. From that experience he wrote a book about the challenge of managing in a bureaucracy, an interesting period piece if one wishes to compare U.S. governmental administration of that time with the present. Juran's conclusion was that the government did not follow proven principles of sound management (*plus ça change, plus c'est la même chose*). It is also likely that he developed his antipathy for zero-defects programs while in his government position: "An important disease of Bureaucracy is the disease of making no errors at all costs." To avoid errors, more administrative layers were necessary, more audits, more reports, and an increased duplication of effort. With the Lend-Lease Administration

Juran did learn one lesson that would make his focus differ from Deming's—that quality was more than statistics, required the involvement of all employees, and was a part of the entire management process.

After the war Juran became an independent consultant on quality control but, like Deming, found interest waning among U.S. manufacturers. He assembled and edited a weighty handbook on quality control that became a standard reference tool on the subject and also led JUSE to invite Juran to Japan in 1954.[4] According to Kaoru Ishikawa, a leading figure in JUSE, Japanese managers and workers struggled trying to understand Deming's ideas on statistical quality control until Juran came and established quality control as a job for everyone. Juran recalled: "I gave the Japanese no secrets. What I told them was what I had been telling audiences in the United States for years. The difference was not what I said but whose ears heard it. . . . The people who attended my first two-day lectures in Japan turned out to be CEOs from the largest manufacturing companies in the country. . . . In the United States, the audiences consisted of engineers and quality control managers. Never before and never since, has the industrial leadership of a major power given me so much of its attention."[5]

Juran felt that the Japanese had known about quality for many years, at least since Taylor's ideas were introduced there, and all that he and Deming had done was to jump-start them in the postwar years. Before World War II "Made in Japan" suggested inferior consumer goods; this was largely because the nation's priority was high-quality military hardware. The best engineers, scientists, and managers were working on airplanes, ships, and weapons while the others were exporting low-quality products. Japan's defeat presented a new obstacle, how to make quality consumer goods for export, and now the Japanese were eager to hear the words of Western experts.

Juran advocated the formation of a company-wide quality committee to oversee the planning and implementation of quality management programs. His approach asked the firm to identify and work on the most critical problems first—he called these the "vital few"—before moving on to resolving the "trivial many" problems. Juran called this the "Pareto principle," although he later admitted that this was an improper attribution to Vilfredo Pareto, a late-nineteenth- and early-twentieth-century economist. (Proper attribution would be to Max Otto Lorenz, who developed the "Lorenz curve," which displays the deviation of a sample from the standard.) Regardless, the Pareto principle has been passed down as an 80/20 rule: for example, 80 percent of the quality problems are caused by 20 percent of the manufacturing operations. By focusing on Juran's "vital few" operations first, a large number of problems could be resolved before management turned to the "trivial many."

Juran placed less emphasis on statistics and developed a control trilogy that focused on quality:

1. Moving from chronic poor to improved performance:
   • Create a climate for change
   • Identify the vital few projects
   • Organize for the breakthrough
   • Do the problem analysis and propose solutions
   • Determine how to overcome resistance to change (Juran advocated participation)
   • Institute the change
   • Institute means to monitor the solutions and correct sporadic problems

2. Establish a control sequence (from vendor relations to customer service)
   • Optimize the cost of quality
   • Employ needed professional staff for quality control
   • Provide a feedback loop to compare outcomes with performance standards
   • Repeat the action cycle by taking corrective action if necessary

3. Formulate an annual quality program
   • Establish objectives for quality
   • Maintain the initiative

Juran's three-part system was aimed at improving quality year after year. Firms began by setting goals, organizing into teams to work on these projects, and working with Juran and his staff through each project. This approach blended statistical analysis with traditional managerial actions of planning, organizing, and controlling. Clients admired Juran's methodical, company-wide approach and were happy with the results as the "vital few" and the "trivial many" problems were solved.

Juran and Deming's paths crossed occasionally but essentially ran parallel as they established their reputations as the leading thinkers of quality control.

Both were at the Western Electric Hawthorne plant; Walter Shewhart was their inspiration; Deming went to Japan shortly before Juran; both became successful consultants; they agreed that zero defects was not a quality goal but a slogan that did not require a company-wide commitment for quality; Juran gave one-day seminars while Deming held longer ones; and both received Japan's Second Order of the Sacred Treasure award in recognition of their work, although Juran had to wait until 1981 for his.

There was mutual respect between Juran and Deming with differences appearing mainly in their view of quality control. Juran felt that Deming was basically a statistician who had spent much of his life without direct corporate experience and responsibilities, while Juran had risen through the ranks at Western Electric and had more of a managerial viewpoint. Deming felt that the Baldrige Award was too numbers driven, but Juran saw possibilities for management to think of the Baldrige criteria as benchmarks: "Learn where you stand and where you go from there. Some people may be dismayed by the results. Don't worry. You've got plenty of company."

Despite their differences, Deming and Juran set the tone for a renaissance in quality control that can help firms remain competitive in a global economy. Others have followed in their footsteps. Armand V. Feigenbaum is a widely known quality consultant with extensive executive-level, worldwide experience in quality management. He saw quality as a general management responsibility, affecting all operations and carrying a tremendous cost if not done well. Feigenbaum coined the phrase "Total Quality Control" (TQC). The most flamboyant of the leading U.S. quality experts is Philip B. Crosby, who noted that while statisticians were comfortable if the failure rate did not exceed 5 percent, even one failure could be disastrous in national defense or air traffic control. Crosby became well known as an advocate of zero defects. In Japan there was Kaoru Ishikawa, the son of a prominent Japanese industrialist, who helped JUSE keep its focus on quality in the early 1950s; Genichi Taguchi, who developed Nippon Telephone and Telegraph's quality control program and later found some U.S. clients; and Ichiro Ueno, an expert in value added manufacturing, son of Yoichi Ueno who helped bring scientific management to Japan in the early 1910s.

The continuing lesson will be that quality has a price, but a lack of quality carries an even greater price. Though acronyms abound, such as QC, SQC, CWQC, TQC, TQM (for Total Quality Management, a phrase coined by the Department of Defense), it is important to remember that the one constant in all of these is the letter Q.

TAIICHI OHNO

Quality is one facet of efficient and effective production, and now we turn our attention to Taiichi Ohno, who learned how to incorporate quality into a total company philosophy at Toyota Motors. Ohno illustrates how good ideas can be made into better ones through study and constant refinement. Ohno was born in Dairen, Manchuria, in February 1912. In 1932, after graduating from the department of mechanical engineering at Nagoya Technical High School, he joined the Toyoda Automatic Loom Works in the plant where the firm manufactured looms.

The Toyoda Automatic Loom Works was the product of the inventive and entrepreneurial genius of Sakichi Toyoda, who perfected Japan's first power-driven loom and held numerous patents for automatic looms and textile production. Kiichiro Toyoda, Sakichi's eldest son, was in charge of loom production but held a far deeper interest in engines and automobiles. Kiichiro was a mechanical engineer who had studied at the University of Tokyo, and he set aside a portion of the loom-making factory to experiment with engines. When Sakichi sold his patent rights, he provided 1,000,000 yen to Kiichiro to further his research.

Kiichiro Toyoda began buying and testing engine parts made by foreign companies, including buying a new 1933 Chevrolet and disassembling it to study its parts. These were the modest beginnings of a Japanese strategy to reverse-engineer what others had produced, so that these products could be analyzed and improved. General Motors and Ford had assembly plants in Japan, so a decision for Toyoda to move into automobile production was considered risky. Kiichiro, however, built a system of suppliers who could make the parts he wanted, the way he wanted them made, and was able to convince Toyoda's board of directors to form Toyota Motor Corporation in 1937. (Toyota is an alternate reading of the two logo graphs with which the family name is written.) In a country of limited natural resources, Kiichiro's goal was to establish Toyota cars as fuel-efficient vehicles that would match Japanese streets and Japanese wallets.

World War II changed Toyota's target from supplying the consumer sector to making vehicles for the war effort. Toyota struggled to find the raw materials, parts, and labor to keep its operations going. As the war brought Allied bombers to the homeland, all of Toyota's factories were leveled—Toyota was a company of three thousand employees who had no place to work. During the war, however, Kiichiro Toyoda found help in the form of a young man, Taiichi Ohno, who arrived just in time to reestablish Toyota as a competitive force in the automobile industry.

Just-in-Time

Taiichi Ohno's first supervisory position was in the loom shop, where he was put in charge of a large number of female employees. His youthful appearance did not convey the impression that he was old enough to be a manager so he grew "a prominent mustache to have a more authoritative air."[6] Facial hair was not in fashion in Japan, so his distinctive appearance earned him the nickname "Mr. Mustache."

In the chaos of war Kiichiro Toyoda was looking for good managers for the motor works, where scarce materials, conscripted workers, and demanding schedules were severe problems. The loom-making shops had been converted to making automobile and truck parts, and it was there that Kiichiro saw a young man with a mustache following a time-honored Toyoda family tradition—*genchi genbutsu shugi*, meaning "learning by careful observation."[7] Sakichi Toyoda had used this method in his inventions, and it had become part of the Toyoda culture.

Ohno's implementation of this practice involved carrying a piece of chalk with him as he roamed the workshop. Whenever a machine was not performing as expected, he would draw a chalk circle on the floor around the machine and tell the supervisor to stand inside the circle and to watch carefully until he understood what was wrong. It was expected that this focus on problem spots, followed by corrections in the process, would gradually lead to overall better performance. This practice became known as *kaizen*, striving for continuous improvement by careful observation and analysis. *Kaizen* became a slogan for the Japanese and others and was based on a simple axiom—one can learn more by watching and listening than by talking.

While *kaizen* apparently evolved from a Toyoda family practice, it appears that Ohno was able to make other advancements by adapting ideas from Henry Ford. Ohno devoted a book chapter to Ford and his theory of waste. According to Henry Ford:

> My theory of waste goes back of the thing itself into the labor of producing it. We want to get full value out of labor so that we may be able to pay it full value. It is use—not conservation—that interests us. We want to use material

to its utmost in order that the time of men may not be lost. Materials cost nothing. It is of no account until it comes into the hands of management.

Saving material because it is material, and saving material because it represents labor might seem to amount to the same thing. But the approach makes a deal of difference. We will use material more carefully if we think of it as labor. For instance, we will not so lightly waste material simply because we can reclaim it—for salvage involves labor. The ideal is to have nothing to salvage.[8]

Value-added manufacturing begins at least as early as Ford, although he may have recalled from Benjamin Franklin's *Poor Richard's Almanac* the adage "Waste not, want not." Neither wasted effort nor wasted material nor wasted time added value to a product or a service.

The reduction of waste was central in Ohno's thinking, and he identified seven kinds of waste and what to do instead:

- *Overproduction.* Make no more than is needed, to avoid added inventory stockpiling costs.
- *Delays.* Eliminate waiting and idle machines by balancing the workload better, or by using more flexible employees and general-purpose equipment.
- *Unnecessary transportation.* Plan workplace layout and flow to eliminate unnecessary material handling.
- *Faulty work processes.* Question the process. Is it necessary? What value does it add to the desired result?
- *Excess materials.* Use just-in-time inventory management to eliminate stockpiling.
- *Wasted motions.* If the motions cannot be simplified and made more economical, automate.
- *Defective materials and defective products.* Implement quality control and fail-safe procedures.[9]

In the machine shop department Ohno was responsible for the manufacture of the components that fed Toyota's assembly line. He observed that the employees wasted a great deal of time waiting for their machine to finish its task. When a part was completed, the worker would carry it to the next station, where that worker was waiting also. Ohno rearranged the workplace in an L shape so that a worker could start one machine while the other was running the same operation, and then switch back to the first machine while the second one ran. Later, improving on this, he put each worker in charge of three machines, arranged in a U shape. The results of his experiments were less idle time and labor waste. But these machines were making parts that were being fed into the assembly line, and on the line, Ohno could not use the same methods to reduce waste.

The feeder lines in his section pushed parts toward the assembly line, creating stockpiles of parts along the line. Ohno's answer was to develop a system whereby the assembly process would *pull* the parts to it in the quantity needed at the time they were needed. Ohno provided two equally plausible accounts of what inspired his system of just-in-time manufacturing. In an interview, Ohno said that he learned it all from Henry Ford's book *Today and Tomorrow*.[10] In that book Ford described the inventory system at his fully integrated River Rouge plant:

> Our finished inventory is all in transit. So is most of our raw material inventory. When production stands at 8,000 a day, this means that our various factories manufacture and ship enough to make 8,000 complete cars. We know just how many machines and employees it will take to reach a given figure at a given time, and how to take care of seasonal demands without the danger of becoming overstocked. . . .
>
> The average shipping time between the factory and the branches is 6.16 days, which means that there is an average of a little more than six days' supply of parts in transit. This is called the "float." If production is at the rate of 8,000 cars a day, there are parts enough in transit to make more than forty-eight thousand complete cars. Thus, the traffic and production departments must work closely together to see that all the proper parts reach the branches at the same time—the shortage of a single kind of bolt would hold up the whole assembly at a branch. . . . This method does away with filling out shipping orders. Instead, they are printed and books are kept on one master part only.[11]

Ford's "float" would be the materials and parts in process on their way to the point of use. Rather than being stored in inventory, they were in transit.

A second account by Ohno used the example of an American supermarket, witnessed by Ohno personally on a visit to the United States in 1956. While combining supermarkets and automobile manufacturing seems odd, Ohno was able to make the connection for his just-in-time system:

> A supermarket is where a customer can get (1) what is needed, (2) at the time needed, (3) in the amount needed. Sometimes, of course, a customer may

buy more than he or she needs. In principle, however, the supermarket is a place where we buy according to need. Supermarket operators, therefore, must make certain that customers can buy what they need at any time. . . .

From the supermarket we got the idea of viewing the earlier process in a production line as a kind of store. The later process (customer) goes to the earlier process (supermarket) to acquire the required parts (commodities) at the time and in the quantity needed. The earlier process immediately produces the quantity just taken (restocking the shelves).[12]

The paperwork behind Toyota's just-in-time system used *kanban* pieces of paper contained in rectangular vinyl envelopes listing the part number of each piece and other information related to how to process the work, including production quantity, time, method, sequence or transfer quantity, transfer time, destination, storage point, transfer equipment, container, and so on.

In time, the entire system of just-in-time production became known as *kanban*. In this system, the tag serves to alert someone about something that needs to be done. When one part (or a standard-sized container of the same part) is used at any point in the production process, the card is returned to the supplier, indicating the need to replenish the supply. The card moves backward from site to site as each station needs to be resupplied. The goal is to replace exactly the amount that has been consumed—no more and no less.

A perfect system would have no inventory, each part arriving at the exact moment it is needed, but that is very difficult to achieve. What *kanban* does is pull the parts as needed, rather than pushing inventory, having it be stockpiled, and tying up money in idle inventory. Henry Ford gave dollar figures to compare the previous inventory method with his new system incorporating a "float": "If we were operating today [1926] under the methods of 1921 . . . [our] investment in raw material and finished goods [would be] not far from two hundred million dollars. . . . [Instead] we have an average investment of only fifty million dollars . . . [and our] inventory is less than it was when our production was only half as great."[13]

At Toyota, Ohno adapted any method that would help eliminate waste. Waste did not add value; waiting employees, idle machines, and stockpiled inventory were portions of the production process that created nothing useful. Many of the ideas he used were those that Frederick Taylor and the Gilbreths would have used in similar situations to eliminate waste and reduce fatigue. Ohno commented that "time is the shadow of the motion," indicating that Taylor's time study and Frank Gilbreth's motion study used different solutions to attack the same problem—wasted human efforts.

Ohno was careful, however, to caution that Toyota's production management system might not be applicable in other settings: "We have a slight doubt whether our just-in-time system could be applied to foreign countries where the business climates, industrial relations, and many other social systems are different from ours."[14] Among those differences would be:

- Japan's Ministry of International Trade and Industry, which provides institutional direction, dampens internal competition, and attempts to manage external competition
- The Japanese financial system, which enables decisions to be for the long term rather than for quick payouts
- The Japanese *keiretsu*, the "family" of linked enterprises that resembles a fully integrated system
- The cross-holding of shares of other companies by *Keiretsu* members, promoting mutual trust and protection
- Enterprise unions (at company level), which enable Japanese management to be more flexible in job assignments and in paying different wages for the same work to different individuals (such as pay based on seniority)
- Location of suppliers near assembly points, enabling more predictable delivery schedules for Japanese manufacturers

Although differences existed, Ohno's just-in-time inventory system and other advances at Toyota in production management had an impact on business practices in other countries. Managers began looking to Japan for ideas such as buying or making parts as they were needed rather than periodically buying in quantity. The inventory was pulled by what was needed, not pushed by what could be made.

Poka-yoke

Poka-yoke sounds like an international folk dance but in reality it was another clever adaptation of a Western idea about production. Credit for *poka-yoke* appears to belong to Taiichi Ohno, although an industrial consultant, Shigeo Shingo, played an important role in its development and its implementation in other workplaces. Sakichi Toyoda had invented devices that monitored the flow of raw material through his looms to measure output. Ohno was attempting to make a similar monitoring device for the machinery in his shop when one of Toyota's employees returned from a visit to a Ford factory. Ford Motor was using a limiting switch that turned machines off after a particular amount of output. Ohno's insight was to develop a machine that could monitor the operations as well as the output of a machine.

From this idea, Ohno's engineers experimented and gradually developed a means for machines to stop themselves when a process was finished or a malfunction occurred. The employee did not need to watch each machine, but could focus on the exceptions, that is, those that had stopped. Ohno added signal lights (*poka-yoke*) that would flash on when problems developed, enabling the employee to go directly to the problem.[15]

Shigeo Shingo was an industrial consultant on productivity improvement who credits his career choice to his reading Taylor's *Principles of Scientific Management* and the works of Yoichi Ueno and others who had brought scientific management to Japan. Shingo worked closely with Ohno in developing Toyota's system of rapid changeovers of dies used to make a part. Whereas Ford Motor, for instance, would emphasize long runs of a particular part, Toyota stresses small lot sizes of parts and quick setups. Shingo's contribution was called "Single-Minute Exchange of Die" and reduced the changeover time from hours to minutes, enabling less inventory and increased efficiency.[16]

To minimize human error in assembly, Shingo also suggested that the parts be designed so they would fit only one way—the correct way. For example, he recommended beveling a part so it fitted only one way, designing a wall plug so it cannot be inserted incorrectly, and so on. This type of *poka-yoke* would be particularly helpful to those of us who are instructionally challenged when we encounter those "some assembly required" toys at gift-giving time.

In 1953 Taiichi Ohno was promoted to general manager of manufacturing at Toyota. He continued to zealously attack the evil of waste in all its forms, and some of his strategies led others to consider "Mr. Mustache" eccentric. For example, when workers made too many parts, he suggested they take them home at the end of their shift, since they would not be needed until the next day. Eiji Toyoda, the managing director for manufacturing, was fully supportive of Ohno because he had seen proof of his methods. Eiji, an engineer, had spent a year at Ford Motor Company in the United States and brought back their employee suggestion system. He installed it at Toyota and encouraged all employees to root out waste and find ways to improve operations.

The tandem of Eiji Toyoda and Taiichi Ohno also started the policy that any employee could halt the entire assembly process if a problem occurred. Once the problem was found and fixed, the line would proceed. This practice developed out of the early record that Toyota had for poor quality. *Kaizen* was not enough, as too many automobiles either needed reworking after assembly or had to be brought back to dealers for repairs. Neither just-in-time inventory management, *poka-yoke*, nor any of the other techniques had led to the desired level of quality. These were techniques to produce more cars, but not necessarily better ones. This moment in history brought Toyota to W. Edwards Deming and statistical quality control.

Taiichi Ohno's initial reactions to Deming's methods were not favorable. He thought the statistics were too complicated for line workers; too many records had to be kept; frequent meetings were a burden; and he knew that the engineers were somewhat skeptical about how practical Deming's ideas were. However, Toyota's executives continued to push the idea of quality control—it was, in fact, a must if the company was to gain the image it sought in the market place.

Ohno became a convert, although a gradual one, as he saw that just-in-time and quality control were wholly compatible. Total quality control sought to eliminate defects at the source, and just-in-time sought to minimize inventory; together, they attacked quality and quantity problems at work stations in the production process. Just-in-time would fail if the delivered parts were defective and replacement parts had to be reordered. If both quality control and just-in-time were in place, only defect-free components would enter when they were needed and in the quantity necessary.

As Toyota's quality improved, it became a fierce competitor in a global industry characterized by intense rivalry. In 1965, Toyota received the Deming Prize for quality, a reward for a long-term commitment to driving out waste, to *kaizen*, to just-in-time, and to total quality control. Outside Toyota, people referred to it as the "Toyota production system"; inside Toyota, it was more commonly referred to as "Mr. Mustache's methods," a bow to the accomplishments of Taiichi Ohno.

12

GURU

We end where we began—with the importance of invention and innovation for business success in a competitive environment. The questioning process is one of seeking solutions to problems or issues, and it is vital that the right questions be asked. This attitude is an ingredient of technological innovation as well as important for finding better ways of doing tasks, finding new markets, or opening new opportunities. Our subject is Peter F. Drucker, undoubtedly the most widely quoted management writer, recognized by academics and practitioners alike.

PETER F. DRUCKER

I first met Peter Drucker through his writings and from hearing about him from my father, who had worked with him for some years.[1] My first physical meeting with him, in the fall of 1970, was the result of my dragging doctoral dissertation work. My subject was the decentralization of the General Electric Company in the first half of the 1950s. Harold F. Smiddy, General Electric's vice president, had spearheaded the restructuring of the company, my father had been a member of the team, and Peter Drucker was the major outside consultant. During an interview, Smiddy suggested I speak to Peter and handed me his business card with an indecipherable scrawl on the reverse (Drucker would recognize the intent, which was to introduce me as a friend). I made my way to New York University—not far from the Federal Reserve Bank of New York, where I then worked—where Peter was to teach a graduate class. I waited outside the classroom for him to appear, introduced myself, handed him Smiddy's card, and asked if I could sit in on his class. After class he asked me if I would like to be his research assistant. I wasn't attending NYU—I was completing work at the University of Oklahoma. However, it made no difference to Drucker, and so I signed on. This was the beginning of a long and valued friendship with this very European, very warm, brilliant man.

Among the more than two dozen major books Drucker has written there is one autobiographical work, *Adventures of a Bystander*.[2] Although Drucker is so often right, he errs with this title—a bystander he is not. His insights and work have a wide influence on leaders and organizations throughout the world. He sees the forest but can envision the individual trees. He once told me, "I have a limited point of view: I see the entire organization before I see the pieces—and that is the only way to see it."

Drucker was born on November 19, 1909, in Vienna, Austria, to Adolph and Caroline Drucker. The family was very prosperous, and as a youth, Peter met Sigmund Freud and Joseph Schumpeter, who was a family friend. His grandmother had performed on the piano for Johannes Brahms, and her last public performance was under the baton of Gustav Mahler in 1896. Drucker's father was an economist and a senior government official in Vienna who emigrated to the United States in 1938 and was professor of international economics first at the University of North Carolina, Chapel Hill, and later at American University. After retiring from teaching economics at age seventy, he taught European literature at the University of California at Berkeley for a few years. Adolph Drucker died in 1967 at the age of ninety-one.

Peter's mother, Caroline, was one of the first women in Austria to study medicine. She also attended many of Freud's lectures, studied his work at length, and pronounced him the most important man in Europe, but had major intellectual disagreements with many of his concepts. Despite their different interests and field of expertise, it is her personality, not Adolph's, that family members see in Drucker.

Peter moved to Germany in the fall of 1927 as a clerk in an export firm in Hamburg and then went to Frankfurt fifteen months later as a securities analyst for a merchant bank. After the stock market crash, he joined a newspaper as a financial writer, began teaching law, and completed his doctoral degree in international law. His first book, on Friedrich Julius Stahl, a conservative politician, was published in 1933. The book was immediately banned by the Nazis. One step ahead of the SS, Drucker moved to London and a job with a merchant bank.

In 1937 he came to the United States as a reporter on the American scene for a few British financial institutions. He carried with him his unfinished manuscript for *The End of Economic Man,* which predicted the end of capitalism, at least in Europe. He began teaching at Sarah Lawrence College, but promptly changed to a position at Bennington College, where he taught philosophy, government, and religion. He was at Bennington from 1942 to 1949. In 1950 he moved to New York University in New York City, where so many of his early clients would be found. Since 1971 he has been at Claremont College, where he is professor of management in the Peter F. Drucker Graduate School of Management. He may be the only professor in the world to teach in a school named after himself—but that is yet another indication of the respect and pervasive nature of his work in the field of management. Demonstrating his intellectual range, he also served as professorial lecturer in Oriental art at Pomona College from 1979 to 1985.

His first consulting job came while he was still at Bennington, after Donaldson Brown, the controversial vice president of General Motors, had read Drucker's *The Future of Industrial Man.* Brown's invitation for Drucker to study GM gave Drucker an entrance to the inner workings of the highest levels of the biggest company in the world. It also led to a very close association with Alfred P. Sloan Jr., GM's longtime chief executive.

I once asked Drucker how he worked his way up the corporate ladder to become the consultant to top management. "I started at the top," was his reply. This first consulting project led to his book *Concept of the Corporation,* a book that GM (at least those at the top of the corporation) regarded as negative and hostile. But others read it with great interest and it would open numerous executive doors: Ralph Cordiner and Harold Smiddy at General Electric; General George C. Marshall; Presidents Eisenhower, Kennedy, and Johnson; and most of the major executives in the United States, Europe, and Japan. The book also became required reading at GM's own General Motors Institute in Flint, Michigan (now a private college, GMI Engineering and Management Institute).

Drucker was no more a bystander than Alfred Sloan Jr., but he never managed a large firm (or a small one, unless you count his one-person consulting business, which is over a half century old), he never ran a government post, and he never earned a teaching degree. But he has stood as a leader in each of these fields—"as a critic, not as an actor," he says. Kenneth Boulding called him the "foremost philosopher of American society." Drucker is also the foremost philosopher of world management practice.

He is bespectacled, slender, above average height (six feet tall), a walker, and a former mountain climber. Not, he admits, the kind that scales the sides of cliffs, but a consummate wanderer of mountainsides. He is also an unabashed phoneholic whose distinct Austrian accent makes it superfluous for him to say, "This is Peter Drucker." He has an intellectual wit par excellence, with a caustic, sarcastic dry humor. He and his wife of over half a century, Doris, are the parents of three daughters (Kathleen, Cecily, and Joan) and one son (Vincent). Drucker studied with John Maynard Keynes and was greatly influenced by General George Marshall, who frequently used him for special assignments during World War II. On one assignment, Peter learned that he needed to be more than a bystander when he was told to go look at an old cavalry general running a pilot school for the air corps. Upon his return Peter told Marshall that the man was incompetent. Marshall asked what Peter had done about it. "I am just reporting my findings." "You should have relieved him of his command!" said Marshall. "But I have no authority!" replied Drucker. "You were told to investigate the situation and should have fixed the situation." "But I have no idea what to do with him after I fire him." Marshall said, "That's my problem, not yours."

Drucker's *The Practice of Management* was the book that set him on the top rung. It is a classic and the very best book in management literature. Books by Frederick Taylor and the Gilbreths were read by practitioners in the earliest years of this century, and Drucker has served modern practitioners in the same way. He is remarkably consistent: Each new book is insightful, provocative, original to him, and startlingly applicable for the future. Readers are also coming more and more to realize that what he often calls management is a description of leadership. He writes of maintaining the organization by setting a course for the future—and that is leadership.

Peter is a cosmopolitan who writes about the activity that most captures the imagination of America: business organizations. He has the manners of old Europe and the thoughts of a man completely oriented to the future, a future he more often than not accurately predicts. Peter once said that he is "not a consultant but an insultant" because "I long ago learned not to be nice, because people do not hear you when you hint." Yet most people know him as a warm, delightful, charming gentleman. His first words typically are a warm greeting to an old friend, a catching up on your recent personal activities, an inquiry about you, your family, and mutual friends. He has the gift of making you feel like the center of attention. Although small talk is not his specialty, he can engage in it with great flair.

One of my favorite times spent with him was a chance meeting on the sidewalk in the Wall Street area of New York, not far from his NYU office. He wanted to talk and invited me to his office, which, with his transition to Claremont College, he had not used for quite some time. I accompanied him first to a florist to purchase a few dozen roses. At his Trinity Place office he saw one secretary after another; each received a hug, a kiss, the gift of a rose, and then a short but very personal conversation with each. He wanted to know how husbands and children were doing, and he recalled them by name. One's son had broken a leg in football that fall; another was a senior in high school and Peter asked if he could help him get into the college of his choice. These secretaries truly loved Peter. I know the same warmth exists between him and the staff at Claremont, and he has their most dedicated loyalty. I often suspect he learns more about the pulse of America via his colleagues (and I don't mean the faculty) than he does from all the data he reads. As a onetime financial journalist, he still reads enormous quantities of data with much vigor. Data, especially demographic data, are his security blanket, but his love of people colors his daily life.

Management by Objectives and Self-Control

Most fads die a quick death after much fanfare. Management by Objectives (MBO) was a fad in the 1960s, though it developed a number of problems, mainly because the concept was improperly used. Today the concept is even more popular, but with far less fanfare—perhaps the secret to its current success.

Drucker did develop the concept, there is no doubt about that. As the story was related to me, Harold F. Smiddy and Peter Drucker had already developed a good relationship in the late 1940s. They had first met after World War II, probably as early as 1946 when Smiddy, who was a partner in Booz, Allen and Hamilton's New York office, approached Drucker after reading the book about GM. Between 1946 and 1948 the two met many times; in 1948 Drucker took a consulting assignment with the Chesapeake and Ohio Railroad and asked Smiddy to join him. But Smiddy declined, having decided to join the General Electric Company. Peter eventually would become the prime consultant on the GE project and Smiddy's most trusted sounding board, a position Drucker would duplicate with hundreds of executives in the next half century. MBO as it is understood today was conceptualized by Drucker and first put into practice by Harold Smiddy and his staff at GE.

The concept of MBO, according to Drucker, was

> management by objectives and self-control. . . . It substitutes for control from outside the stricter, more exacting and more effective control from the inside. It motivates the manager to action not because somebody tells him to do something. . . . but because the objective needs of his task demand it.[3]

The implementation of MBO was, according to Drucker, dependent on getting agreement about what was to be accomplished. MBO is a vehicle to produce results, not an end in itself. What it does is to help bring forth diversity by exposing different beliefs, basic dissents, and different approaches to getting the job done: "It is understanding that different people, all employed in a common task and familiar with it, define objectives and goals differently, see differently, see different priorities, and would prefer very different and incompatible strategies." A manager would not want to make a decision until an understanding was reached about the complexity, risk, and difficulty of setting objectives.

Issues could be better understood through informed dissent: "Informed dissent is essential where people of good will and substantial knowledge find out how differently they view the same problem, the mission, the same task, and the same reality." Drucker pointed out that Mary Parker Follett had observed many years ago that people who seem to differ on what the answer is usually disagree on what the right question is. MBO was a process for teasing out differences and exposing the multiple objectives and the complexity of the decision making process.

The basic difference in Drucker's philosophy was that others took for granted that the objectives of a job are known when in fact they are risk-taking decisions and anything but known or given. To Drucker, objectives were something you look at first. Unless you did, you could not plan, let alone organize, select people, or measure results. Drucker understood that objectives of a business or even a management position were anything but obvious, yet were at the heart of real managing.

Drucker also stressed the need to define key areas for setting objectives and evaluating results. Drucker mentioned eight of these key areas: market standing (measured against the market potential); innovation (in products, services, or in improving how these products and services were made or delivered); productivity (a yardstick as a target for "constant improvement"); physical and financial resources (defining needs, planning, and acquiring); profitability (for rate of return on investment); manager performance and development (managing by objectives and self-control); worker performance and attitude (employee relations); and public responsibility (participating responsibly in society).

Drucker built management as a discipline and managing as a practice around objectives that were needed in key performance areas. Others may have used a concept similar to MBO earlier, but it took Drucker to put it all together, think through its underlying philosophy, and then explain and advocate it in a form others could use.

Questions

As one of the top organization consultants, Peter Drucker does not give answers. He asks questions. From what appears to be simple questions come profound answers, because Drucker asks the *right* questions. Also, Drucker has a facility for getting his clients to give the answers themselves. For managing an organization, Drucker advocates centering on the needs of the future, for there are no answers in the past, and one can do very little to affect the present. Long before the phrase "strategic management" was coined, Drucker said: "The decisions that really matter, are strategic. They involve either finding out what the situation is, or changing it, either finding out what the resources are or what they should be. . . . The important and difficult job is never to find the right answer, it is to find the right question."

The "right" questions sounded easy, but the answers were often difficult to express. Drucker's famous questions were:

What is our business?

Who is the customer?

What does the customer buy?

What is value to the customer?

What will our business be?

And what should it be?

In essence, Drucker anticipated what became known as the "marketing concept" when he said the purpose of a business is to create a customer.

In analyzing a firm's product mix, Drucker provides a short list into which each product might be categorized. In typically catchy but simple phrasing, the list includes: Today's Breadwinners; Tomorrow's Breadwinners; Yesterday's Breadwinners; Investments in Managerial Ego; and Cinderellas (or Sleepers), to name a few. The money and organizational talent should be placed in Tomorrow's Breadwinners; Yesterday's Breadwinners need systematic abandonment, so as not to drain resources. Drucker felt the major difficulty with shedding yesterday's products is that so many people seem to have such warm feelings toward yesterday.

Drucker pointed out that knowledge is a perishable commodity and must be replenished by "knowledge workers" as the world demands change. Innovation was necessary to meet change successfully and he viewed society and business as in a constant state of creation, growth, stagnation, and decline. Abandonment of stagnating or declining ventures was innovative, according to Drucker, because it freed up resources for another innovative step. What kept the organization from failing was its ability to perform an entrepreneurial task of innovating—finding a new or better product, creating new customers or new uses for old products, and making, pricing, or distributing the product or service in a more competitive way.

The Sayings of Chairman Peter

Peter Drucker is so much a man of the Old World—yet he is always at the forefront in thought about the newest of global developments. In fact, he anticipates many trends and develops concepts anew. It would be impossible to list even a small part of the important observations that Drucker has written about management and organizations in the last half-century. A *Wall Street Journal* article he writes every few months has kept him in the minds of world executives, and the breath of topics he covers in these columns is amazing. His pithy insights, often one-liners, are enough to open new vistas for practicing managers.

On overworked executives: "Don't be proud of an 80 hour work week," he says, "80 hour work weeks are not a sign of performance—but a sign of poor planning."

On time management: "What would happen if this were not done at all? . . . Which of the activities on my time log could be done by somebody else? . . . [Ask your coworkers] what do I do that wastes [your] time without contributing to your effectiveness?" Drucker notes that "another common time-waster is malorganization. Its symptom is an excess of meetings. Meetings are by definition a concession to deficient organization for one either meets or one works. One cannot do both at the same time."

On social responsibility: "Management has failed if it fails to produce economic results . . . [and] if it has not supplied goods and services desired by the consumer at a price the consumer is willing to pay. It has failed if it does not improve or at least maintain the wealth producing capacity of the economic resources entrusted to it." There could be noneconomic consequences of managerial decisions, such as improved community well-being, but these were by-products made possible only by an emphasis on economic performance. For Drucker, economic results took priority and social or noneconomic objectives could be pursued only if the primary objectives had been attained.

Drucker was an early enthusiast of teamwork, but he saw a huge difference between committees and a team. If meetings needed to be scheduled often, then you had committees; team members interacted of their own accord, and there was no need to schedule meetings. The mere grouping of people together or the anointing of a team by an executive did not make a team. Teams grow and evolve. They develop because two or more people respect the ability of the others.

John Tarrant has collected some 150 "sayings of Chairman Peter" and they reveal why he is the most quoted modern management writer:

Far too much reorganization goes on all the time. Organizitis is like a spastic colon.

Reorganization is surgery. One doesn't just cut.

So much of what we call management consists in making it difficult for people to work.

We know nothing about motivation. All we can do is write books about it.

Management says the first job of the supervisor is human relations. But when promotion time comes they promote the fellow who puts in his paperwork.

Graduate school faculties are made up of people who have never been out working in organizations, who have never found out about the brilliant marketing strategy that doesn't work because the consumer does not behave the way you think he ought to.

Ignorance of the function of management is one of the most serious weaknesses of an industrial society—and almost universal.

When a subject becomes totally obsolete, we make it a required course.

If a government commission had worked on the horse, you would have the first horse who could operate his knee joint in both directions. The only trouble would have been that he couldn't stand up.

I was lucky. When God rained manna from heaven, I had a spoon.[4]

But Peter F. Drucker's contributions far exceed his aphorisms. When he fled Germany he had seen fascism firsthand and was full of pessimism about capitalism in the *End of Economic Man*. About this same time his Austrian economist colleague Joseph Schumpeter predicted the fall of capitalism in his book *Capitalism, Socialism, and Democracy*. But they were both wrong. Capitalism did not die but was rejuvenated through innovation, a customer orientation, and better management. Capitalism enjoyed its renaissance because of people like Peter Drucker, who asked the right questions.

NOTES

INVENTORS

1. Eli Whitney, quoted in Harold C. Livesay, *American Made: Men Who Shaped the American Economy*, Boston: Little, Brown and Company, 1979, pp. 45–46.

2. Robert S. Woodbury, "The Legend of Eli Whitney and Interchangeable Parts," *Technology and Culture*, vol. 1, no. 3 (Summer 1960), pp. 235–53.

3. Denison Olmsted, *Technology and Society: Memoir of Eli Whitney, Esq.*, New Haven: Durrie and Peck, 1846, p. 49.

4. Thomas A. Edison, quoted in Matthew Josephson, *Edison*, New York: McGraw-Hill, 1959, p. 435.

5. Thomas A. Edison, quoted in Jonathan Hughes, *The Vital Few*, Boston: Houghton Mifflin, 1966, p. 173.

6. Frank L. Dyer, Thomas C. Martin, and William H. Meadowcroft, *Edison: His Life and Inventions*, New York: Harper and Brothers, 1929, vol. 2, pp. 975–1009. Edison also had 1,239 patents in other countries besides the U.S.

MAKERS

1. Norbert Lyons, *The McCormick Reaper Legend*, New York: Exposition Press, 1955.

2. J. Leander Bishop, *A History of American Manufactures from 1608 to 1860*, Philadelphia: E. Young and Company, 1864, vol. 2, p. 390.

3. William T. Hutchinson, *Cyrus Hall McCormick*, New York: Century, 1930, vol. 1, p. 255. Also useful is the *Dictionary of American Biography* (Dumas Malone, editor), New York: Charles Scribner's Sons, 1933, vol. 6, pp. 607–9.

4. Andrew Carnegie, *The Autobiography of Andrew Carnegie*, Boston: Houghton Mifflin, 1920, pp. 70–71.

5. Andrew Carnegie, *The Empire of Business*, New York: Doubleday, Doran, 1933, p. 100.

6. Harold C. Livesay, *Andrew Carnegie and the Rise of Big Business*, Boston: Little, Brown, 1975, p. 141.

7. John J. McCusker, *How Much Is That in Real Money? A Deflator of Money Values in the Economy of the United States*, Worcester, Mass.: American Antiquarian Society, 1992, pp. 329–32.

8. Andrew Carnegie, *The Gospel of Wealth and Other Timely Essays*, New York: Century, 1901, p. 15.

9. Charles E. Sorensen, with Samuel T. Williamson, *My Forty Years with Ford*, New York: W. W. Norton, 1956, p. 116.

10. David A. Hounshell, *From the American System to Mass Production, 1800–1932*, Baltimore: The Johns Hopkins University Press, 1984, p. 224.

11. Horace L. Arnold and Fay L. Faurote, *Ford Methods and Ford Shops*, New York: Engineering Magazine, 1915, p. 20.

12. Henry Ford in collaboration with Samuel Crowther, *My Life and Work*, Garden City, N.Y.: Doubleday, Page, 1922, p. 175.

13. Peter B. Petersen, "The Light Before the Dawn," *Journal of Managerial Issues*, vol. 5 (Spring 1993), p. 33.

14. With due credit to Harold C. Livesay, *American Made: Men Who Shaped the American Economy*, Boston, M.A.: Little, Brown, 1979, pp. 176–77.

SELLERS

1. Michael B. Miller, *The Bon Marché: Bourgeois Culture and the Department Store, 1869–1920*, Princeton: Princeton University Press, 1981, pp. 25–27.

2. Stephen N. Elias, *Alexander T. Stewart: The Forgotten Merchant Prince*, Westport, Conn.: Praeger, 1992, p. 15.

3. Elias, *Alexander T. Stewart*, pp. 16–36; Harry E. Ressequie, "Alexander Turney Stewart and the Development of the Department Store, 1823–1876," *Business History Review*, vol. 39 (Autumn 1965), pp. 301–22.

4. Robert Hendrickson, *The Grand Emporiums: The Illustrated History of America's Great Department Stores*, New York: Stein and Day, 1979, p. 38.

5. Elias, *Aexander T. Stewart*, p. 79.

6. Policy quotes are from Boris Emmet and John E. Jeuck, *Catalogues and Counters: A History of Sears, Roebuck and Company*, Chicago: University of Chicago Press, 1950, pp. 248–49. With permission of the University of Chicago Press.

7. Richard S. Tedlow, *New and Improved: The Story of Mass Marketing in America*, New York: Basic Books, 1990, pp. 272–73.

8. James C. Worthy, *Shaping an American Institution: Robert E. Wood and Sears, Roebuck*, Urbana: University of Illinois Press, 1984, p. 28.

9. Emmet and Jeuck, *Catalogues and Counters*, pp. 51–53.

10. Quoted in ibid., p. 184.

11. David M. Potter, *People of Plenty: Economic Abundance and the American Character*, Chicago: University of Chicago Press, 1954, p. 80.

12. Worthy, *Shaping an American Institution*, p. 59.

13. Robert E. Wood, quoted in Emmet and Jeuck, *Catalogues and Counters*, pp. 339–40. With permission of the University of Chicago Press.

14. Worthy, *Shaping an American Institution*, p. 17.

MOVERS

1. Anonymous, "John Henry," quoted in *The Great Machines: Poems and Songs of the American Railroad* (Robert Hedin, editor), Iowa City: University of Iowa Press, 1996, pp. 11–13.

2. Albro Martin, *James J. Hill and the Opening of the Northwest*, New York: Oxford University Press, 1976, p. 33.

3. James J. Hill, *Highways of Progress*, New York: Doubleday, Page, 1910, p. 162.

4. Robert Sobel, *The Entrepreneurs: Explorations Within the American Tradition*, New York: Weybright and Talley, 1974, p. 138.

5. Hill, *Highways of Progress*, p. 166.

6. Joseph G. Pyle, *The Life of James J. Hill*, New York: Doubleday, Page, 1926, vol. 2, p. 28.

7. Hill, *Highways to Progress*, p. 131.

8. Maury Klein, "A Hell of a Way to Run a Railroad," *Audacity: The Magazine of Business Experience*, vol. 1, no. 1 (Fall 1992), p. 26.

9. George Kennan, *E. H. Harriman: A Biography*, Boston: Houghton Mifflin, 1922, Vol. 1, p. 17.

10. Lloyd J. Mercer, *E. H. Harriman: Master Railroader*, Boston: Twayne Publishers, 1985, pp. 46–47.

11. Jonathan Hughes, *The Vital Few: American Economic Progress and Its Protagonists*, Boston: Houghton Mifflin, 1966, p. 375.

12. Klein, "A Hell of a Way to Run a Railroad," p. 21.

13. Kennan, *E. H. Harriman*, Vol. 1, p. 296.

14. Martin, *James J. Hill*, p. 320.

15. Justices Harlan and Holmes quoted in ibid., pp. 518–19.

16. Alfred D. Chandler Jr., *The Visible Hand: The Managerial Revolution in American Business*, Cambridge, Mass.: Harvard University Press, 1977, pp. 173–74.

17. John Moody combined the Hill-Morgan lines such that they comprised 47,206 miles of track and were capitalized at $2,265,116,350, making those lines the largest of all groups. Using Moody's 1903 data, Harriman's lines would be fifth of the six groups in miles of track and fourth of six in capitalization, certainly not the dominant American railroad system. See John Moody, *The Truth About the Trusts*, New York: Moody, 1904, p. 439.

18. Harriman, quoted in Kennan, *E. H. Harriman*, vol. 2, p. 353.

COMMUNICATORS

1. Samuel I. Prime, *The Life of Samuel F. B. Morse*, New York: D. Appleton, 1875, pp. 5–6 and 18–25.

2. Quoted in Nathan Rosenberg (ed.), *The American System of Manufactures*, Edinburgh: Edinburgh University Press, 1969, p. 368.

3. Philip Dorf, *The Builder: A Biography of Ezra Cornell*, New York: Macmillan, 1952, p. 118.

4. Robert L. Thompson, *Wiring a Continent: The History of the Telegraph Industry in the United States, 1832–1866*, Princeton.: Princeton University Press, 1947, p. 315.

5. Thomas A. Watson, *Exploring Life*, New York: D. Appleton, 1926, p. 78.

6. Robert V. Bruce, *Bell: Alexander Graham Bell and the Conquest of Solitude*, Boston: Little, Brown, 1973, p. 141.

7. See George David Smith, "Forfeiting the Future," *Audacity: The Magazine of Business Experience*, vol. 4, no. 3 (Spring 1996), p. 26; Matthew Josephson, *Edison*, New York: McGraw-Hill, 1959, p. 141.

8. Watson, *Exploring Life*, p. 107.

FINANCIERS

1. *Tontine*, after the Neapolitan banker Lorenzo Tonti, meant an annuity shared among a number of persons, with the death of each beneficiary causing the annuity to be passed along to the survivors until the there was only one survivor. Today, such a tontine, if legal, would eventually be in the hands of the Internal Revenue Service.

2. In Greek mythology, Mephistopheles was a cunning, devious devil. In Johann Wolfgang von Goethe's *Faust*, Mephistopheles was the one who bargained for Faust's eternal soul.

3. Jay Gould, quoted in Maury Klein, *The Life and Legend of Jay Gould*, Baltimore: The John Hopkins University Press, 1986, p. 72.

4. Jay Gould, quoted in Julius Grodinsky, *Jay Gould: His Business Career, 1967–1892*, Philadelphia: University of Pennsylvania Press, 1957, p. 44. Details of the Erie wars can be found in ibid., pp. 38–53, and in Klein, *Gould*, pp. 76–87.

5. "Financial Policy of the Administration," *New York Times*, August 26, 1869, p. 11.

6. Quoted in Kenneth D. Ackerman, *The Gold Ring*, New York: Dodd, Mead, 1988, p. 155.

7. Ackerman estimated Gould's profits at "$10 to 12 million"; *Gold Ring*, p. 276. Klein, *Gould*, p. 115, says Gould "came up empty" and "the gold scheme had collapsed." Grodinsky, *Gould*, p. 79, says "Gould failed in gold speculation." In 50-plus pages of Gould and Fisk's testimony before the House Investigating Committee, they were *never* asked the key question of whether or not they had profited. See United States House of Representatives, Forty-First Congress, Second Session, "Investigation of Gold Panic in New York, 1869; Testimony of Jay Gould, James Fisk, and others," House Report 31, Washington, D.C.: U.S. Government Printing Office, 1870 (Serial Set 1436).

8. Klein, *Gould*, p. 119.

9. Ibid., pp. 205–7.

10. Grodinsky, *Gould*, p. 284.

11. Quoted in Klein, *Gould*, p. 11.

12. Mira Wilkins, *The Emergence of Multinational Enterprise: American Business Abroad from the Colonial Era to 1914*, Cambridge, Mass.: Harvard University Press, 1970, pp. 201–7.

13. Vincent P. Carosso, *The Morgans: Private International Bankers, 1854–1913*, Cambridge, Mass.: Harvard University Press, 1987, pp. 433–34.

14. Jonathan Hughes, *The Vital Few: American Economic Progress and Its Protagonists*, Boston: Houghton Mifflin, 1966, p. 448.

15. Frederick Lewis Allen, *The Great Pierpont Morgan*, New York: Harper and Brothers, 1949, p. 220.

16. *Money Trust Investigation Hearings*, quoted in Carosso, *Morgan*, pp. 632–33.

17. Andrew Sinclair, *Corsair: The Life of J. Pierpont Morgan*, Boston: Little, Brown, 1981, p. 229.

WORKING SMARTER

1. "Micromanaging from the Grave," *Business Week*, May 15, 1995, p. 34.

2. Charles D. Wrege and Ronald G. Greenwood, *Frederick W. Taylor, the Father of Scientific Management: Myth and Reality*, Homewood, Ill.: Business One Irwin, 1991, p. 35.

3. Frederick W. Taylor, *The Principles of Scientific Management*, New York: Harper and Row, 1911, pp. 33–34. Taylor also wrote *Shop Management*, New York: Harper and Row, 1903.

4. Robert P. A. Taylor (Stevens Tech's benefactor), quoted in Daniel Nelson, *Frederick W. Taylor and the Rise of Scientific Management*, Madison: University of Wisconsin Press, 1980, p. 105.

5. Peter F. Drucker, *The Age of Discontinuity*, New York: Harper and Row, 1968, p. 271.

6. Edna Yost, *Frank and Lillian Gilbreth: Partners for Life*, New Brunswick, N.J.: Rutgers University Press, 1949, p. 81.

7. Frank B. Gilbreth Jr. and Ernestine Gilbreth Carey, *Cheaper by the Dozen*, New York: Thomas Y. Crowell, 1948, pp. 135–37.

8. Lillian M. Gilbreth, "Why Women Succeed in Business," *North American Review*, vol. 226 (August 1928), pp. 158–66.

9. Michael Y. Yoshino, *Japan's Managerial System*, Cambridge, Mass.: MIT Press, 1968, p. 21.

10. Koji Taira, "Factory Legislation and Management Modernization During Japan's Industrialization, 1886–1916," *Business History Review*, vol. 44, no. 1 (Spring 1970), p. 84.

11. Elizabeth G. Hayward, *A Classified Guide to the Frederick Winslow Taylor Collection*, Hoboken, N.J.: Stevens Institute of Technology, 1951, p. 6.

12. Yoichi Ueno, quoted in Ronald G. Greenwood, Regina A. Greenwood, and Robert H. Ross, "Yoichi Ueno: A Brief History of Japanese Management 1911 to World War II," in K. H. Chung (ed.), *Academy of Management Proceedings*, San Diego, Calif., 1981, p. 108.

13. Ueno, quoted in Greenwood, Greenwood, and Ross, "Yoichi Ueno," p. 108.

14. Lillian M. Gilbreth, "A Taylor Society Delegate's Report" [of the World Engineering Congress in Tokyo], *Taylor Society Bulletin*, vol. 15, no. 1 (February 1930), p. 40.

15. Peter B. Petersen, "The Light Before the Dawn: The Origin of Quality Japanese Products During the 1920s," *Journal of Managerial Issues*, Vol. 5, no. 1 (Spring 1993), p. 35.

16. Ichiro Ueno and Susumu Takamiya, "Yoichi Ueno," in L. F. Urwick and W. B. Wolf (eds.), *The Golden Book of Management*, New York: AMACOM, 1984, p. 361.

ORGANIZERS

1. William C. Durant, quoted in Alfred D. Chandler Jr. (ed.), *Giant Enterprise: Ford, General Motors, and the Automobile Industry*, New York: Harcourt, Brace and World, 1964, p. 63. See also Lawrence R. Gustin, *Billy Durant: Creator of General Motors*, Grand Rapids, Michigan: W. B. Eerdmans, 1973, pp. 133–43.

2. Thomas R. Navin, "The 500 Largest American Industrials in 1917," *Business History Review*, vol. 44, no. 3 (Autumn 1970), pp. 369–71.

3. Peter F. Drucker, *Concept of the Corporation*, New York: John Day, 1946, p. 46.

4. Alfred P. Sloan Jr., *My Years with General Motors*, Garden City, N.Y.: Doubleday, 1963, p. 443. Sloan remained as honorary chairman of GM's board until 1956. Before his death in 1966, at age ninety-one, his philanthropy enabled the Sloan School of Management at his alma mater, MIT, and, with his longtime colleague Charles Kettering, the Sloan-Kettering Cancer Center.

5. William B. Wolf, *Conversations with Chester I. Barnard*, Ithaca, N.Y.: New York State School of Industrial Relations, Cornell University, 1973, p. 14.

6. Chester I. Barnard, *The Functions of the Executive*, Cambridge, Mass.: Harvard University Press, 1938, pp. 165–66.

7. Barnard, *Functions*, pp. 282–83.

MOTIVATORS

1. Ronald G. Greenwood, Alfred A. Bolton, and Regina A. Greenwood, "Hawthorne a Half Century Later: Relay Assembly Participants Remember," *Journal of Management*, vol. 9, no. 3 (Fall 1983), pp. 222–24.

2. Alfred A. Bolton, "Relay Assembly Test Room Participants Remember: Hawthorne a Half Century Later," *International Journal of Public Administration*, vol. 17, no. 2 (1994), p. 367.

3. Bolton, "Relay Assembly Test Room Participants Remember," p. 365.

4. Richard C. S. Trahair, *The Humanist Temper: The Life and Work of Elton Mayo*, New Brunswick, N.J.: Transaction Books, 1984, pp. 304–5.

5. Trahair, *Mayo*, p. 337.

6. Peter F. Drucker, *Adventures of a Bystander*, New York: Harper and Row, 1979, p. 314.

7. Fritz J. Roethlisberger and William J. Dickson, *Management and the Worker*, Cambridge, Mass.: Harvard University Press, 1939, p. 160.

8. Charles D. Wrege, "Review of 'The Hawthorne Myth Dies Hard,'" unpublished manuscript, August 1, 1979; quoted in Greenwood, Bolton, and Greenwood, "Hawthorne," p. 220.

9. Edward Hoffman, "Interview with Abraham Maslow," *Psychology Today*, vol. 26 (January–February 1992), p. 71.

10. Abraham H. Maslow, "A Theory of Human Motivation," *Psychological Review* vol. 50, No. 4 (1943), pp. 370–71, 374–75, 379, 382.

11. Abraham H. Maslow, *Eupsychian Management: A Journal*, Homewood, Ill.: R. D. Irwin, 1965, pp. 6–7, 18, 32, 35, 72, 75, 122, 125, 126, 261.

12. *Allama Sir Abdullah Al-Mamun Al-Suhrawardy* (1949), quoted in MOW International Research Team, *The Meaning of Working*, New York: Academic Press, 1987, p. 4.

13. Frederick I. Herzberg, "Happiness and Unhappiness: A Brief Autobiography," in A. G. Bedeian (ed.), *Management Laureates: A Collection of Autobiographical Essays*, Greenwich, Conn.: JAI Press, 1993, p. 5.

14. Frederick Herzberg, Bernard Mausner, and Barbara B. Snyderman, *The Motivation to Work*, New York: John Wiley and Sons, 1959, p. 113. With permission of JAI Press.

15. Frederick Herzberg, "One More Time: How Do You Motivate Employees," *Harvard Business Review*, vol. 46, no. 1 (January–February 1968), p. 59.

16. Frederick Herzberg, *Work and the Nature of Man*, New York: Thomas Y. Crowell, 1966.

17. J. Richard Hackman and Greg R. Oldham, *Work Redesign*, Reading, Mass.: Addison-Wesley, 1980.

18. Victor H. Vroom, *Work and Motivation*, New York: John Wiley and Sons, 1964.

19. Whiting Williams, *Mainsprings of Men*, New York: Charles Scribner's Sons, 1925.

20. Edwin A. Locke and Gary P. Latham, *A Theory of Goal Setting and Task Performance*, Englewood Cliffs, N.J.: Prentice-Hall, 1990.

LEADERS

1. Nicolò Machiavelli, *Discourses on Livy*, trans. Alan I I. Gilbert, reprinted in *Machiavelli: The Chief Works and Others*, Durham, N.C.: Duke University Press, 1956, vol. 1, p. 203.

2. Nicolò Machiavelli, *The Prince*, trans. Luigi Ricci, New York: New American Library, 1952. Due to the numerous editions of *The Prince*, these references are from (in order) chapters 18, 25, 19, 6, and 18.

3. Mary Parker Follett, *Freedom and Coordination: Lectures in Business Organization*, London: Management Publications Trust, 1949, pp. 52–56; Henry C. Metcalf and Lyndall Urwick (eds.), *Dynamic Administration: The Collected Papers of Mary Parker Follett*, New York: Harper and Row, 1940, p. 262; and Mary Parker Follett, *Creative Experience*, London: Longmans, Green, 1924, p. xii.

4. Warren Bennis, "Thoughts on the 'Essentials of Leadership,'" in Pauline Graham (ed.), *Mary Parker Follett: Prophet of Management*, Boston, Mass.: Harvard Business School Press, 1995, p. 178.

5. Douglas McGregor, "On Leadership," in John D. Glover and Ralph M. Hower (eds.), *The Administrator: Cases on Human Relations in Business*, 4th ed., Homewood, Ill.: Richard D. Irwin, 1963, p. 719.

6. Douglas McGregor, *The Human Side of Enterprise*, New York: McGraw-Hill, 1960, pp. 33–34. With permission of the McGraw-Hill Companies.

7. McGregor, *Human Side*, pp. 47–48. With permission of the McGraw-Hill Companies.

8. Peter Drucker, quoted in William F. Dowling (ed.), *Effective Management and the Behavioral Sciences: Conversations from Organizational Dynamics,* New York: Amacom, 1978, p. 223.

9. Abraham H. Maslow, *The Journal of Abraham Maslow* (Richard J. Lowery, ed.), Brattleboro, V.T.: Lewis Publishing, 1982, p. 345.

10. Douglas McGregor, *Leadership and Motivation: Essays of Douglas McGregor* (Warren G. Bennis, Edgar H. Schein, and Caroline McGregor, eds.), Cambridge, Mass.: MIT Press, 1966, p. 125. With permission of the MIT Press.

QUALITY SEEKERS

1. Homer Sarasohn, quoted in Robert C. Wood, "A Lesson Learned and a Lesson Forgotten," *Forbes,* vol. 143, no. 3 (February 6, 1989), p. 71.

2. Cecelia S. Kilian, *The World of W. Edwards Deming,* (2nd ed.,). Knoxville Tenn.: SPC Press, 1992, p. 6.

3. W. Edwards Deming, *The New Economics for Industry, Government, and Education,* Cambridge, Mass.: Massachusetts Institute of Technology, Center for Advanced Engineering Study, 1993, p. 94. Also, W. Edwards Deming, *Out of the Crisis,* Cambridge, Mass.: Massachusetts Institute of Technology, Center for Advanced Engineering Study, 1986.

4. Joseph M. Juran (ed.), *Quality Control Handbook,* New York: McGraw-Hill, 1951.

5. Joseph M. Juran, "Made in U.S.A.: A Renaissance in Quality," *Harvard Business Review,* vol. 71, no. 4 (July–August 1993), p. 43.

6. Yukiyasu Togo and William Wartman, *Against All Odds: The Story of the Toyota Motor Corporation and the Family that Created It,* New York: St. Martin's Press, 1993, p. 115.

7. Togo and Wartman, *Against All Odds,* p. 116.

8. Henry Ford, in collaboration with Samuel Crowther, *Today and Tomorrow,* Garden City, N.Y.: Doubleday, Page, and Company, 1926, p. 91.

9. Taiichi Ohno, *Toyota Production System—Beyond Large-Scale Production,* Cambridge, Mass.: Productivity Press, 1988, pp. 19–20. Originally published as *Toyota seisan hōshiki,* Tokyo: Diamond Publishing Company, 1978.

10. Taiichi Ohno, quoted by Norman Bodek in Henry Ford (in collaboration with Samuel Crowther), *Today and Tomorrow,* 1926, reprint Cambridge, Mass.: Productivity Press, 1988, p. vii. See also Peter B. Petersen, "The Light

Before the Dawn: The Origin of Quality Japanese Products During the 1920s," *Journal of Managerial Issues*, vol. 5 (Spring 1993), p. 33.

11. Ford, *Today and Tomorrow*, p. 114.

12. Ohno, *Toyota Production System*, p. 26. Cambridge, Mass.: Productivity Press.

13. Ford, *Today and Tomorrow*, p. 108.

14. Taiichi Ohno, quoted in Andrew Mair, *Honda's Global Local Corporation*, New York: St. Martin's Press, 1994, p. 34.

15. Togo and Wartman, *Against All Odds*, p. 130.

16. Shigeo Shingo, *A Study of the Toyota Production System from an Industrial Engineering Viewpoint* (trans. Andrew P. Dillon), Cambridge, Mass.: Productivity Press, 1989.

GURU

1. The first person in this narrative refers to Ronald G. Greenwood, a student, research assistant, and longtime friend and follower of Peter Drucker.

2. Peter F. Drucker, *Adventures of a Bystander*, New York: Harper and Row, 1979.

3. Peter F. Drucker, *The Practice of Management*, New York: Harper and Row, 1954, p. 136.

4. John J. Tarrant, *Drucker: The Man Who Invented the Corporate Society*, Boston: Warner Books, 1976, pp. 257–58, 260, 262, 264.

INDEX